CHANGE IN THE AMERICAN WEST

EDITED BY STEPHEN TCHUDI

Change in the American West

Exploring the Human Dimension

UNIVERSITY OF NEVADA PRESS

RENO · LAS VEGAS

Published by the Nevada Humanities Committee and the University of Nevada
Press. The Committee logo is derived from a petroglyph representing a human
hand at Rattlesnake Well, Mineral County, Nevada, carved ca. A.D. 800–1200.

University of Nevada Press, Reno, Nevada 89557 USA

"Elephants" by Patrick Lane from *Selected Poems* (Toronto: Oxford University Press,
1987), copyright © 1987 by Patrick Lane, is reprinted on pages 3–4 by permission of
the poet.
Unless otherwise noted, all photos by Kit Miller copyright © 1996 by Kit Miller; all
photos by T. H. Watkins copyright © 1996 by The Wilderness Society.

Library of Congress Cataloging-in-Publication Data

Change in the American West : exploring the human dimension / edited by
Stephen Tchudi.
p.   cm.
ISBN 0-87417-288-8 (alk. paper)
1. West (U.S.)—Civilization.   2. Social change—West (U.S.)   3. Humanities—West
(U.S.)   4. West (U.S.)—Poetry.   I. Tchudi, Stephen, 1942–
F595.C47   1996
978—dc20
                                                                                96-30675
                                                                                CIP

The paper used in this book meets the requirements of American National
Standard for Information Sciences—Permanence of Paper for Printed Library
Materials, ANSI Z39.48-1984. Binding materials were selected for strength and
durability.

First Printing
05 04 03 02 01 00 99 98 97 96   5 4 3 2 1

Halcyon, previously an annual journal of the humanities, is now a book imprint
published by the Nevada Humanities Committee and the University of Nevada
Press through a grant from the National Endowment for the Humanities. *Change in
the American West* continues as volume 18 of the publication.

As the ancient bird,

the halcyon,

calmed the waters

in the face of winter gales

so can the humanities

calm our fears and launch

us on our quest

CONTENTS

About the time the essays in this volume on "Change in the American West" were completed, the Microsoft Corporation launched its new computer operating system, "Windows 95." Sifting through the public relations hoopla, National Public Radio commentator John McChesney remarked on the process of change and evolution in computer software and hardware. He noted that despite the appearances of regularity—version 5.3 of a program faithfully follows version 5.2—computer evolution is often less systematic than it might appear. Windows 95 contained a number of idiosyncratic features to allow users of previous versions of Windows to run their old programs. Thus the '95 edition could not be an entirely clean design, for it had to accommodate past history.

McChesney likened the development of the new system to the evolution of a coral reef, where polyps randomly but systematically attach themselves to existing structures, creating a reef that follows patterns that are generally but not specifically predictable.

The coral reef metaphor seems appropriate for the theme of this volume on "Change in the American West." As tempting as it might be to offer tidy formulae on the Western past and future, the writers here have chosen to look at some of the individual elements and events that have led to that curious "reef" we label "the West." ("Which West?" one might properly ask.) Could one have predicted that the Western frontier, virtually untracked and uncharted at the beginning of the nineteenth century, would be declared closed by Frederick Jackson Turner by 1893? Could a historian or poet looking at Turner's allegedly closed frontier have prophesied the concept of a Las Vegas or Los Angeles one hundred years later? Our writers have chosen *not* to take such a long-odds gamble. Rather, they offer particular instances of and insights into the complex processes of change.

In his lead essay, Ted Chamberlin asks us to consider the role of the humanities in a changing West. In a wide-ranging essay that discusses the humanities in both classical and contemporary worlds, he argues compellingly for studies that center themselves concretely in the *yard*, "grounded in the urgencies of the everyday and the gritty particulars of place," as opposed to the "ivory and ivied" *tower*. Chamberlin urges us to search for "a sense of meaning and value which will be founded on an understanding of what is permanent both in human nature and in the natural world." By examining the particulars of human experience, he suggests, we can move toward more general principles that help us understand both change and constancy.

Three of the writers in this collection look to the arts in the nineteenth century for reflections of what Westerners were thinking and changing. In an essay linking technology and the arts, Lee Scanlon discusses the arrival of the transcontinental railroad in Salt Lake City and the impact of now-mobile theater companies' content and comments on community mores. Sheri Crawford examines the origins of Giacomo Puccini's opera "The Girl of the Golden West" in the writings of David Belasco and discovers strong elements of "progressive" thinking in both, even when that thought is displayed in the context of traditional Western themes of rugged individualism and vigilante justice. June Johnson Bube discusses women's roles in the dime novels of that past century, and, like Crawford, finds that in contrast to traditional stereotypes such as the barmaid or the schoolmarm, writers of fiction about the West were exploring changing and individualized roles for women.

Three writers focus on the theme of change as it is revealed in the quintessential Western issue of *water*. Wesley Reid examines the evolution of water rights in Nevada's Walker River basin and explains how changing language and rhetoric have literally shaped the channels of water and figuratively shaped channels of power and control. Dorothy Zeisler-Vralsted traces the development of an irrigation system and resulting boosterism in the Columbia Basin of Washington, while Katrine Barber looks to the writing of Edward Abbey and Leslie Marmon Silko as a way of understanding environmental "mythologies" surrounding the controversial Glen Canyon Dam.

The people of the West are architects of change or, to sustain our metaphor, the individual polyps who consciously or accidentally create the structures and patterns of change. In an essay on Basque-American history, William A. Douglass describes issues and problems in sustaining a cultural identity in a rapidly changing West.

Kit Miller presents the stories of working people of the West, specifically, workers in Nevada's casinos, whom she regards as "the fabric of the American community" and whose stories "reflect how work life is changing" in the American West today.

Two other writers in this collection look at institutional and community change in the West. Michael Green offers us a "personal history" of his years as a young journalist at the *Valley Times* of North Las Vegas, and in doing so, explores Western political, journalistic, and economic power struggles over a quarter of a century. Jon Christensen interviews a nonfiction writer, an editor, a historian, and an urban theorist, who speculate about the past and future of that unpredictable but understandably Western phenomenon, the city of Las Vegas.

Writing for a previous volume in the *Halcyon* series, editor Thomas Wright remarked on precedent set by the founder and first editor, Wilbur Shepperson, who offered readers "a varied menu" of essays in the sphere of the public humanities. *Change in the American West* supports and extends that tradition, presenting the implicit argument that one can discuss the humanities—yard or tower—in diverse genres and media. For example, in an essay discussing the work of Terry Tempest Williams, Cheryll Glotfelty shows that traditional "boundaries of form" in fiction and nonfiction are being dissolved as humanists seek new ways to describe responses to the Western experience. Such boundaries are dissolved in this collection, as well. The reader will find a memoir of life in a changing North Dakota town (Teresa Baumeister), a photo essay and prose-poem on the changing Utah desert (Tom Watkins), fiction about Western stereotypes and current realities (Paul Morris) and poetry on phenomena as varied as the seasons in the Nevada desert (Laurie Macfee), the demise of the Virginia & Truckee railroad (Bill Cowee), weed abatement on the loneliest road in America (Shaun Griffin), and the ways in which we go about "Writing Our Story" (Bill Abrams).

"The world has a way of insisting on itself," writes Ted Chamberlin, and we need ways to understand and resist this "overwhelming pressure." The humanities provide a means by which we can take events and processes that may seem "appallingly incoherent, unstable, and sometimes even insane" and respond to them with "intelligence and courage." The imaginative work of humanists in

this volume is intended to offer just that sort of perspective on the
unwieldy but uniquely fascinating theme of "Change in the American West."

STEPHEN TCHUDI
University of Nevada, Reno

Bury the Dead and Pay the Rent
Practicing the Humanities in
the Changing West

An old friend of mine has lived a life that chronicles the changes that have taken place this century on farms and ranches throughout the country. He left school at fifteen, when his father became ill, and for sixty years he has raised cattle and pigs, grown barley, oats and—when hybrids and herbicides came along—some corn, and filled the hay mow with sweet-smelling alfalfa. He worked the fields with horses until 1952, when he bought his first tractor. Electricity came that year too, bringing many good things with it—lights in the barn, some leisure time, a fridge and freezer and a radio, a way for the kids to do homework in the evening. But he still thought the hay was better stooked by hand, and he treated his tractors like working stock. Indeed, he lived a life of many contradictions. Born into a community where cooperation was a way of life—he and his neighbors shared land, labor, and equipment—he was also fiercely competitive, proud of his own cattle and crops and of the horses he bred, raised, and showed in local fairs and international exhibitions—first Clydes and Percherons, then hackneys, and for the past twenty-five years some of the best hunters and jumpers in Canada.

But now he can't do it all anymore—and if he can't do it all, he says, he won't do any of it. His kids have tried to work the farm into their lives, but haven't been able to. The last time I spoke with him, he talked about selling. And I thought about farm auctions. Those of you who have been to one will know the scene: the family there in the background, leaden-hearted, watching while their past is laid out for everyone to pick over, knowing that their future depends on how much they sell during the next two or three hours. Bury the dead and pay the rent. The men of the family try not to cry, but few succeed. The women, who are stronger, try not to bid on a favorite item, much more precious than the family heirloom they held back—something bought thirty years ago when the youngest child was born, or twenty years ago when a sister died, or ten years ago when the old man stopped drinking, or five years ago when the first grandchild came along. They are hoping with all their hearts that their neighbors will find a way to pay more than they can afford for livestock and equipment they don't really need, and which they look on as partly their own anyway since they have helped raise and repair them. Meanwhile, the auctioneer shows all the tricks of his trade, humoring the friendly vultures circling about the yard with lighthearted comments about the bits and pieces of a lifetime of laughter and tears, and trying to sell things that are both priceless and worthless.

What do the humanities make of this, other than a social document or a sentimental drama? How do those of us who study and profess the humanities deal with *this* past, and *this* present; and how do we connect all this to the future? One of the central claims made by the humanities has always been that they help us live our lives. I think it's time to ask whether they do, and how they can.

There's a song by the great Jamaican reggae musician Bob Marley entitled "Duppy Conqueror," which begins "Yes, me friend, me friend, him set me free again." It is about breaking free from the power of a duppy, a ghost or spirit of the dead whose burial rites have been incomplete. The spirit wanders homeless, ready to be captured by others with evil on their minds. Instead of being an ancestral protector, the duppy becomes an evil presence, performing the will of the obeah-men, who in the rhetoric of Marley's song are the politicians and judges who represent the corrupt society of contemporary Babylon.

Although the image is located in Jamaican language and beliefs, it conveys a universal warning about the price we all pay, one way or another, for failing to come to terms with our past. And it conveys something of the promise, which I believe we must take more seriously than we do these days, that the humanities—in this case, songs and stories—can help us do so. In a poem entitled "Elephants" (*Selected Poems* 1987), the Canadian poet Patrick Lane brings this closer to home with a story set in the interior of British Columbia, where I grew up, at a time when the future meant roads and hydroelectric dams and the obliteration of Indian villages and of Indian gravesites . . . or all but a few, for the tourists.

The cracked cedar bunkhouse
hangs behind me like a grey pueblo
in the sundown where I sit
to carve an elephant
from a hunk of brown soap
for the Indian boy who lives
in the village a mile back in the bush.

The alcoholic truck-driver
and the cat-skinner sit beside me
with their eyes closed
all of us waiting out the last hours
until we go back on the grade

and I try to forget the forever
clank clank clank
across the grade
pounding stones and earth to powder
for hours in mosquito darkness
of the endless cold mountain night.

The elephant takes form—
my knife caresses smooth soap
scaling off curls of brown
which the boy saves to take home
to his mother in the village

Finished, I hand the carving to him
and he looks at the image of the great
beast for a long time
then sets it on dry cedar
and looks up at me:
                What's an elephant?
he asks
so I tell him of the elephants
and their jungles. The story
of the elephant graveyard
which no one has ever found
and how the silent
animals of the rain forest
go away to die somewhere

in the limberlost of distances
and he smiles

tells me of his father's
graveyard where his people have been
buried for years. So far back
no one remembers when it started
and I ask him where the graveyard is
and he tells me it is gone
now where no one will ever find it
buried under the grade of the new
highway.

These images—from Kingston and Kamloops—passed through my mind as I stood several years ago in a small aboriginal camp just north of Alice Springs, in central Australia. I had gone there to find out what was happening with aboriginal rights, and I was visiting with a group of aboriginal men and women from across Australia who had gathered to discuss what to do about their homelands, which were haunted by restless spirits. They talked about many things, but in the evening, after a day of dealing with details, they talked about their ancestors, some of whom were resting uneasily as museum exhibits or skeleton curiosities, appropriated as someone else's heritage, part of an imperialism that turned aboriginal ancestors into artifacts—and duppies into evil presences. Other ancestors of these men and women had been lost from sight; many had died alone and unremembered. The land where their spirits remained had fallen into other hands, and the spirits wandered homeless. So, in a sense, did many of their descendants, those with whom I was sharing a meal around cooking fires set in old oil drums and talking around open fires under a clear and surprisingly cold desert sky.

This was a gathering of the Federation of Land Councils, an organization of state and territorial organizations that was playing an important part in getting some land back into aboriginal hands. Oscar Wilde said that our obligation to history is to rewrite it. These folks were in the process of doing just that. Or more exactly, of writing themselves—and speaking themselves—into European and Australian history. And they were doing something else: insisting that their country belongs to them, not in a proprietary way, but in the way we all belong to our history and our heritage. Willy nilly. Whether we like it or not. For in a paradox that is at the heart of human experience, and of the humanities, we are *possessed* by what *belongs* to us—the land, our language, our hopes and our fears, our songs and our stories.

When he was asked by Aunt Sally whether anybody had been hurt by the explosion on the Mississippi riverboat, Huck Finn replied, "No. Killed a nigger." "Well, it's lucky," said Aunt Sally, "because sometimes people do get hurt." Australia's founding legislation, passed in 1901, outdid even Aunt Sally, proposing that "in reckoning the numbers of people of the Commonwealth, or of a State, or other part of the Commonwealth, Aboriginal natives shall not be counted." This section was not amended until 1967, and although it was surrounded by complicated legal fictions within which it had a kind of justification, in the final analysis it represented a simple belief: Aborigines are not to be counted, because they do not count.

In the beginning—that is, a mere two hundred years ago—there was nothing at all in Australia. That was the seafaring theology of the first Europeans to arrive in the eighteenth century. *Terra nullius* was the description—in Latin, still for some the language of empire—of the land that had been discovered. There is nobody at home, it meant, or more precisely, this *is* nobody's home. The continent belongs to no one and therefore becomes the property of anyone who claims sovereignty over it. The British immediately did just that, at first in 1768, when Captain Cook sailed up the east coast of Australia waving the flag, and later on January 26, 1788, at Sydney Cove, when Governor Phillip raised the Union Jack.

Two hundred years later, the aborigines of contemporary Australia are preempting these European notions of sovereignty and taking as given that they are the original sovereigns of the land, the landowners. Underlying title, they assert, is aboriginal title, not crown title. The settlers who had come in recent times—which is to say in the past couple of centuries—are therefore their tenants.

But the aborigines are responsible landlords, with no wish to throw tenants out onto the street. They know too well what that's like. They do want to negotiate the rent, however, including the back rent. Two hundred years' worth. In a nice turn of phrase, Pay the Rent was the memorable slogan of aboriginal sovereignty that had wide currency while I was in Australia, and it caught the determination of aborigines to count for something in Australian affairs.

It also caught something else of immediate relevance in the

American West—something that reminds us that we should not feel too superior, for the humanities conspire every day in acts of categorical dispossession: the categories that literary studies and history embrace, for example, which routinely privilege written over oral traditions—actively discrediting the latter, and by implication those whose heritage it is. Or political science, which presumes a strict separation of material and spiritual values (our much ballyhooed separation of church and state), and which consequently views the expressions of spiritual beliefs that are central to every affirmation of political sovereignty by aboriginal peoples as either ostentatiously romantic or embarrassingly primitive. (This is the same political science, ironically, that seems to be quite comfortable with our effectively saying "In God We Trust" every time we make a cash transaction.) We could extend this kind of catalog, sadly, throughout most of the contemporary academy. Defying these categories should be something more than a hazardous career decision for the younger members of the profession.

"The tongueless man gets his land took," says a Cornish proverb. Constitutions should give tongue to the dispossessed instead of merely giving them names. So should the humanities, for the humanities have always provided our central *constitutional* texts, defining for us who we are and where we belong. (That's why curricular issues generate such controversy in the community, although we may not think of them this way.) It is too often the case that the more liberal and progressive people are, the more likely they are to imprison or exclude others by their definitions of them and by the ways in which—to use another analogy from Huck Finn—they describe Indian territory as something out there, rather than right here.

When I speak of the humanities, I don't mean only the professional disciplines of the arts and sciences. I mean all of the activities we engage in, as individuals and as communities, that give meaning and value to our lives. The stories we tell: stories of the origin and purpose of things; of causes and effects and sequences of events; of what holds us together and keeps us apart. The institutions we establish and the covenants we enter into: secular and sacred; large and small. The ways in which we organize our communities: how we lay out the land, our patterns of ownership (of stories, as well as of land), the buildings and roads we construct, the spaces we make open, or closed; the priorities we give to health care, education, law and order, commerce, clean air and water, the arts . . .

and, just as important, the ways in which we divide these up in our minds. These are part of the humanities; and according to them we live our lives, practicing subsistence—trying to live within our means, with a sense of spiritual as well as material fullness—and exercising sovereignty—using our intelligence and imagination to create an understanding of ourselves, individually and collectively, as human beings.

These—the humanities—also reflect a set of complementary wisdoms: those of the *yard,* and those of the *tower.* All societies require specialists, charged with responsibility for consolidating the conditions for survival and maintaining the sources of power. In recent years, by which I mean the past several hundred, some of us have gotten into the habit of distinguishing between specialists who work in the yard and those who work in the tower, between those who make themselves useful by concentrating on the particulars of the here and now, and those who set themselves above and beyond the everyday and dream—wonderfully, but worthlessly—about universals. The idea of what I call the *yard* resonates with the authenticity of the people, grounded in urgencies of the everyday and the gritty particulars of place; the *tower,* especially in its nineteenth-century ivory or ivied versions, rises up with an authority that is heightened by the privileges of detachment and contemplation.

A presumed antagonism between the yard and the tower plagues the academy these days. However, it is a false opposition, and we should know better, for it reflects an ancient dichotomy between particulars and universals and is part of an old, old story—a story of ideas and things rooted in place and time, on the one hand, and those that transcend time and place. *Both,* we should know by now, are necessary for subsistence and survival, and *both* become sites of power and centers of sovereignty.

The argument goes back a long way. In the relatively short memory of European civilization, it goes back to Boethius, in prison near Milan in the year 525 A.D., in the dark end days of the Roman Empire, writing a book called *The Consolations of Philosophy,* which became a medieval best seller. But this is not some dusty old issue. It is around us constantly, this issue of particulars and universals: in the arguments about standards determined here or elsewhere, about advice coming from those directly involved or those distant and detached, about practice and theory, about local and literary language. It is there in the contradictions between individual and collective rights and between local laws and those of supposedly higher standing. Civil disobedience rests its case upon this distinction, which received eloquent expression in Martin Luther King's famous letter from Birmingham Jail, when he answered charges that his actions were untimely, that he was an outsider, and that he was disobeying a particular law of the land, with an appeal to the universals of justice and freedom. It is there, this tension between particulars and universals, in the continuing argument about whether the humanities are centered in the yard or in the tower, whether they should be rooted in everyday experiences or set above and beyond them, whether they are generated at home—in *this* place—or away, in some *other*, separate place. At the still point, or in the turning world.

Sometimes we become convinced that we must choose one or the other—choose *between* the yard and the tower, between the practical and the theoretical, between particulars and universals, between the secular and the sacred, between the worthy and the worthless. It is a debilitating preoccupation, about a foolish choice, between false alternatives. It is a choice between being isolated and being overwhelmed, between being marooned on an island and drowned in the sea. Nobody should have to make that choice. The humanities should ensure that nobody has to, and should point out that ultimately nobody can. The humanities have not been doing their job.

Admittedly, it isn't always easy. High in the Rockies up in British Columbia, there's a town—more like a curve in the road—called Canal Flats. It's hard to find on the map, harder still to recognize when you get there, having asked directions from the north, say, following the river (and the Shuswap Indians) up through Death Rapids to the dry benchlands and the low-lying marshes where the glacial waters of Finley Creek and the hot springs of Fairmont come together on the flats at the headwaters of the Columbia; or coming from the south, following the Kootenay River (and the Kutenai Indians) up from Montana past the flats to the headwaters high in the sawtooth mountains of the Rocky Mountain trench. These two great rivers pass within about a hundred feet of each other, going in different directions, at Canal Flats. The Columbia runs north in Canada to a place called Boat Encampment, at the head of what we used to call the Big Bend, and then sweeps south through the northwest United States twelve hundred miles to the sea. The Kootenay heads south to the United States, just passing by the rolling country and rodeo towns of Montana and Idaho, when it turns north again to Canada and the lake country of the east Kootenays. I spent much of my youth there, and I grew up on these rivers, running the length of the Kootenay several times by canoe, and once—once was enough—the dangerous Big Bend. I came away with a powerful sense not only of this natural heritage but of the ways in which it has shaped the lives of those who lived within it.

It is sometimes said—Giambattista Vico said it first—that we should think of God as a verb, not a noun. For me, these rivers were pure verb. There have always been folks who want to turn them into nouns. Maybe naming rivers *is* our first mistake, our original sin. In any case, this belief of mine led to my first serious, and my first unsuccessful, venture as a humanist in the early '60s. Along with many others—most of them very unlikely protestors from the town of Revelstoke—I tried to get arrested by lying down in front of the bulldozers that were about to begin work on the Mica Creek dam, the first in what would eventually become a large hydroelectric project (rivalling those lower down the Columbia), stretching from High Arrow to Kinbasket Lake and flooding some of the greatest wilderness areas in the Northwest. It was accompanied by the Libby Dam and other smaller projects on the Kootenay, backing the waters up into the valley of the Purcells. We didn't get thrown in jail—they walked the cats around us—and, of course, we didn't stop the dams. But we did talk a lot about how, in Thoreau's wonderful words, "in wildness is the preservation of the world."

A couple of years later, living in Vancouver and living off my indignation, I went to hear the Weavers—with Lee Hays, Ronnie Gilbert, Eric Darling, and Pete Seeger. To me, their songs represented all that was progressive and promising about the world, and they embodied the possibilities of resistance in our actions and revolution in our attitudes. I wouldn't have missed them for the world. Then Lee Hays led off with Woody Guthrie's classic, "Roll On, Columbia." And I didn't know whether to laugh or cry.

This song was one of twenty-six that Guthrie wrote under the sponsorship of the Department of the Interior and the Bonneville Power Authority. He came to the Northwest out of the dust bowl and the depression, with a deep sense of the plight of the dislocated and the dispossessed. In bewildering ways, he ignored the situation of Native Americans, some of whom had been dislocated and dispossessed by the very projects he celebrated. But he did so from within an ambivalent ideology of oppression and opportunity: a

belief that institutions, not individuals, are the major agents of dispossession and dislocation, and that institutions (especially those
generated by government initiatives) will provide the main remedy.

So Guthrie celebrated the promise of the hydroelectric projects
of the Bonneville Power Authority, whose most powerful image at
the time was the Grand Coulee Dam. Guthrie's song about it, with
that title, caught the complex confusion between what the Northern
Irish poet Seamus Heaney once called territorial piety and imperial
power. Guthrie sings of the river flowing through canyons "like a
prancing, dancing stallion," but he also draws our attention to the
dam, "the biggest thing yet built by human hands." Uncle Sam,
Guthrie explains, invited the river to roll along, but also to "do some
work for me."

It doesn't take a literary critic to recognize the insignia of natu-
ralness, sovereignty, and independence, each of them associated
with the river, and of ingenuity, inspiration, and industry, corre-
spondingly identified with the government and the dams and developments they sponsor. The power of the Columbia, mighty and
majestic, is not so much controlled as it is "harnessed," the way
one might harness horses or oxen—which become, like the river,
no less themselves for being made useful to humans. In this image,
the Columbia becomes a useful river, like the Nile, but it remains a
great river, also like the Nile. It is a modern river, but it is one that
somehow retains the ancient aura of the wilderness. In the regions
of the imagination—although not in the regions of the Northwest
now, as anyone who knows the river will quickly add—it is both
wild and civilized, both a part of nature and a part of us.

But there is more, especially when we come to think about the
powerful iconographic tradition of rivers like the Columbia, with
their larger-than-life status. Mountains and oceans sometimes share
this, and so does the weather—the sun and the wind and the rain
and the snow. Although all of these can be harnessed to human use,
they remain ultimately beyond human control and beyond human
capriciousness. "As long as the rivers flow" goes the promise of
many of the Indian treaties, perhaps in some measure out of a cyni-
cal conviction that this is one of the few things likely to last longer
than the next administration, but more profoundly signaling a belief that where other sanctions (such as those of the Bible) are not
shared, this is one of the few rhetorical gestures that brings together
a sense of natural and supernatural authority. Stop the rivers, goes

the underlying logic, and something unthinkable will happen, because something both unnatural and unholy has been done.

Yet the projects that Guthrie celebrated held promise of controlling the drought and the flood, those twin scourges of the settled world, and part of that same overwhelmingly natural world. And this brings us to one of the venerable parables of European settlement in the Americas: turning a wasteland—sometimes construed as a wilderness—into a garden, or making the desert bloom. There is a powerful Judeo-Christian rhetoric at work here, in which the land that brings forth plenty is deemed to be blessed by God, while the land that does not is cursed. One of the markers of divine disfavor is the barren land. In Islam, too, which like Judaism is preeminently a religion of the desert, the water hole is a blessed place.

As the aborigines of Australia might say, Guthrie sang in the water holes, celebrating the dams that would "run the great factories and water the land" of the Northwest, so that "rich farms would come from the hot desert sand." He sang (in his words) "at all sorts and sizes of meetings where people brought bonds to bring the power lines over the fields and hills to their own little places. Electricity to milk the cows, kiss the maid, shoe the old mare, light up the saloon, the chili joint window, the schools and churches along the way." He sang a praise song to the people and to hydroelectric projects that, in the words of "Roll On, Columbia," would "turn the darkness to dawn." And a great wild river into a tame and turgid lake.

The problem is not so much *where* humanists stand on this but *how* the humanities help negotiate between these differing imaginative allegiances. That's what they are; and we *do* need to make choices—choices between verbs and nouns, as it were. The humanities cannot make these choices for us—they are often asked to, although that is not their role—but they *can* help us understand where the choices lie: partly by showing us how chronicles of events—stories and songs—are also ceremonies of belief; and partly by reminding us that every genuine choice is in some measure caught up in relationships between the ways in which we *see* the world and the ways in which we *say* things about it.

The Gitksan peoples of the northwest of British Columbia have lived in the mountains fishing and hunting and farming and trading for thousands of years. There is a story among them that tells of changes to one of the river valleys, nearby the mountain called

Stekyooden, across from the village of Temlaxam. It was once the center of their world, one of those paradisal places of peace and prosperity that bring blessings and that shape the lives of the people who live there.

This valley nourished the Gitksan people so well that they became unmindful of their good fortune and forgot the ways that the mountains and the rivers and the plants and the animals had taught them. The spirit of the valley, a grizzly bear called Mediik who lived by Stekyooden, warned them and gave them many signs of his anger; but they ignored these warnings, until he finally became so enraged that he came tearing down from the top of the mountain—grizzlies running uphill resemble a freight train impersonating a gazelle; but their front legs are short, and they sometimes tumble coming down—and he brought half the mountain with him, covering the valley floor and the village of Temlaxam and all the people there. Only a few survived, those who were out hunting in the high country or berry picking on the opposite slopes or doing the hard work that makes for an easy life.

This was just about seven thousand years ago. Over time, the people returned to the valley, and although never the rich and fertile home it once had been, it always held its place in their history; and they remember the great grizzly and the lesson he taught them. Today the stories of the Gitksan move out from that valley like spokes from the center of a wheel or branches from a tree or children from their parents. It is the center of their lives, the place they came from, and the place to which they return their thoughts and their thanks. Their claims to the territory around arise from the claims that the valley has on them, and the story of the grizzly and the slide confirms both claims.

Several years ago, when the Gitksan finally were forced to assert their claims in the courts of the new people in the valley, the Canadian people, they told this story. They told it with reluctance, and they told it with all the ritual that it required; for the stories and songs that represent their past—the Gitksan call them *ada'ox*, which is a word that includes both the medium and the message of their history—are in every sense ceremonies of belief as well as chronicles of events.

So are all stories, as they realized. They also realized that the story of the grizzly and the sacred mountain called Stekyooden and village of Temlaxam, which in their minds confirmed the presence of their people in that place for millennia, and certainly far longer than any Europeans could claim, might not be believed by the judge, schooled as he was in stories of a different sort. So their leader, Neil Sterritt, suggested they draw on another story line to confirm their own. He had geologists drill under the river that still runs through the valley and take a core sample and analyze it. The geologists discovered that sixty feet down there was clay that matched the clay high up on the mountain slope, exposed where the grizzly had taken down the hillside—or where the earthquake had produced the slide that brought down half the mountain. And the sample was dated *exactly* when their story said the grizzly grew angry with the people in the Kispiox valley.

The court was inclined to see the scientific story as confirming the legendary one. However, Sterritt and the elders of the Gitksan were at pains to persuade the judge that *each* story was validated by the *other;* that neither had a monopoly on understanding what happened; that the story line of geology was framed by a narrative just as much the product of invention and discovery as the story told by their people; and that each storyteller's imagination—whether telling of tectonic plates or of grizzly outrage—was engaged with a reality that included much more than the merely human. The story of the grizzly is a very old one, hardened on an anvil of ancient tellings and tested by memories that contested and disputed it for much longer than our seismic and sedimentary theories. Each story is as true as the other. Both sorts of stories are necessary for us to live our lives.

The humanities can help us put them together by showing us how stories and songs mediate between these truths, mirroring the mind as they make sense of the world and displaying both the ordinariness of human existence and the extraordinary powers that surround and affect us. Beyond this, the humanities can remind us of the dignity of the everyday, the strangeness of the familiar, the extravagance of the orderly, and the bountiful grace of limits. They can show us how we understand any convention—local or literary, social or cultural, scientific or mythical—not by learning it in isolation but by seeing where it meets the world. The humanities can— and they do—educate our imaginations in the ways of the world, often by showing us other worlds and other ways.

There's an old cowboy song called "When the Work's All Done
This Fall." I first heard it when I was five or six, living in Calgary
in the late 1940s, sung by a local singer named Stu Davis. There's
some uncertainty about who wrote it, although it was first published in the *Stock Grower's Journal* in Miles City, Montana, in 1893.
It was also said to have originated on a stock trail out of Deadwood,
Wyoming. (Whatever its provenance, it has been a perennial favorite—recently, for example, it has been recorded in versions as different as the country pop style of Michael Martin Murphey and the
traditional folk style of Norman and Nancy Blake.) The song tells
of a cowboy who, a lifetime after leaving home to ride the range,
announces that at the end of this season he is going back home to
Dixie with what's left of his wages, instead of doing what he would
usually do, which is spend it all on drinking, dancing, and some
other unmentionable activities.

The song turns around images of home: his brokenhearted
mother's home, which we know cannot be quite the same place
he left long years ago, but to which he plans to return after this
last roundup; his home on the range, one that has held him for so
long; and his final home, which he refers to (in a familiar figure of
speech) as the "new range" to which he will soon be called by his
Master. The wanderer dreaming of home, of which this song is an
example, is of course an old theme. In the Americas, it takes forms
as different as the great old French Canadian folk song that begins
"Un Canadien errant, banni de ses foyer" (a wandering Canadian,
banished from his home), and the question posed by the Barba-
dian poet Kamau Brathwaite, reflecting on the rootlessness of West
Indian blacks: "Where then is the nigger's home?" he asks in one of
his poems, "Postlude/Home," "In Paris, Brixton, Kingston, Rome?
Here, or in heaven?"

However slight its ambitions (and we don't want to presume too
much just yet on that count), "When the Work's All Done This Fall"
belongs in that tradition. It belongs in the tradition of the humanities, that is to say, for the humanities have always been about home
—home, which, it turns out, is almost never on a map. Then again,
as Ishmael said in *Moby Dick*, "true places never are."

The song also turns around another notion, one that is not stated
in so many words, but rather in so few rhymes. Let me try to explain. The chorus of the song goes like this:

After the roundups are over and after the shipping is done,
I am going right straight home, boys, ere all my money is gone.
I have changed my ways, boys, no more will I fall;
And I am going home, boys, when the work's all done this fall.

The night after he announces this, the cowboy is out riding herd when a storm comes up. The cattle stampede; he tries to head them off. His horse stumbles in the dark, falls on him, and he is fatally injured, although he dies only after giving away his possessions to his mates in a formal—and formulaic—ritual that is familiar from Homer to Merle Haggard. The final verse of the song tells the words that are carved on the wooden board that marks his grave.

Charlie died at daybreak, he died from a fall
And he'll not see his mother when the work's all done this fall.

Now one of the things that I remember thinking first about this song was that the fellow who wrote it must have been pretty short on rhymes. Both in the chorus and in the final verse he rhymes *fall* and *fall*—a sure thing, I know, but too simple, rather embarassingly so. Just what you'd expect out on the Spotted Wood Trail. Yet there's method in this monotony, for he makes us immediately aware of the several meanings of "fall" that he is using. In the chorus, *fall* refers both to the season—a season of harvest, of the roundup and ship- ping of cattle—*and* to the sinner who leads a life of low living. (As the first verse has it, "I am an old cowpuncher and here I'm dressed in rags./I used to be a tough one and go on great big jags.") The final verse presents another pair: his fall from the horse, and the season again—but this time a season of death, of another kind of roundup. As a result, the song resonates with the various meanings of *fall*— figurative and literal, literary and local, secular and sacred.

It turns out that poets do this sort of thing all the time. Do what? Well, play with words and with rhymes. Take another song, right from the heart of the poetic tradition in English—William Blake's opening "Song of Innocence."

Piper sit thee down and write
In a book that all may read
So he vanished from my sight
And I pluck'd a hollow reed.

Here, of course, *read* and *reed* are spelled differently; but they sound the same, and again the effect is achieved because the poet draws our attention, by what at first seems an awkwardness, to the kind of riddling that poetry has delighted in for millennia. So perhaps this old cowboy song isn't so silly after all. Certainly its links, in its own tradition of story and song, with an essentially poetic play of language, are reinforced every weekend in spring, summer, and fall by rodeo announcers, the best of whom make rap musicians sound tongue-tied.

It turns out that there are a lot of other familiar elements in the song. For one thing, it belongs in a venerable poetic tradition commemorating the dead, in verse that has often become extraordinarily *popular.* Many of these poems celebrate not the powerful and the privileged but what Thomas Gray (in his elegy written in another yard, a country churchyard) called "the short and simple annals of the poor." Furthermore, poetry in English has a long tradition—from the medieval border balladeers and the Scots Chaucerians through Robert Burns and William Wordsworth to Walt Whitman and William Carlos Williams—of using vernacular language, the language of speech, in literature. This reminds us that one of the sources of poetry *is* speech; and speech certainly shapes this song, to the extent that some of the words—for instance, *done* and *gone,* which are rhymed in the first two lines of the refrain—recall the speech of an earlier time, for the slight awkwardness of what is to our contemporary ears a near rhyme (*done* and *gone*) alerts us to the fact that their vowels would have been pronounced the same. This song also resists the fashionable assumption that speech is the only begetter of poetry, for it includes another reminder: that one of poetry's venerable sources is the epigraph, words written on the tomb. Indeed, they are the original duppy conquerors, such words, burying the dead (and sometimes paying the rent as well), charms to keep the spirits appeased.

There's much more that we could mention about this song—about its rhythms, its rhetoric, its refrain, its images, its catalogs and namings. We need to find ways of talking about such songs, other than to turn them into documents about plain folks or popular culture. For there's something else at issue here. These are the songs and poems that have held a place in people's hearts for generations—many of our parent's hearts, for example. How can I look down from the tower with such condescension on my mother and my father, walking the yard with their carefully folded poems in their purse and pocket, which they would bring out and read—or recite by heart— with a mixture of sentimentality and seriousness that was normally reserved for holy writ? Like the scriptures, these poems gave them lines to live by. My love of poetry comes from them, I am sure of that, and from them came a memory of verse as well. Does my vocation, do the humanities, have no room for what gave them courage and comfort? And what about some of the songs our teenage children listen to? These are the same children who begin school loving words and numbers and end up hating poetry and mathematics—something that has always seemed to me one of the really remarkable achievements of the educational system in which many of us play a central role. I sang old Anglican hymns for years—I sing fewer now, but they are hard-wired into my consciousness— and they were in quatrains, tetrameter and trimeter that are exactly those of this cowboy song, and often much *less* subtle and sophisticated and no less sentimental. Two of the best poets writing in English now—Seamus Heaney, whom I have already mentioned, and the 1992 Nobel Laureate, Derek Walcott, from the West Indies—remind us every chance they get of the profound influence that Methodist hymns and the Catholic liturgy had on them. The Jamaican poet Lorna Goodison tells of her housekeeper, a woman who perhaps had never heard of Ireland, and certainly not of William Butler Yeats, singing "Down by the Salley Gardens" as she worked in the kitchen—and giving her a sense as she was growing up of the possibilities of language, and of literature, and I guess of love as well.

I don't want to make "When the Work's All Done This Fall" out to be more than it is, and I am not wanting to claim it as a masterpiece—after all, it's only been around a hundred years. I know that many of us, myself included, will decide that we much prefer the poetry of Gary Snyder or Tom Wayman or Pattiann Rogers or Lorna Crozier or Joy Harjo or Simon Ortiz or any number of other wellknown contemporary poets writing in the West. On the other hand, we want to be very careful before we dismiss poems just because they are popular. This song does have some interesting features. Part of its appeal *is* essentially literary, holding us with structure and style as much as subject, and making us aware (paradoxically in some of its apparent awkwardnesses) that these are inseparable anyway. This is what works of literature typically do all the time, showing us that how we say things shapes the way we see them,

and perhaps even determines what we see. Recognizing this pro-
tects such songs from what is the most serious menace they face
from those of us in the humanities: turning them into quaint cultural illustrations of race or class or gender or region or whatever,
looking through or around or behind them rather than *at* them and
acknowledging them for neither more nor less than what they are—
imaginative expressions that emerge out of, and return us to, both
life *and* literature, the life and literature we *all* share.

Some years ago, I guided a big-game hunting party in the southeast of British Columbia with an Indian by the name of Camille
Joseph. He was chief of the Kutenai band, a man with a wonderful
sense of humor and a legendary reputation—his nickname, mis-
spelled on the wall of bush cabins throughout the Kootenays, was
Kemeal the Prophet. He was supposed to be able to predict the
weather and the ways of the woods. On our first morning out, he
came running back from the creek near where we were camped
with exciting news for the hunters, a wide-eyed group from Louisi-
ana. "I've just seen a grizzly," he said breathlessly. Then, after a long
silence filled with the unspoken authority of his Indian heritage, he
added, "I recognized it from some pictures I once saw in a *National
Geographic* magazine."

Sometimes I think about what the humanities—or at least my
small corner of them—might make of these comments of Camille's
these days. Ironic self-reflexivity comes to mind, with a footnote
about how his post-modern intertextual play of signifiers and sig-
nifieds cleverly questions the status of experience through a decon-
structive problematizing of both individual cognition and cultural
hegemonym that generates, in its defiantly aboriginal positionality,
a space of post-colonial interrogation. I guess there was some of that
there. I'm sure there was. But there was also something else. A few
days later, as we were walking out to check on the horses, Camille
told me where he *had* first met a grizzly—not in *National Geographic*,
of course, but not up Bear Creek, either. His first encounter, he
said—with the seriousness of someone for whom hunting was a
way of life—had been in a story told him by his father and repeated
many times. He first learned how to hunt, he added, not from going
out in the woods but from listening to his father, over and over
again. Listening with a disciplined attention to the text that would
exhaust a roomful of new critics. Camille's imagination was highly
educated in the realities of hunting before he ever walked up the

trail. He knew, better than most of us, that we are moved by imaginative representations of the world before we are ever moved by the world. That's where we learn the lessons of survival, and of power.

The world has a way of insisting on itself, of compelling us to accept the terms of its sometimes vicious and always temporary social, economic, or political categories, of hypnotizing us into the delusion that its elements are permanent, its priorities immutable. We submit to that world by accepting its demands, and in doing so we move closer and closer to what Thoreau once described as a life of "quiet desperation," in which we are always under pressure to react to what is happening outside ourselves, or elsewhere. That's if we are lucky. If we are unlucky, we become violent, or go mad. Or we surrender to the first thing that offers us survival of any sort, or any sort of power.

It is only through the imagination that we can resist this overwhelming pressure. It is in this sense that *all* stories and songs are, in their way, resistance stories. Confronted with situations and events that are appallingly incoherent, unstable, and sometimes even insane, they help us respond with intelligence and courage, to tranquilize them in our minds, to create for ourselves a sense of meaning and value that will be founded on an understanding of what is permanent both in human nature and in the natural world, and that will give us some center of belief from which we can move out to live with others. These—and their representation in the traditions of the humanities—are the true duppy conquerors, keeping body and soul together.

The Transcontinental Railroad and Its Impact on the Salt Lake Theatre

May 1869 marks a crucial time in the development of the United States. It was the year the transcontinental railroad was completed, joining east and west with a dramatic time-saving travel device that would eventually transform the face of the nation. Further, the following five years were critical to the Mormon society in its Rocky Mountain stronghold as well as important years in the development of the United States. For the Latter-day Saints, or Mormons, it was a period that saw the final years of the man termed "the American Moses," Brigham Young, and marked a period when the isolated nature of the Salt Lake valley was broken. With their isolation ended, Mormons had to contend with a flood of nonbelievers who scoffed at and challenged fundamental beliefs of the Mormon Church. It was a period when the Church itself had to deal with the first strong evidence of internal schism following the death of its founder, Joseph Smith, some two decades earlier. It was, in addition, a time of national economic strain featuring depression and bank failures following the Civil War. It was a time when the federal government began to involve itself in what became a constitutional issue of the rights guaranteed under the First Amendment: freedom of religion as it was practiced in the Utah Territory. With the end of the war, and with Utah lying astride the gold and wagon trails to California and Oregon, it was easy for the U.S. government to focus on the territory and Mormon religious practices, especially polygamy. The first of the court trials of Mormon leaders began in this period. It was, in short, a time of great change for the Mormons and the nation as well.

The theater, local as well as national, could not avoid being influenced by these sweeping changes. The Salt Lake Theatre, built in 1862, had been dedicated by Daniel H. Wells, of the First Presidency of the LDS church, and in the dedicatory prayer the theater

was dedicated as a "safe and righteous habitation . . . for the benefit of [the] Saints." He then concluded the prayer with a warning
that the building must never be used for wicked purposes: "Suffer
no evil or wicked influences to predominate or prevail within these
walls, neither disorder, drunkenness, debauchery or licentiousness
of any sort or kind; but rather than this, sooner than it should pass
into the hands or the control of the wicked or ungodly, let it utterly
perish and crumble to atoms; let it be as though it had not been, an
utter waste, each and every part returning to its natural element"
(Tullidge, 743). These utterances, more than any other, helped form
the dramatic taste and offerings of the Salt Lake Theatre. But with
the coming of the railroad, the Saints' dedication to the theater
would be sorely tried.

Because of its isolation, the Salt Lake Theatre saw very few
notable actors or actresses in its early years. The offerings were provided primarily by the Deseret Dramatic Association, a local stock
company. The association, like other stock companies of the period,
organized its players along what were termed "lines of business,"
or specific character types. There was the leading man, the leading
lady, a juvenile or light comedian, second lady or leading juvenile, first and second heavy, first and second old man, old woman,
an eccentric comedian, singing chambermaid, walking gentlemen,
walking lady, responsible utilities (both men and women, basically
spear-carriers with lines) and utilities (both men and women who
were basically spear-carriers period). Each of these roles had specific character types and the approach was probably the strongest
influence on acting style during the period.

This reliance on local talent was required in part by the war, but
equally as responsible was the available mode of travel, the stagecoach, which connected Salt Lake City with Denver on the east and
with Sacramento on the west. The passage from Denver to Salt Lake
covered 592 miles and included forty-six stops (Root, 303). From
Salt Lake to Sacramento the distance was nearly 800 miles, with
some sixty stops. Travel time from Salt Lake to Denver or California varied according to the weather, the temper of the Indian
nations, and the quality of coaches and their drivers. The average
coach traveled at about four miles an hour. The entire trip from the
Missouri (where to many, civilization in the United States ended) to
the Pacific took an average of twenty-three days, and was probably
best summed up by an anonymous traveler who said, "I know what

Hell is like. I've just had twenty-four days of it" (Moody, 124). Since actors, or any travelers for that matter, paid an average fare of about fifteen cents a mile and were restricted to only twenty-five pounds of baggage, one can easily see actors' or anyone's reluctance to traverse the wilderness for whatever money the Saints might be able to pay.

Between 1863 and 1869 only five actors and actresses visited the Salt Lake Theatre. They were Thomas A. Lyne, Mr. and Mrs. Selden Irwin, George Pauncefort, and Julia Dean Hayne.

Thomas A. Lyne had been converted to Mormonism while working in the professional theater in Philadelphia. He went west to Nauvoo, Illinois, where he practiced his profession among his fellow Mormons. When Joseph Smith was killed, Lyne chose not to go west, but sixteen years after the Saints had established themselves in the Salt Lake Valley, he traveled there and stayed until his death in 1890. His performances were in pieces familiar to the Saints: *Pizzaro, William Tell, The Stranger,* and *Damon and Pythias.* These were all staples of mid-nineteenth-century American theater, nothing new or provocative. The Irwins introduced a whole new set of dramas, including *The Lady of Lyons, Ingomar the Barbarian, Octoroon, The Corsican Brothers,* and *Colleen Bawn,* all of which were received with welcome enthusiasm. In 1864 George Pauncefort, a British actor, played briefly with the Mormon company, and while not introducing any new dramas, he did introduce an apparently lighter spirit. "George Pauncefort breathed upon the Salt Lake stage a lighter atmosphere. The somewhat Puritanic spirit which had hitherto prevailed in our theatre was dispelled, without a shock to the families of apostles, bishops and elders who filled the parquette for the plays now introduced were still chaste, though of a lighter order" (Tullidge, 747).

But the first major star to visit the Salt Lake Theatre prior to 1869 was Julia Dean Hayne. While offering no new approaches to the theater, her professional skill was quite impressive, so much so that both Edward Tullidge and Edward Sloan, local writers and critics, wrote plays for her. The memory of her visit lingered long in the Salt Lake Valley. She apparently returned the affection with which she was held, as she noted in her curtain speech at her final appearance:

> It is seldom I lose the artist in the woman, or permit a personal feeling to mingle with my public duties; yet, perhaps, in now taking leave I may be pardoned if I essay to speak of obligations

which are lasting. . . . To President Young, for very many cour-
tesies to a stranger, lone and unprotected, I return those thanks
which are hallowed by their earnestness; and I trust he will permit me in the name of my art to speak my high appreciation of the
order and beauty that reign throughout this house. (Gates, 276)

But the majority of performances continued to be carried by the
Deseret Dramatic Association.

The theater season prior to the arrival of the railroad varied little
and centered around the April and October conferences of the Mormon Church. Traditionally the fall and winter season would open
sometime in September and close in either February or March; then
the spring and summer season would commence in late March and
continue until June or July. Sometimes there would be a second summer season, running through August, but it was usually the result
of a troupe or "star" passing through and asking for an engagement.

As the completion of the transcontinental railroad neared, the
anticipation of theatergoers grew, as noted in the March 12, 1869,
edition of the *Deseret Evening News* (the newspaper owned and operated by the LDS church): "Our theatregoers may now look confi-
dently forward to entertainments of more than ordinary excellence
at the Theatre. The completion of the railroad greatly facilitates the
acquisition of first-class talent of this description from the East, and
Salt Lake City is very likely to become a point of attraction to theatrical stars. To meet the wants of the time . . . Messrs. Clawson
and Caine [managers of the theater] have Miss Lockhart, Mr. Herne
and Miss Lucille Western, all three being acknowledged as artists
of great ability"(3). In the months to come the audiences were not
to be disappointed.

With the completion of the railroad, the Salt Lake Theatre was
virtually inundated by a galaxy of stars of varying magnitude. The
number of performances rose to 250 during that first year of what
might be termed "railroad theater."

Actually, the first visit of the "railroad stars" proved to be a mixed
blessing to the Salt Lake audience. On March 10, 1869, James A.
Herne, a few years away from his destined eminence as a prominent
American playwright, opened in the title role of *Rip Van Winkle.* The
play ran for six consecutive nights—a very unusual occurrence, for
the Salt Lake Theatre seldom gave that many performances of a
single play over an entire season. Herne, who was appearing with

his former sister-in-law, Lucille Western (he had divorced her sister Helen two years earlier), also played in *East Lynne, Leah the Forsaken, Our American Cousin, Lucretia Borgia,* and what was to become a center of controversy, *Oliver Twist.*

Oliver Twist opened March 22, 1869, and the program described it as "Dicken's Moral Picture of Life as it is in London" (Pyper, 169). Western appeared in the role of Nancy Sykes, Herne played Bill Sykes, and the members of the Deseret Dramatic Association took supporting roles, including local favorite Phil Margetts as the Artful Dodger and John S. Lindsay as Fagin. In the words of George Pyper, the performance was "one of the wildest sensations of the day." But Lindsay best describes the performance:

> In the scene where Bill Sikes [*sic*] . . . kills Nancy . . . , both Herne and Miss Western sought to make the murder as realistic and blood-curdling as possible. . . . To carry out the realism of the beating a pad was made of wet towels; these Herne struck with a piece of board, making a sickening thud which Lucille accompanied with a scream, each one growing fainter until it became a groan, then Bill steals across the stage and off at an outer door and Nancy almost dead, drags herself on till she gets to the centre of the stage, her face completely hidden by her disheveled hair; when she gets to position centre she turns her face which has been covered from the audience, throws her hair back and reveals her face covered with stage gore. On this occasion the picture was so revolting that several women in the audience fainted— everybody was shocked.

"The Great Salt Lake Stage Controversy" was under way. Clarissa Young Spencer, one of Brigham Young's daughters, notes only that "Father declined to allow the play to be repeated" (Spencer, 160). Lindsay, in his autobiography, corroborates this. Pyper, writing well after the event, credits Brigham Young with saying: "If I had my way I would never have a tragedy played on these boards" (168). Unfortunately, while this may make good dramatic copy, Brigham Young actually made the statement in 1862 at the dedication of the theater (Widtsoe, 243). There are, apparently, no direct quotations from the Mormon president at the time of the visit of Herne and Western. But obviously something was said somewhere, as the theater managers, Hiram B. Clawson (a son-in-law of Brigham Young) and John T. Caine noted in the *Deseret Evening News:*

Learning on Sunday afternoon, from parties whose opinion we respect, that portions of the play of "Oliver Twist," produced at the Theatre Saturday evening, and advertised for repetition this evening, was distasteful to the feelings of the community, we immediately determined, either to so alter the piece as to relieve it of the objectionable features, (which mainly consisted in acting it so true to life as to render it repulsive to refined feelings) or to withdraw it from the stage. After consulting Miss Western and Mr. Herne, we determined to withdraw the play as neither they nor the management has any disposition to enact plays that would cause an unpleasant feeling or offend the most sensitive of our patrons.

Another bill has been substituted for this evening which will be found every way worthy of the patronage of the Public. Very respectfully,

> Clawson & Caine
> Lessees and Managers
> (March 27, 1869)

The substituted bill consisted of a performance of the farce *Handy Andy* and of *The Heart of the Stage, or The Actress of Padua*.

The closest Salt Lake officialdom came to condemning the performance was an editorial in the *Deseret Evening News* by editor George Q. Cannon, who was also a member of the First Presidency of the Mormon Church:

A well-conducted, properly managed Theatre is an agency that can be used very effectively for the education and improvement of the people. On the stage, the manners, styles, modes of living etc., of those of past generations and of other nations, can be portrayed so historically true that all classes, but especially the young, may derive much information therefrom. It is an excellent and interesting method of teaching history, of inculcating fine moral sentiments, and imparting lessons that must have a permanent effect upon those who hear them.

The representation of a drama that gives truthful delineations of historical incidents and scenes cannot fail to afford instruction, even to the most careful student of history, and to give a better understanding of the times and the people among whom the events are supposed to have happened. This is especially the case if the surroundings—the costumes, the scenery, etc., are in historical keeping with the incidents. (April 1, 1869)

Cannon then mentioned having seen performances in London by the English actor Charles Kean in a series Kean referred to as "Shakespearean revivals." Cannon told how effectively and vividly these scenes recreated history in plays such as *Henry VIII,* more so than any of his readings had ever done. He then commented on the influence of the stage, in general:

> The representations of historical plays upon our stage in this city have been attended with one excellent effect which we have had occasion to notice. Young people, not familiar with the history of the period in which the dramas have been laid, have been stimulated to ask questions and to read history to obtain a more thorough knowledge of the personages and scenes in which they had become interested at the Theatre. In this respect they have done much good; and though in such dramas anachronisms may occasionally occur, a further familiarity with the histories soon correct these. But while we are convinced that information has been diffused and general intelligence promoted among us, through the agency of the Theatre, yet it is in the enlarged knowledge of language, in the correct and various methods of giving of expression to thought which it has given, that we perceive the greatest improvement. Slang phrases are still too common, but there has been a great change in this respect among the rising generation. The stage has had a refining influence, and in the conversation of the young people we are of the opinion that the language used is more comprehensive and select than it would have been, had the Theatre not been made an institution among us. (Ibid.)

But Cannon finally got to the point of this extended essay, which was a response to the presentation of the Herne and Western version of *Oliver Twist.* He first pointed out that nothing should be performed on the stage that could be objectionable in language or morals. If, he noted, the leaders of the Church in their public pronouncements are held to strict accountability, so too should the stage, whose influence should be "pure, healthy and elevating." Cannon described the stage as a "school" where lessons on deportment, manners, and the like are given. The stage, he pointed out, should never sink beneath the dignity of its profession, that profession apparently being education. Foul language, especially using the name of Deity, must be avoided, as well as oaths, vulgarity, and double entendres. He also attacked over-acting: "The mouthing, the contortions of countenance and the rolling and blinking of the eyes, which some performers fall into, are bad habits which make a disagreeable impression upon the audience, and detract from the interest felt in the artist and the performance. A performer who places a proper estimate upon the power of the eye, in attracting and enchaining an audience, will correct these faults. Such will also be attentive to gestures that they be modest and expressive" (ibid.). Cannon then took time to comment on what he described as "obsolete and antiquated pronunciation of words," before concluding his comments: "It is not in the spirit of captious criticism that we allude to these things. We fully recognize the difficulty that managers and performers have to contend with. They deserve credit for what they have accomplished. We desire to see them perfect in their professions, and the Theatre a school which old and young may attend with profit and delight" (ibid.).

As criticism of the stage and its performers, this editorial must rank as one of the gentlest ever written, especially in what became the continuing war between religion and the theater. Cannon's editorial reads like nothing so much as William Hazlitt's essay, "On Actors and Acting," first published in 1817. There is no way of knowing if Cannon had read Hazlitt, but there is certainly a correlation between Hazlitt's philosophy and that of the Mormon playgoer of the nineteenth century.

The wonderful gift of the transcontinental railroad had brought the first of its mixed blessings to Salt Lake City. In the following months the Salt Lake Theatre stage saw roughly 250 performances, which was more than the preceding seven seasons combined. And while the *Deseret Evening News* had glowed with anticipation of "first-class talent . . . from the East," it was talent from the West that captured the Mormon theater audience in the fall of 1869.

Having sought talent where it was available, the Salt Lake Theatre management had been in contact with Lawrence Barret throughout the early months of 1869. Barret, working in California, though not yet of the stature he was to enjoy in later years, was nonetheless a legitimate star. By June it was clear he would not be able to come to Salt Lake, but he had suggested a fellow actor, John Brougham. By July, business in Salt Lake was drying up and the theater management again requested Barret's attendance. He responded that he still could not come but now recommended a Neil Warner. Caine and Clawson contacted Warner and offered him, through someone named MacDougall, the following "contract":

> 2 weeks commencing September 10th. This time we most willingly place at the disposal of Mr. Warner if however, it would not interfere with any other arrangement, we would prefer putting his opening a week later say Sept. 17 as we think the weather would be much cooler, the nights longer and the busy season of Harvesting entirely through by that time, and consequently more beneficial to Mr. Warner as there would be a probability of larger houses. We submit this for your consideration, act as you deem best and advise us accordingly. We offer Mr. Warner the following terms. Share equally the gross receipts after $275 nightly for two weeks and ½ clear benefit on the eleventh night. The Internal Revenue tax of 2% to be deducted in all cases before division.
>
> These are better terms than we have given to any *Star*. Our sharing terms have usually been after 300 to first class stars— and after 400 for lesser lights. We are even willing to make a difference in terms to great artists, among which if we can believe the encomiums of the press which are abundantly backed up by Mr. Barret and other gentlemen who we cannot help but believe, we must without a doubt place Mr. Warner. . . . If Mr. Warner accepts terms please telegraph which date he will open upon. (Young, Letter-book, 69)

Thus were negotiations begun to bring the first internationally experienced actor to visit the Salt Lake Theatre since George Pauncefort played there in 1864.

Neil Warner, whose real name was William Burton Lockwood, was thirty-eight years old when he arrived in Salt Lake City. He had debuted in Brighton, England, seventeen years earlier and had been acting ever since. He had toured Australia, New York, and San Francisco, where he had been favorably received by press and public.

Prior to Warner's actual arrival, the *Deseret Evening News* had been puffing his engagement in Salt Lake with liberal quotes from the San Francisco reviews of his performances. On September 13, 1869, Warner opened in Salt Lake with Shakespeare's *Richard III*. The Salt Lake critics waxed ecstatic: "luminary of the first magnitude"; "far superior to any personation"; "acting was superb"; "To say he is a great artist scarcely speaks sufficiently strong"; "wonderful natural powers." After the initial performance he followed *Richard III* with *Richilieu* and concluded his first week with plays that were in the stock company's repertoire, *Ingomar the Barbarian, A New Way to Pay Old Debts,* and *Othello.* The critics lauded most of his performances, but noted that the visit had been anything but a financial success. In the second week Warner presented more of the roles in the company's repertoire, and then on September 25, 1869, he played *Hamlet.* If the critics had waxed ecstatic over his Richard, they went into orbit over his Hamlet. The major critics of the time were John Lyon of the *Deseret Evening News* and Edward Tullidge of the *Salt Lake Daily Telegraph.* Both Lyon and Tullidge now used terms like *genius* and *perfection.* Both noted that Warner finally had a nearly full house for a performance. On October 11, 1869, Warner was given a benefit in response to a public demand by the city's leading citizens. He reprised the role of Sir Giles Overreach in *A New Way to Pay Old Debts* and then left town, never to return.

Why was such an apparently good actor not better received, in terms of audience numbers? The low attendance can be attributed to three things: the changing nature of the actor and his art, the dated acting style of the local stock company, and the limited audience base. But it is particularly clear that the new acting styles and dramas were presenting a challenge to the Salt Lake theater actors and audiences. The Deseret Dramatic Association, which was largely self-trained, would find it increasingly difficult to adjust to the expectations of the advancing wave of actors and actresses. Indeed, with the arrival of the railroad the Deseret Dramatic Association would change forever. Slowly at first, but inexorably, all of the leading "lines of business" were being handled by hired professionals. While the local people were still being paid, and without doubt considered themselves professional, they had never acted anywhere else, and were strictly a homegrown product. Among the newcomers were Annie Lockhart, Annie Ward, Mrs. C. DeBar, W. T. Harris, and, in early 1870, Kate Denin and John Wilson, all professional, non-Mormon actors. As an example of the changing nature of the stock company itself a brief biography of Kate Denin should suffice.

Kate Denin had been born in Philadelphia in 1837. She began, as a juvenile actress, at the Chatham Street Theatre in Philadelphia. In the early 1850s she toured the country playing Romeo to her sister Susan's Juliet. She became a stock star with the Boston Museum Company in the early 1860s, toured Oregon with George B. Waldron in the 1870s, was a member of Charles Frohman's company in the 1880s, and was playing a character role in New York when she died in 1907. Her obituary in the *New York Times* noted that she had played in nearly every theater in America and Australia and had acted with Edwin Booth, Charles Keene, John McCullough, Edward A. Sothern, and others (February 6, 1907). Denin also had as many husbands as she had theatrical companies. She was married to C. K. Fox, whom, according to Franklin Graham, she deserted the day after the wedding; then she married a Sam Ryan, whom she apparently deserted when she eloped with a Mrs. Vincent's young husband, an actor whose stage name was John Wilson, from the Boston Museum Company (Graham, 178). This was certainly a significantly different life-style than the Salt Lake audiences were used to, polygamy notwithstanding.

Meanwhile, criticisms continued to mount over the performances, or lack of performances, of members of the stock company, including Phil Margetts, who, with others, was frequently taken to task for not knowing his lines or for what might best be described as endemic failures, such as occurred in a performance of *Rob Roy* on December 30, 1869:

> But we could hardly reconcile, as incidental to the piece, such sudden transitions of dialect, first speaking good English and at the next scene speaking broken Scotch, as several of the subordinates exhibited. We fully appreciate the difficulty which an actor has to battle against and the great amount of practice necessary to enable him to play a character in which the Scotch or other dialect is required to give that degree of force and naturalness to the part which the author intends to convey. If an actor is called upon to play a Scotch part and does not feel himself fully competent to do justice to the dialect, it would be infinitely better, instead of making futile attempts to pronounce Scotch, to say whatever he has to say in pure English, that one may be enabled to form some conception of the piece that is being played. (*Deseret Evening News,* December 31, 1869)

The first half of the 1869–1870 season began to draw to a close with benefits for the various members of the company, including farewell benefits for John S. Lindsay, who was leaving for greener pastures, and John T. Caine, who was resigning as manager of the

theater to go into business with Edward Sloan as associate publisher of a new newspaper, the *Salt Lake Herald*. Further evidence of
erosion of the local stock company surfaced in an incident involving Margetts and money, described in a February 28, 1870, letter
addressed to Margetts and jointly signed by Clawson and Caine:

Bro. Philip Margetts
Dear Sir:–
We have been rather astonished during the past week to hear
from more than one source that you were blustering and talking
around town about the time of the termination of your engagement with us asserting that you were engaged to the end of the
term of our lease of the Theatre, viz. March 1st, that you were entitled to a salary to that date that you calculated to make a demand
for it, etc. etc. . . . We have never refused to pay a just claim held
against us—if you can establish that we owe you another week's
salary (which we deny) we hope to be able to pay it. We think
it very unkind that any remarks of the character we have heard
should emanate from you. . . . We have always paid your salary
faithfully every week, according to agreement—not only so but
frequently have advanced pay to accommodate you. On your last
benefit but one, we gave you within a fraction of half the receipts
of the house. When we were only under obligation to give you a
third, and many other little favors which we never would have
named but for the seeming ingratitude of your talk about town.
. . . [A]nd what are our thanks? Misrepresentation and abuse.
    We do not wish to dwell further upon this matter it is too dis-
agreeable[. W]e have said this much to let you know that all
though we have been in Theatrical business several years, we still
have *feelings* and fully appreciate the kind treatment of our brethren. (Young, Letter-book, 83)

Shortly after this letter, on March 26, 1870, the *Mormon Tribune*
began publication with Tullidge as assistant editor. The *Mormon
Tribune*, which began life as the *Utah Magazine*, was the voice for
several disaffected Mormons, including Tullidge, in what became
known as the Godbeite movement, the first major schism in the
Mormon Church since its trek to Utah in 1847. Several Mormons—
William S. Godbe, Amasa Lyman, T. B. H. Stenhouse, and other
prominent businessmen—had begun clamoring as early as 1869 for
the Mormon Church to become active in mining and, especially, in

business with the so-called "Gentiles," or non-Mormons. Brigham Young, since the arrival in Utah Valley, had steadfastly refused to allow the Church and Church members to engage in mining, fearing that the pursuit of mineral riches would lead the faithful away from the building up of Zion. When Godbe and his associates refused to change their views or follow the dictates of the Church, they were excommunicated. They established their version of Mormonism, called the New Movement, which failed. But their publication of the *Tribune* was to become one of the strongest non-Mormon voices in the territory.

Meanwhile, the theatrical season bumped along with nothing new or compelling until May 3, 1870. On that date the famous, or perhaps notorious, Leo Hudson was in town. Hudson was an *equestrienne,* one of several such "actresses" who made their living recreating sensational dramas of the time that incorporated riding a live horse on the stage. Probably the most famous of this school of performers was Adah Isaacs Mencken.

One of the great attractions was Hudson's performance in *Mazeppa,* in which she appeared in flesh-colored tights, tied to the back of her horse, Black Bess. Since this was pointed out in the advance publicity, John Lyon went to particular pains to note that there would be nothing offensive about her performance.

> In the presentation of "Mazeppa" there will be nothing to offend the sensibilities of the most delicate and refined. The way this piece has been presented in some places, and the reputation of some who have attained notoriety in the personification of the chief character, may have led some to anticipate that an approach to the nude drama would be attempted in placing it upon the boards of the Salt Lake stage. But we are assured that there will not be the least approach to anything unchaste or indelicate. (*Deseret Evening News,* May 2, 1870)

While in Salt Lake City, Hudson played four nights, presenting three performances of Byron's *Mazzepa* (at least the concept of the play was his) and one performance of *Rookwood, or the Life and Adventures of Dick Turpin.* Lyon had little to say of her performances, except to describe them as "sensational trash."

Following Hudson's "horse operas," the Salt Lake stage offered occasional entertainment by the stock company, including benefit performances, such as one for Margetts "upon his retiring from the stage." (This was one of at least three announced benefits for Margetts's retirement from the stage. He always came back.)

Meanwhile, in these intermittent entertainments, Lyon wrote one of his most biting criticisms of the local stock company:

> On Saturday evening there was a moderately good house to witness the variety bill offered on the occasion. Of the style or character of the performance we can not say much that is commendatory. We have seen "Handy Andy" played better. . . . We think the credit of the Theatre will suffer by their continuance. The one on Saturday evening week—was intolerable [sic] boshy, but it was very much superior to that on Saturday evening. The wild beast scene was extremely ridiculous. Our Theatre has gained an enviable reputation for the high class of its performances, and at this late date, it is too bad to introduce such trashy affairs.
>
> (*Deseret Evening News*, June 17, 1870)

The 1869–1870 season came to a close in early August 1870 with two performances by the Duprez and Benedict Minstrels before what Lyon described as the largest audiences he had seen in some time.

This first "railroad" season had meant a great deal to Salt Lake City. First, and most obviously, the audiences had been given an opportunity to see stars and troupes still fresh from triumphs around the country. The theater was able to present new stars to its audience and at the same time exposed the Mormon culture to the contemporary mores and fashions of the rest of the nation—mores and fashions that clashed with the Mormons' more conservative views. But it was becoming clear that Salt Lake City and its standards were at variance with the contemporary drama.

The theatrical season of 1870–1871 brought more changes to the normal routine of the Salt Lake Theatre. For one, there were no visiting professional actors or actresses starring on the stage until mid-December; for another, the theatrical season ran virtually continuously from mid-September until late July. It was a period of turmoil for the theater management and one of a briefly arrested decline for the local stock company.

The season began with *The Hugonot*, followed four days later by *William Tell*, starring the aging Thomas A. Lyne. Four days after that Lyne starred in *Damon and Pythias*. Those three plays marked the beginning, zenith, and end of the management team of Margetts and Bowring. Their plays had failed to please the critics, but more important, they had failed to draw audiences. Their brief fling at management seems, in retrospect, to be an effort to recapture a past no longer of interest to the present.

In a brief note of September 7, 1870, Clawson acknowledged receipt of a note from Margetts and Bowring and in reply accepted their release from managing the theater. On this same day, Sloan, writing in the *Salt Lake Herald,* shed a little more light on the problems of the two managers:

> We regret to learn that Messrs. Margetts & Bowring, the new lessees of the Theatre, have been forced through lack of patronage, to bring the fall season to a premature close. The scarcity of money in the community, and the lack of available attractions have doubtless contributed much in bringing about this result. . . . As it is we are left entirely without amusements, though we may have one of the finest theatre buildings in the country. We have heard it hinted also that members of the company and other employees were rather exacting in the salaries they demanded and required a kind of pay which their services would not draw into the house. We deplore this, as it manifest a spirit of selfishness anything but commendable. But such is human nature all the world over.

If the latter was true, it is somewhat ironic that Margetts, who had been a leader in the battle with Brigham Young to establish wages for the actors in the stock company in 1867, should himself be a victim of salary demands three years later.

The theater resumed the season again on September 21, 1870, with Sloan noting that he was not sure who was in charge but that John C. Graham was apparently responsible for getting the troupe together to form a season. (*Salt Lake Herald,* September 7, 1870.)

The struggling season continued with the stock company playing dramas out of their available repertoire and even introducing some new plays, but always to slim houses. Finally, on December 14, 1870, the Jack Langrishe Troupe, operating out of Denver, arrived to play the Salt Lake Theatre, or break the monotony, as John S. Lindsay described it (93). But even so, when the troupe concluded its visit on December 21, 1870, it was to a comparatively empty house, which may explain why the troupe never returned to Salt

Lake. Over the next months five other actors and actresses arrived to play before the Mormons, including Charles W. Couldock and his daughter Eliza, who would return in May 1871.

But when traveling stars came to visit, they continued to bring what can best be described as ill-chosen or deliberately provocative dramas. Milton Nobles came to the Salt Lake Theatre in January 1871 to present *Wine Works Wonders* to the teetotaling Mormon audience. The *Salt Lake Herald* commented, "Mr. Milton Nobles was not happy in his selection of 'Wine Works Wonders' for his first appearance. The piece is too lugubrious for a successful comedy and too light for a heavy drama, and hasn't 'blood and thunder' enough for a melodrama; while its morality is execrable" (January 18, 1871). Following Nobles's visit, the stock company resumed playing, sporadically, through early March. In that month visits were made by such stars as Rose Evans, who played the title role in *Hamlet,* and a Marietta Ravel, whose theatrical talent was limited to tight-rope walking. (Nevertheless, the critics noted with some discomfort that Ravel played to nearly full houses in each of her eighteen performances.) But the most interesting was the visit of Arthur McKee Rankin and his wife, Kitty Blanchard, and the play they *didn't* perform.

> "Oliver Twist" was in our repertoire, [Rankin said,] but [Brigham Young] insisted on cutting it out. We were quite anxious to play it. I had an interview with him and he said that a play where there was a realistic scene of a brute killing his mistress, and in a most brutal way, was dangerous for prospective mothers to witness. I could not controvert such an argument and we did not produce the play.
>
> He was very gracious and courteous about the whole affair and did everything to make our stay pleasant. (*Deseret Evening News,* July 26, 1913)

Rankin's comments in this article, which appeared the year before his death, also included observations on the Salt Lake Theatre:

> We were very agreeably surprised at what we found in the theater. . . . And what a wonderful company it was! Our pieces were beautifully put on. Beyond question the theater was one of the best constructed in the United States.
>
> The "props" belonging to the theater were the most complete

that one could imagine. These with the wardrobe and library were estimated to be worth nearly a million dollars.

The stage manager [W. T. Harris] was a man of wonderful resources and I was struck particularly with his handling of the light effects. Each act was perfect in that respect and what was more remarkable, he had no gas to modulate the effects with, as the entire house was lighted front and rear with coal oil. (Ibid.)

The season was now half completed, and houses were barely making expenses for the actors and actresses. And if the performers at times were not interesting, the audience certainly was. During April, Sloan took the Salt Lake audience to task for eating peanuts during performances, as well as for bringing babes in arms to the plays. These kinds of distractions were a continuing problem. Through the years, editorials appeared against squeaking boots, drinking, and love-making as well. The highlight of the theatrical season was the visit of John McCullough, Edwin Adams, and Helen Tracy in July 1871. They brought nothing new in the way of plays, but their performances in the classics, especially Shakespeare, were very well received. As John S. Lindsay said, "The wise thing for the managers to have done would have been to close the season with that extraordinary engagement" (104). But the stock company performed until July 24, 1871, when the season officially closed.

The season of 1870–1871 may be said to end a chapter in Mormon history. It was the last year in which the Church would enjoy relative peace from its enemies, for in October 1871, Brigham Young himself would be indicted on charges of "lewd cohabitation," the first overt attempt by the federal government against the Church's practice of polygamy. It had been a time of great turmoil in the theater company itself. During the season, nearly sixty different actors and actresses, excluding visiting stars and troupes, appeared in speaking parts. By season's end, more members of the local stock company had departed, including Lindsay and Margetts. Because of a paucity of records, it is extremely difficult to assess a specific cause to the turnover in personnel, but undoubtedly money, or the lack of it, was at the base. But perhaps the most destructive element in the erosion of the local stock company in the long run was a lack of any apparent development or training for those aspiring to the theater. And since money was not an incentive, and as the theater had no other but a local outlet, it became an erosion by attrition.

This erosion meant that other professionals, at higher salaries, must be hired, thus contributing to the financial problems and locking the theater in a downward money spiral it would fight for several years. At the same time, other incidents would pile upon each other until by the mid-1880s the Mormons would be virtually disenfranchised as American citizens.

The 1871–1872 season would be marked more by what happened off-stage than on. Tullidge, who had been quiescent for some time, came to life late in the season and became a vociferous, almost strident critic of what he alleged to be immoral, illegal, and unethical practices of the Church's administration of the theater. It is apparent that anti-Mormon forces had begun to focus on the theater as a battlefield. Controlled by the Mormon Church, it seems to have become a symbolic rallying point.

In October 1866, D. J. King Robinson had been shot to death after being summoned from his home late at night, ostensibly to treat someone with a broken arm. A motive for the murder of Robinson—a non-Mormon—was proposed by some as an indication of a Mormon policy of extermination. To others it was a case of accidental homicide by parties unknown who had intended only to "rough up" Robinson for his part in land speculation and alleged claim jumping. Regardless of the motive, no one was ever convicted of the murder and the crime remains unsolved.

However, in December 1871, several city police officers and several leading Mormons, including Brigham Young, were arrested on murder charges, specifically for the Robinson murder case. The theater became part of the trial when Caine and Graham, theater managers, were called by the defense to refute key testimony of the leading prosecution witness who said he had witnessed the crime while his way home from a performance at the theater. Caine, referring to the bound volumes of playbills that the theater had stored, showed that there had been no performance at the theater on the night of October 22, 1866. Later, the chief prosecution witness admitted committing perjury and the murder charges were dropped. But Brigham Young continued on trial in what was the first of many such attempts to circumscribe the Mormon religious practice of polygamy.

Early in 1872, another publication began under the aegis of Graham. *Footlights* was devoted primarily to theater and other entertainments. Graham used the paper as a voice for the theater against

Tullidge, who continued to call for another theater, free from the constraints of the Mormon Church. A theatrical benefit for Lyne prompted another skirmish in the continuing battle. The benefit appears to have come about because of a letter of March 4, 1872, that was published the following day in the *Salt Lake Tribune:* "Learning that you (Lyne) intend to change your vocation [we] would be pleased to show our appreciation of your talents as an actor by attending a dramatic entertainment for your benefit. We should have been pleased to enjoy one of your specialities at the theatre, but as the public are well aware that the Salt Lake Theatre has long been closed to you, we would suggest a night of dramatic readings at the Liberal Institute" (March 5, 1872). It is no accident that names like Raybould, Walker, and Lindsay were signatories to the letter, all of them in one way or another associated with the Godbeite movement. The writer of the letter, probably Tullidge, makes the first of many allusions about the theater being closed to Lyne; however, the facts do not bear him out. Lyne continued to play at the theater from time to time, but he would always trot out the same ancient series of plays. Tullidge had tied his new theater movement to what was essentially a dead horse.

When the benefit was held, Tullidge followed with another shot: "We hope it may be repeated. Lyne and Lindsay are favorites of the Salt Lake public, and we should like to hear them oftener. These gentlemen having been ostracised from the Church Theatre in consequence of their heterodox views, we think that if a cosmopolitan theatre were opened in which they could have a fine opportunity, it would be liberally patronized" (*Salt Lake Tribune*, March 12, 1872).

Within a year, Tullidge would have his wish with not one but two additional theaters competing for the Salt Lake audience. Meanwhile, Tullidge continued to rail about the inadequacies of the theater: "The Theatre, especially, needs better lighting, one half the effect of all plays produced being lost through its present dingy appearance occasioned by lack of light. The introduction of . . . Gas would greatly enhance the pleasure of all attending the Theatre" (*Salt Lake Tribune*, May 15, 1872). But Tullidge saved his largest blast for the following week:

> One of the very best possible methods of breaking the "one-man power" and reducing the power of the priesthood to a minimum is to break down all the church monopolies. . . . Who caters to

theatrical taste? Brigham, and it is he who decides the character of the plays the Salt Lake public shall witness at the Theatre, and what not. Now we assert that his condition of things is the acme of centralization of power, and our list of monopolies is scarcely commenced. What we want in all the enterprises is *competition* and, in the matter of a theatre, we think there is a fine chance for a successful competition. . . . Gentile money is as acceptable at the Box-office as any other. The non-Mormon population is increasing here so rapidly that a new theatre is demanded. (*Salt Lake Tribune*, May 22, 1872)

If Tullidge anticipated a response, he got it the next day, not from the *Deseret Evening News* or even the *Herald*, but rather from Graham and *Footlights*. Graham defended the theater as a source of pride and pleasure to the Salt Lake audience, regardless of religion. He then took Tullidge to task for asserting that some actors had been banished from the Salt Lake stage:

We have a strong desire to learn from the writer of the article referred to, who the "best actors" are that have been "banished" from the boards of this Church Theatre for disagreeing with the principles of the Gospel. We claim to be pretty well informed in regard to the history of the drama in this city, and we can answer without fear of successful contradiction, *not one*. . . . Let the Methodists build a Theatre and perhaps the Episcopalians may call it monopoly. Let the Episcopalians build one and the Catholics may call it monopoly. Let either build one and the "NEW MOVE" may call it cosmopolitan; but let the Mormons build a Theatre or anything else, then and only then, is it monopoly. (*Footlights*, May 23, 1872)

Both Graham and Tullidge fired a few more rounds in this skirmish, theoretically about theater.

Perhaps one reads more into the events of the spring and summer season than can be adequately supported by the facts, but there are some interesting points: Tullidge's allusions to continuing problems of management in almost all of his writings; and the alleged banishment of John S. Lindsay and his strange reappearance in the final production of the season, not to mention his own silence on the matter in his autobiography. What is very clear is that the events of the time had intruded into the theater itself, and it, too, had become a warring ground between Mormon and non-Mormon.

The penultimate season discussed here began August 7, 1872, and ran until July 30, 1873. It was a normal season in that it was divided, once again, into the traditional fall and winter, spring and summer seasons. It was a theatrical season of almost unparalleled activity as more than 230 performances were given, the majority (200) in the fall and winter alone. Gas lighting was introduced to the Salt Lake stage; the local stock company continued its erosion and change; productions of four different homegrown playwrights were offered; and the theater was sold to a trust group headed by Clawson and Caine.

George Reynolds, one of the theater managers, noted in February 1873 that the theater finally had some competition.

> Since I last wrote to you I regret to say we have been doing but poor business. There have been numerous, I might say almost unprecedented, reasons for this. The principal of which are the bad weather and the horse disease. The first prevented our patrons, especially the ladies, from walking to the Theatre, the second put an entire stop to their riding. . . . There is still another reason: a Melodeon or Music Hall has been opened on Main St. where I am told brazen women dance lewd dances. This hall is well attended. (Young, Letter-book, February 5, 1873)

The melodeon or music hall was the Bowery, a dance hall cum saloon operated by a Mr. Dudler. There is no indication of when it opened; the letter is the first mention of its existence. Tullidge, who chronicled its brief career in the pages of the *Tribune*, visited it for the first time in March and wrote: "We made a visit to this place of amusement last evening. A splendid bill was prepared to honor St. Patrick's Day. The audience was sufficiently large to be quite satisfactory to the energetic management. We were gratified to see so marked an improvement in the character, acting and singing of the various artists" (March 18, 1873). The only performers Tullidge identifies with the Bowery were a Carrie Chapman, a "flat-foot stepper," and a Mr. McCarthy. The Bowery's life was short. The *Salt Lake Tribune* reported on March 31, 1873, that it was to close April 1 because the owner wished to convert it into a saloon.

Prior to the short life of the Bowery, there had appeared the Salt Lake Theater Comique, which would be located upstairs at the

Brewer & Bemis Saloon (also known as the Omaha Saloon). The only performance was mentioned on February 18, 1873, and included McCarthy and Chapman, who would continue their careers briefly at the Bowery. These were the only attempts at competition with the Salt Lake Theatre in the period of this study.

The theatrical year of 1873–1874 began with high hope and ended in financial failure. The season included the visit of one of the great actor-playwrights of the nineteenth century, Dion Bouccicault, and the dissolution of the Deseret Dramatic Association. The final week of the 1874 spring season consisted of a weeklong series of benefits in which a visiting combination or company of actors and actresses agreed to perform for a week, without pay, so that the theater might recoup its financial losses.

The five-year period of this study, although turbulent, was like a calm summer day compared to the years ahead for the Territory of Utah and its Mormon founders. The advent of the railroad had proved a bittersweet experience. It had brought hundreds of actors and actresses from around the world to introduce themselves and their art to the Saints. The clash of cultures produced both good and bad for Mormons and non-Mormons. It certainly elevated the taste in both drama and style of the audience while challenging some fundamental beliefs the audience retained in and about itself. It introduced the Salt Lake audiences to the concept of the "combination," or traveling theatrical, troupe that eventually contributed to the demise of the local stock company all across the nation. The Deseret Dramatic Association would disband in 1875.

The railroad had impact on other aspects of the Utah Territory economy as well. What had once been a primarily agricultural community with local industries, possible because they had no competition, now virtually disappeared. The railroad effectively ended such local industries as cotton and silk manufacturing. In addition, when the first wagonload of silver arrived at the railroad, it became abundantly clear that mining would soon be a major industry in the state. The railroad, as noted historian Leonard J. Arrington observes, "marked the territory's entry into the mainstream of American economic life." (Arrington, p. 175). The railroad also brought immigrants in an ever greater flow, both Mormon and non-Mormon, including several religions that thought it was time to send missionaries to the Mormons.

But the real challenge came from the political front, where bill after bill was introduced into Congress aimed specifically at the Mormon practice of polygamy. The railroad brought political visitors by the score, including Vice President Colfax and U.S. Senate Chaplain Dr. J. P. Freeman in 1869, who became active in the national battle against the Mormons.

Prior to the railroad's arrival, George Q. Cannon had told the Saints, "We are told—openly and without disguise, that when the railroad is completed there will be such a flood of so called 'civilization' brought in here that every vestige of us, our church and institutions, shall be completely obliterated."

Perhaps Brigham Young had the best long-term view of the situation: Mormonism "must indeed be a ——— poor religion, if it cannot stand one railroad" (Arrington, 174).

REFERENCES

Books

Arrington, Leonard J., and Davis Bitton. *The Mormon Experience: A History of the Latter-day Saints.* New York: Vintage Books, 1979.

Gates, Susan Young, and Leah D. Widtsoe. *The Life Story of Brigham Young.* New York: MacMillan Company, 1931.

Graham, Franklin. *Historic Montreal.* 2d ed. Montreal: John Lovell and Son, 1902.

Lindsay, John S. *The Mormons and the Theatre.* Salt Lake City, Utah: Century Printing, 1905.

Moody, Ralph. *Stagecoach West.* New York: Thomas Y. Crowell, 1967.

Pyper, George D. *The Romance of an Old Playhouse.* Salt Lake City, Utah: Seagull Press, 1928.

Root, Frank A., and Wiliam Elsey Connelley. *The Overland Stage to California.* Columbus, Ohio: Long's College Book Company, 1950.

Spencer, Clarissa Young. *Brigham Young at Home.* Salt Lake City, Utah: Deseret News Press, 1990.

Tullidge, Edward W. *History of Salt Lake City.* Salt Lake City, Utah: Star Printing Co., 1886.

Widtsoe, John A. *Discourses of Brigham Young.* Salt Lake City, Utah: Deseret Book, 1977.

Newspapers

Deseret Evening News, 1865–74.

Footlights, 1871–73.

New York Times, 1865–1874.

Salt Lake Herald, 1870–74.

Salt Lake Tribune, 1870–74.

Unpublished Material

Salt Lake Theatre Collection. Latter-day Saints Church Archives, Salt Lake City.

Young, Brigham. Letter-books, 1868–1875. Latter-day Saints Church Archives, Salt Lake City.

On the Demolition of the Virginia & Truckee Engine Shops

"The paths of glory lead but to the grave."
—Thomas Gray *Elegy Written in a Country Churchyard*

It's the land you won that now betrays you,
the dirt beneath your brown tracks valued
more for apartments than pigeon roosts
and hollow-shelled historical derelicts.

Proud structure, magnificent largesse,
the faces of each sandstone block hewed
into walls of character, wet with summer
sweat, sealed against the winter wind.

Decorated in herringbone patterns of pine
the giant bay doors slump, strain to fall in
on themselves, empty windows blind to decay,
the glass shattered from their frames long ago.

Developers cast lots, number the wooden bones
and round shouldered arcs of yellow stone
from the prison quarry. Arthritic joints open,
lay exposed by the failure of rotted mortar.

Masons fitted the rock tight, the arches
barely sag. Silent walls stand stoic,
upright, charcoaled by the soot-breath
of engines, by a fire the black night

transients got too cold and flame
too hot for the dry truss timbers.
A natural skylight opened into the shops.
Days later, corrugated tin sheets

on the roof blow off in a gale like
cinnamon shreds of juniper bark.
Your ghosts sing in the wind, rusty
metal bangs like hammers, screeches

like a steel winch that extracted corroded
boilers, tipped out the red water as blood
from the neck of a slain animal hung
in chains. Ghosts—the slow whistle

of the Washoe Zephyr through vacant
window sills and locked doors shrunk
on their hinges. Ghosts—chuffing gusts
rumble from throats of fallen smoke vents.

There's no longer room for things old,
no pride in buildings that stand past
their purpose, past inevitable obsolescence.
Who remembers the craft after the stones

disassemble? Who eyes the earth roadbeds
sleeping toward Virginia City? Old builders
give way to developers whose children are already
born and placing one glorious block atop another.

The Spirit of Progressivism in Puccini's
Girl of the Golden West

Within the fading memories of the closing frontier, Puccini's *Girl of the Golden West* premiered in 1910. It became the New York Metropolitan Opera's popular opera until World War I, because responsive audience approval and the public's deeper appreciation outweighed many music critics. Contrary to published criticisms, the opera not only offered a veristic portrayal of a mining community but also reflected the reform movements of the early twentieth century. The opera addressed the contemporary issues of xenophobia and loyalty, lynch law and vigilantism, literacy, the status of women, gambling, and prohibition within the context of the early gold rush of 1848–1849.

Its story derived from the experiences of popular playwright David Belasco, whose script provided Puccini with the plot outline of *The Girl of the Golden West*. Although critical opinion classified Belasco's account as romanticized fiction, his story complements the honest perceptions of philosopher and historian Josiah Royce, whose 1886 publication *California* covered the early statehood days. Royce and Belasco are not contrasting products of California's gold rush, as some historians have believed (Clendenning, 36). These two sons of pioneers had much in common, from personal experiences to a conscientious approach to presenting a truthful depiction of the tumultuous days in the Sierra Nevada mining camps.

The opera's plot takes place during the interregnum when Mexican territory became the new state of California. It may be helpful to understand how Belasco and Royce perceived the event, since they were growing up there at the time. Although Royce did not collaborate on the opera, the plot and its actions give voice to his similar insights. To appreciate the significant connections of Belasco's play and their striking parallels with Royce's interpretations, I want to offer background to establish their philosophically linked perspectives.

Growing up in the West

Both Royce and Belasco lived in San Francisco and attended Lincoln Grammar School. Belasco, the son of a British-born Portuguese father and a mother from the Azores, was born in 1853 in San Francisco; Royce grew up in San Francisco, but was born in California's active mining community, Grass Valley, in 1855. Belasco enjoyed San Francisco's gambling houses, opium dens, hospitals, morgues and saloons during his Bohemian youth (Winter 1:3). For a few years the Belascos lived in a mining community in the Caribou Mountains during British Columbia's gold rush. His father, Humphrey Abraham, dealt in merchandise, trading tobacco and fur with miners, hunters, and Indians (Winter 1:20).

When the Belasco family returned from Canada they moved within a block or two of Josiah Royce's home, south of the Market district, known today as the inner Mission (Langley, 91; Winter 1:11–12). Belasco's father became a licensed fruit merchant; Royce's father was a fruit vendor (Langley). The two families—with fathers in the produce business and living within a few blocks of each other—sent their sons to the newly dedicated Lincoln Grammar School in 1866.

Youth and Education

Biographers agree that Royce enjoyed a precocious childhood and advanced rapidly in school (Winter 1:33). Royce's precocity and Belasco's intellectual maturity probably left them both as school outsiders (Winter 1:33; Hine, *Royce*, 53–54). Lincoln, a militarily regimented academy, enrolled 906 boys in sixteen classes. "Each class [was] in two divisions according to the proficiency of the pupils" ("A Day at Lincoln School in 1866," 2). Both boys were small in stature, and the introverted Royce seemed to lack social skills. The boys found great satisfaction in elocution, declamation, and Shakespearean recitation (Winter 1:1; Hine, *Royce*, 53–54).

Some evidence points to their attendance at events and activities; however, no irrefutable proof exists that they even knew each other at school. They shared facilities, their fathers were in the same business, and they lived near each other; nonetheless, the question remains as to what degree daily attendance at school, common interests, physical proximity, and diminished stature might have brought them together.

Belasco's theatrical genius as an actor, playwright, director, and producer of plays and operatic productions and Royce's passion for Greek tragedy, oratory, and debate also could have tied them together at Lincoln. Lincoln's forensic clubs introduced them to the issues of their day. A debate in 1869 was titled "Was the Mexican War justified or not?" The debaters impressed one young girl visiting the school. In her diary, Fannie Cheney described the flamboyance of "one boy who declaimed [who] would make a far famed actor I think" (Cheney, 67–69). Regardless of whether Belasco or Royce were debaters on that day, the repercussions of the Mexican War dominate Royce's writings and Belasco's story.

Another subject deeply etched upon the minds of Royce and Belasco was anarchism. The assassinations of Presidents Lincoln in 1865, Garfield in 1881, and McKinley in 1901 may have linked memories of political turmoil and general lawlessness. Their grammar school was dedicated to the recently slain Lincoln, and their student newspaper published an essay on vigilantism and assassination in its June 1869 issue. The article, with the byline "J.R.," is titled "Is the Assassination of Tyrants ever Justifiable?" This essay equated the senseless assassination of a president with lynchings in early mining communities. Both create anarchy and "encourage violence and disregard of human life, and greatly deteriorate the moral sentiment of the people. Assassination is a cowardly act which none but a coward will attempt. The history of mankind has shown that the assassination of the ruler of a nation never does that nation any good" (*Lincoln Observer*, 1). Citing the most famous assassinations in ancient history, the writer invoked the Bible, emphatically stating that no justification ever exists for blood revenge.

Regardless of whether or not Royce wrote the essay, he learned to fuse some of his mother's strict moral instruction into his rhetorical skills. In spite of Sarah Royce's vocal opposition to various forms of entertainment and the theater, Royce regularly wrote reviews of performances while attending the university at Berkeley, where he enrolled in 1870 at the age of fifteen, having graduated Lincoln one year before Belasco. Royce's undergraduate thesis on Greek tragedy, specifically, Aeschylus' concept of justice in the Orestian trilogy, dominated his writings (Hine, *Royce*, 56). Meanwhile, Belasco earned a living as an actor, arriving in Virginia City in 1874, where he became a member of the stock company at Piper's Opera House under Tom Maguire's direction. On the Comstock, he gathered more experiences and stories, "manage[ing] a saloon, a theatre and a gambling house" while also acting in numerous productions (Belasco, *Gala Days*, vii). Royce's father also provided his son with tales of the Comstock, where he ran a livery stable between 1862 and 1865 (Hine, *Royce*, 47).

Both young men moved back East in 1882, Belasco to New York City and Royce to Harvard University (Winter 1:263; Kuklik, 8). They both attended the Chicago Columbian Exposition in 1893, where Belasco's play *The Girl I Left Behind Me* ran throughout the fair and Royce delivered a paper to the American Historical Association (where Frederick Jackson Turner presented his famous thesis on the closing of the frontier). Royce and Belasco may have been too involved with their separate, active professional lives to have had a chance to know each other, but their ideas of progressivism can be seen illustrated in Puccini's opera.

Girl of the Golden West

The heroine of the story is Minnie Falconer Smith, daughter of a businessman in Monterey, the old Mexican capital. She owns the Polka Saloon in Cloudy Mountain, a mining community somewhere in the foothills of the Sierra Nevada. Jack Rance, the sheriff, wants to marry Minnie, and so does half the mining community. A stranger, Dick Johnson, alias Ramerrez, a notorious bandit, comes into town, only to recognize Minnie, whom he had met in Monterey. A posse and a Wells Fargo agent believe that Johnson may be Ramerrez, a highwayman accused of killing a mail carrier.

Condemned by the critics as too romantic, *The Girl of the Golden West* enjoyed a successful debut in the eyes of popular opinion. One reporter even remarked that "women split their gloves applauding"

Piper's Opera House playbill, circa 1880s.

Critics Find Little American Color In Puccini's Opera, "The Girl of the Golden West."

There seem to be few who heard "La Fanciulla del West" who think that Mr. Puccini succeeded in injecting into it any "American local color." He did succeed in getting into "Madama Butterfly" what at least impresses the Occidental as Japanese local color, and in doing it, by the use of Japanese melodies and Japanese instruments, not only skillfully, but also artistically. It may be true, as we have been told, that the Japan of " Madama Butterfly" is a wholly imaginary country, as unreal as the Japan of Gilbert and Sullivan's " Mikado"; but the music at least gives an impression and envelops the stage with an atmosphere. Such an impression and such an atmosphere are lacking in "La Fanciulla del West."

In truth, the elements out of which Mr. Puccini has endeavored to make an opera from Mr. Belasco's drama have failed him in his specifically musical task, the more characteristic they were of Mr. Belasco's own work. The two most important scenes of the spoken drama, the ones that most deeply impressed the spectators of it, and that really made its success, are the two tensely thrilling scenes of the discovery of the hidden bandit, by the dropping of his blood upon the Sheriff's linen, standing beneath him in Minnie's cabin; and the poker game played for the stake of his life in the same cabin. Of these the first is almost ineffective in the opera and goes for little. The thrill of the original melodrama is lost. This is partly because of the lack of the contact between audience and players in the Metropolitan Opera House, that prohibits the concentration of effect gained at the theatre where the play was produced. But it is due even more to the inability of music to deal with such a purely realistic and quickly progressing scene, which addresses itself to the eye and the intelligence of the listeners, and not to their emotions, their sentiments. The whole point of the situation is blunted, rather than sharpened, by the music with which it is invested. Its swiftness is retarded, its concentration is diffused.

The other scene is longer and more psychological, and might lend itself somewhat better, for this very reason, to musical illustration. But here Mr. Puccini confessed his embarrassment at "setting a game of poker to music," even such an unusual game. He gave up trying to find a really musical interpretation or illustration of the situation and resorted to a frankly illustrative or pictorial method. Had he heard "Salome," and did he remember Strauss's extraordinary vivid device to indicate Salome's impatience and suspense as she peers into the cistern where the executioner is fulfilling his task? Puccini, too, chose the double basses to suggest the breathless suspense of the players as they contest for the stake of a man's life—but there is a world of difference in the result. Mr. Puccini's attempt is distinctly unsuccessful and ineffectual. The measure of its unsuccess may be found in the whispered question of one of the audience at the first performance:

"What's that noise?"

The anxious inquirer was informed, and thereupon responded with a sigh of relief:

"Oh, I though it was a steam pipe snapping somewhere behind the stage!"

RICHARD ALDRICH

Excerpt from *New York Times* review of Puccini's opera, December 8, 1910.

(*New York Times,* December 11, 1910). Fifty-two curtain calls did not balance with the highly critical reviews. The front page headlines of the *New York Times* on December 11, 1910, featured the exploits of Pancho Villa and his revolutionaries, who had captured the imagination of Americans, and the review of opening night of Puccini's opera. Villa's Mexican revolution was presumably playing in the minds of the audience as they watched Enrico Caruso create the dual role of Ramerrez and Dick Johnson.

The opera was as veristic as Puccini's other operas—even more so. Belasco as well as Puccini insisted on factual information for the mining community. Although Puccini never visited the West, he captured a view of it through the eyes of Carlo (Charlie) Zangarini, Guelfo Civinini, and Belasco. Puccini had used Belasco's version of another story, Madam Butterfly, and had seen his play *Girl of the Golden West* in 1905 in London. He sought out Colorado-born librettist Zangarini, whose mother taught English there and had sent a book of Indian songs to Puccini (Seligman, 140). Zangarini's collaborator, Civinini, had just attended a famous congress of women in Rome on behalf of an Italian newspaper (Adami, 178). Puccini derived his true-to-life characters and scene from these well-informed contributors. Nevertheless, critics called his portrayals defective and centered their accusations on a disingenuous impression of Western history. One critic discounted the opera as "a long way from any real impression of the time, the place, the characters of this uncivilized American life" (December 18, 1910). Another declared that the various activities in the saloon and gambling scenes possessed "no photographic resemblance to the realities of that far-off time and place" (*New York Times,* December 19, 1910).

Defending his story and characters as "truer than many of the incidents in Bret Harte," Belasco insisted on verisimilitude (Winter 2:205). His story was based on an event that his father had witnessed. The colorful characters were not caricatures of the old West. During the first years of the gold rush, mining communities exhibited international character with "Sydney Ducks" from Australia, Cornish miners, Irish, and French Argonauts. California-born miners of Hispanic ancestry and Mexicans had dominated in the southern mining towns like Sonora (Paul, 26).

Key Intellectual and Political Issues

In Cloudy Mountain, an ethnically mixed community, Minnie displays racial tolerance, unlike the Anglo-Saxon miners; she treats all the miners alike in spite of their problems or any lackings. "Sonora" is from Sonora, northern Mexico; "Trin" (Trinidad Joe) probably gained his nickname from an area formerly in the New Mexico territory; Sid, from Sydney, Australia, is "a ready-made convict from Britain's Australian penal colony" who lies and cheats at cards (ibid., 202). Born "across the ocean," Larkens, a Welshman, and Sheriff Jack Rance are suspicious of outsiders. Happy and Handsome Charlie may be American citizens and label all Mexicans "greasers," not to be trusted.

Many immigrants treated bilingual Mexicans with racial intolerance and considered them inferior. Royce had used a facetious voice as he candidly reported on the stigma and anti-Mexican bias, saying that "a Spanish American in the mines in the early days" and the "native Californian, a born 'greaser' [were] worse off because we hated his whole degenerate, thieving, landowning, lazy discontented race. Some of them were now even bandits; most of them by this time were, with our help, more or less drunkards; and it was not our fault if they were not all rascals, so they deserved no better" (Royce, *California,* 286–87). Johnson/Ramerrez was a victim of that sort of thinking.

On the other hand, Minnie expresses her love for all strangers, exhibiting no xenophobia, and sings of a means of redemption through the highest teacher—love (Puccini, 113). She sings of pure love while aggressively handling the mining crowd's feelings of alienation and loneliness. They are all guests and strangers in a foreign land. Royce documented the "many foreigners rendered desperate and turned into dangerous rascals" (Royce, 284). "Californios," non-Indians of Hispanic descent, were worse off because they could not make a decent living in areas where they and their families had been born (Peterson, 15).

The ceding of Mexican territory, the annexation and seizure of estates of Mexicans in California, meant that many Californios suffered more discrimination. The new immigrants to the area debated and seriously doubted the Californios' allegiance to a new country. Such doubts led to suspicions about the criminal nature and outlaw tendencies of the former Mexicans. Without respect for their property or lives, miners expelled and punished Mexicans with extra taxes. Those who could not afford or refused to pay entered a life of crime to support their families. Whether he became a bandit by necessity or choice, Puccini's Ramerrez, masquerading as Dick Johnson, is not welcome in Cloudy Mountain.

When Johnson/Ramerrez arrives, the sheriff knows instantly that he is a stranger because he orders "whiskey and water—a sure sign he does not belong here." After he warns Johnson that "we don't allow strangers in camp," Minnie vouches for him (Puccini, 39–41). Her voice outweighs even the sheriff's. The community of miners accepts Johnson/Ramerrez because of Minnie's reputation, trusting her judgment over any suspicions the sheriff may harbor against outsiders. The ironic twist is that everyone in the camp is an outsider—except Ramerrez and Minnie.

In the opening act, the miners sing of their odyssey to the West. In search of a Golden Fleece, miners thought of themselves as voyaging, rootless Argonauts. One of their songs at the saloon's card tables obliquely refers to another Trojan story, that of Odysseus and his faithful dog. The miners wonder whether or not their spouses will recognize them or be as faithful as Penelope at the loom (Puccini, 17). Separation from families and familiar traditions force these miners either to adapt to their changing circumstances or to abandon their rugged life-style.

Several of the miners have learned to improve themselves at Minnie's "academy" in the woods. Although she has had only $30 worth of education, Minnie sings of how she loved to read the classics; her appreciation for literacy transformed the camp. "Trin," "Happy," and "Handsome" are literate and are able to read letters from home; "Harry" reads month-old international newspapers. Minnie has taught them not only to read but to write as well (Puccini, 31). It is interesting to note that Congress had passed a literacy requirement for all foreign immigrants; however, President Taft vetoed the law in 1913 (DeSantis, 198).

In Belasco's original script (1905), Minnie recited Dante's canto of Paolo and Francesca to teach the miners how to read (Belasco, 45). However, in the opera she regularly reads and teaches from the Bible, particularly Psalm 51 (Carner, 403). It is impossible to know why the librettists made this change. Perhaps Civinini was influenced by sentiment at the international women's congress he covered in Rome in 1908. In 1904, the General Federation of

Woman's Clubs, headed by Sarah Platt Decker, had announced its repudiation of Dante as irrelevant to the needs of the twentieth-century woman: "Dante is dead. He has been dead for centuries and I think it is time we dropped the study of the Inferno and turned the attention to our own" (Hymowitz, 221).

The status of women was changing. By 1910 several western states had already given women the right to vote. Minnie exercises her voice on any number of matters and does what pleases her. She employs and befriends two Indians and treats them like anyone else. She is not a neurasthenic Victorian female; she can handle a six-shooter like Annie Oakley, cheat at cards like "Doc" Holliday if necessary, read from the Bible like an evangelical reformer, and survive on her wits and ingenuity. The people of Cloudy Mountain respect her as the true center and "heart of the community" (Hine, *Community,* 25). At the saloon she pours whiskey to the miners, who trust her with their gold and their hearts.

Minnie was not a saloon girl "offering affection, warmth and companionship to her miners" (Hymowitz, 181). She personified the extraordinary pioneer woman and closely resembled the "Indiana Girl" whom California pioneer Louise Clappe described in her *Shirley Letters.* Clappe tells us that the Indiana Girl, Mary Stanfield, was the first white woman to reach the site of Rich Bar, one of the most dangerous mining camps in Plumas County. "Under the board floor of the kitchen [of the Indiana House], she hid much gold dust entrusted to her by the miners for safekeeping" (Clappe 2:28). She ran "Pa's hotel," having inherited it from her father, wore miner's boots, and could pack fifty pounds of flour through five feet of snow (ibid., 28–29). This courageous, historic woman could have been a model for the character of Minnie. Royce had praised Clappe's serially published letters as the "best account of an early mining camp" (Clappe, xvi).

Minnie, like the "Indiana Girl," protected the miners' gold and operated her father's inn in Soledad (near Monterey) before owning the Polka Saloon (Puccini, 37). These kinds of women lived and loved passionately but understood their civilizing effect upon others; they were not fictitious inventions of a romantic imagination. They prepared the miners for the day when women no longer would tend to their needs as sister, banker, cook, teacher, and bartending psychologist-in-residence. They were strong women whose exceptional abilities often helped to stabilize volatile camps.

During the winter season of 1849, mining camps were chaotic: Congress's procrastination had prompted miners to "put the new administration into power in December 1849" (Paul, 200). Royce's history echoed other evidence that most mining communities had acknowledged the Mexican *alcalde*, the sole council that handled and arbitrated disputes (Royce, 220; Shinn, 190). The *alcalde* was a combination of justice of the peace, sheriff, mayor, and tax collector until the state law of 1850 officially abolished the office (Caughey, 34–35). Puccini's community of miners was caught in this time wherein each autonomous *alcalde* carried out its own justice regardless of the mining district's organizational structure, ignoring Mexican statutes and laws.

Royce's disdain for the arbitrary powers and "whims of an *alcalde*" had prompted him to question the right of United States citizens to try Mexicans or anyone else before September 9, 1850, when California legally became a state in the Union. Citing a former general and interregnum governor Riley's "probably legally . . . correct view" of Mexican laws, Royce vociferously claimed that necessity's laws and Mexican laws were preferable to self-government (Royce, *California*, 162).

The interregnum in California's mining communities found miners in limbo until the publication and dissemination of vital information about the "new mechanism." Southern mines provided "some of the worst cases of mob law" and "some of the best examples of law-abiding, justice-seeking organization" (Shinn, 208). Popular rule was in the capricious hands of private individuals, rather than Mexico's legal statutes. Mexican laws governed only in theory (Paul, 201). The powers of an *alcalde* were tied to the power of the miners—the *vox populi*.

In Puccini's adaptation of Belasco's story, the miners become what Royce called "their majesties the mob" (Clendenning, 35). The popular voice was often a symptom of mobocracy and a xenophobic reaction to new immigrants who seemed to threaten the community. This opera captures that moment of transition from a community based on beliefs, emotions, and shared experiences to a newly emerging town with different conditions of awareness. It is a pivotal opportunity in California history when the Mexican *alcalde*, with its local magistrate, must transform itself or self-destruct.

Mexicans had been miners long before Anglo-Saxons arrived; some owned estates and rancheros, which were annexed and seized as United States property during the 1850s. Another Belasco play, *Rose of the Rancho* (1906), and Helen Hunt Jackson's popular *Ramona* (1884) both dealt with the unjustified seizure of lands and the government agent sent to investigate an American father and a Spanish mother's claim to land. These situations led to propertyless Californios.

The Progressive Spirit

This transition from territory to statehood was not unlike the changes throughout the country during the Progressive Era at the turn of the twentieth century. The political mood of the nation demanded reform: the call went out for law and order, for corrupt city "bosses" to be replaced with mayors, and for a more direct form of participation in a republic. Campaigns swept over the urban areas as progressive platforms claimed that "bosses" were not personally committed to community needs but practiced back-room deals and self-promotion.

The opera's "boss," Sheriff Jack Rance, was the interim law-and-order official in the community. In the first and second acts, the miners listen to the sheriff when Sid the Australian is caught cheating at faro, a popular frontier card game. Instead of giving in to the crowd and hanging him, Rance restrains them by singing, "Is death so awful? A sudden shock, a gasp, and all is over" (Puccini, 21). He knows a more degrading punishment: pinning the two of spades over the cheating heart of the gambler. Rance gives permission for the camp to hang Sid if he removes it. Belasco may have borrowed the humiliating idea from Hawthorne's *Scarlet Letter,* but critics complained of the stereotyped romantic invention.

When the sheriff calls for a posse to go after Ramerrez, the men are eager to do the sheriff's bidding and make Ramerrez pay; lynching was the usual punishment for most highwaymen (Angel, 107, 115–20). Rance discovers the wounded Ramerrez hiding out in Minnie's cabin but agrees to not disclose his whereabouts when Minnie challenges Rance to a game of cards. The winner would get Ramerrez. Fueled with whiskey, idled by winter snows, the vengeful sheriff wants him dead, not alive, but agrees to keep Ramerrez's hideout a secret. Minnie announces how she "live[s] on chance money—drink money—card money—saloon money. We're all gamblers" (Belasco, 47; Puccini, 85). Living off whiskey and gold, Minnie cheats at poker with the sheriff and temporarily wins Ramerrez. Moral reformers claimed saloons like Minnie's represented the origin of society's problems. Prohibitionists objected to this kind of alcoholic image associated with the sheriff, Wells Fargo agent Ashby, and the miners.

Taking the law into your hands while intoxicated seemed to be a western tradition. The sheriff wanted to capture Ramerrez, who is wanted by Ashby, but his promise to Minnie kept him from disclosing the bandit's location. During the manhunt for Johnson/Ramerrez's whereabouts, Ashby insists that the outlaw be taken alive; however, the agent ultimately surrenders Ramerrez to Rance and the lynch mob. This decision exposes the collusion and tacit approval of the Wells Fargo agent's expedient and less expensive solution to dealing with alleged criminals. Wells Fargo transported most of the gold in the West and advertised "dead or alive" rewards for road agents (Collins and Levene, 63–64). Since many illegal executions in the West took place in the mining communities, lynching mobs functioned in the best interest of Wells Fargo by saving employees' lives, wages, and time, and, most important, the customers' money.

Vigilantism was rampant in the early part of the first decade in California's statehood, and in the early twentieth century organized groups, such as George Creel's Committee of Public Safety, acted like vigilantes as they went about harassing suspicious individuals (Culberson, 152–53). Anyone not exhibiting complete loyalty would be arrested and sometimes lynched. Impromptu justice satisfied most, but the times were changing. The spirit of compromise would transform the community of miners.

When Sheriff Rance calls for revenge on Ramerrez, the miners object, and the sheriff restrains them. Rance, whose hopeless love for Minnie is threatened by the cultivated, charming, well-dressed, but mysterious gentleman, parallels the evil Sheriff of Nottingham, whose arch rival was the good Robin Hood—Ramerrez. Realizing they may not collect a reward if Ramerrez is lynched, the miners' loyalty shifts slowly from the sheriff to Minnie.

The sheriff had given his word to Minnie that he would not divulge Ramerrez's whereabouts, and he keeps his promise. The posse deputized by Wells Fargo agent Ashby pursues Ramerrez as Rance sings of the enjoyment he will have at paying back Johnson/Ramerrez for taking Minnie's heart. The miners voice a unified "we'll hang him" (Puccini, 101). Rance wants revenge, while agent Ashby insists that "justice must be done." Ashby, however, surrenders the prisoner to Rance and the mob, and rides off.

The lynch scene finds the miners, the bartender, and Billy Jackrabbit (an Indian) getting ready to lynch Johnson/Ramerrez. The critics complained that Billy's prominent role in the lynching was unrealistic; he was removed in the next season's performance (*New York Times*, November 19, 1911). Puccini's emotional finale has Minnie and the miners in a vocal duel over the bandit's fate. The miners' ultimate devotion to a greater cause supersedes their first loyalty to blood revenge. The opera's libretto places the miners in a dilemma that is resolved when they recall how Minnie taught them to read and write. They do not yield to the corrupt villainous symbol of dubious morality—the sheriff. They shift allegiance from Sheriff Rance to Minnie because of her veracity and noble character. Royce, of course, had documented one community's loyalty to its longtime trusted members in an *alcalde* trial (Royce, *California*, 327).

In its early days, a mining camp exhibited mobility, individualism, rootlessness, and atomistic behavior. Before it could be a stable community, the camp needed to create a common relation to the center, or what Hamlin Garland called a "cohesive force of co-operative socialization" (quoted in Hine, 112). Minnie fulfills that requirement and validates Royce's definition of loyalty. The community unites under a "willing, practical, thoroughgoing devotion to a cause." They make a conscious choice to serve a cause greater than self-interest or the private self (Royce, *Loyalty*, 17, 97, 118). Royce had described that communal bond:

> The cause to achieve truth outweighs allegiance to the group. The cause, therefore, to which the loyal man is devoted, is something that appears to him to be . . . superpersonal, because it links several human selves, perhaps a vast number of selves, into some higher social unity. You cannot be loyal to a merely impersonal abstraction; and you also cannot be loyal simply to a collection of various separate persons, viewed merely as a collection. (Ibid., 52)

Minnie's relationship to the community provides the "superpersonal" glue, the hope of permanence—a sense of place. Without her leadership, the sheriff's capricious behavior might have destroyed the promise of a stable community. In the final moments of the opera, the miners' conflict of loyalties and their indecisiveness are resolved in favor of a common cause. They put aside selfish needs and vote for what is in the best interests of the whole—the truth.

Minnie succeeds in persuading the miners to listen to reason; her charismatic speech shows that she is more "inner directed"—in tune with her own morality (Riesman, 13–14; Bellah, 49–50). In the frontier, she is "Everywoman" making a living on her own; her job includes sharing the heartache of solitude amid group coercion and peer pressure. The miners, on the other hand, are "other-directed"—responding to conformist pressure and dependent upon others. The camp is a community based on behavioral conformity and social kinship, but Minnie awakens the miners to their ultimate personal responsibility.

Minnie showed the miners how weak and ineffectual they really were. The miners recall the sheriff's irrationality and vindictiveness, abandoning vigilantism and another lynching. Belasco's play had struck another chord with the audience. Between 1901 and 1910, 846 lynchings took place in the United States (DeSantis, 200; Culberson, 152–53). The message in Puccini's opera meant that the "lynching bee" mentality no longer worked against strangers in civilized American communities. The camp's ambivalence is reconciled in the aborted lynching scene when Minnie, paralleling Clio, the muse of history, faithfully recounts every situation in which her sense of responsibility, personal devotion, and loyalty to the community outweighed her personal desires. While leveling a pistol at the miners, she sings of how she taught them to read and write and to be morally responsible. She reminds them of her roles as surrogate mother and sister, and how her leadership provided economic well-being and nurtured the community. Royce had emphasized the importance of "historical memory, as a prerequisite for community" (Hine, 31; Kuklik, 219–20).

In her heroic entry on horseback, pistol wedged between her teeth, Minnie functions as the *deus ex machina*, rescuing Johnson/Ramerrez. Caught between her devotion to the community and her fondness for Johnson/Ramerrez, she makes an existential choice. Removing the noose, she reprimands the xenophobic community. Her redemptive action absolves a chaotic, lawless mining camp so that it can finally evolve into a bona fide community. She ends the blood revenge just as Athena did in Aeschylus' Orestian trilogy. The Furies (the miners) are transformed into the kindly ones. Their blood revenge is traded in for a fair system of justice with required evidence. Mobocracy yields to a higher judge, Minnie, the embodiment of wisdom and justice. Minnie has become the catalytic synthesis in the struggle between tradition and innovation. She pronounces a verdict of acquittal as her superior vote vetoes the community's *vox populi*. The final act's upheaval forces the community to operate under new ethical principles and to progress in their collective spiritual lives.

Offstage After the Opera

The opera's conclusion addressed the volatile issues of the Progressive Era within the context of the frontier. In the final scene of the opera, Minnie and Ramerrez tearfully bid adieu to the snow-capped Sierra Nevada, their home, and head for another frontier in an urbanized metropolis back East. Minnie has surrendered her ownership of the saloon's gambling casino and embraced, by implication, prohibition. Ramerrez must find a real job to support their dreams. Puccini's adaptation of Belasco's interpretation of the frontier experience seems to incorporate many of Royce's ideas of community at every point in the story. No doubt Royce might have enjoyed the opera and shouted *bravo* to its triumphant finale.

Offstage, in the real world of pre–World War I, progressive reformers gave women the right to vote, made gambling temporarily illegal in Nevada; prohibition arrived shortly thereafter. In the midst of a nation purifying itself from "yellow" and "black" perils, more nativist legislation insulated the United States from the rest of the world. A close colleague of Royce's had initiated a radical transnational movement and "a kind of dual citizenship," which he hoped would counter excessive Americanism (Lasch, 357). Unfortunately, fierce opposition blocked any chance that a divided loyalty could ever be truly American. Consequently, a new wave of xenophobia and undiluted loyalty diminished quotas for non-Anglo-Saxon immigrants, and the Sedition and Espionage Acts questioned everyone's loyalty.

The promise of a better American life may not have been kept for Minnie and Ramerrez. Like the gold rush days in the Sierra Nevada, the good life was still a gamble. The near-tragic ordeal at Cloudy Mountain might have strengthened their chances of survival, but taking a risk in the new urban frontier presented overwhelming odds. If Minnie and Ramerrez had been able to walk off stage and onto New York City's streets, they could expect political and social difficulties in their pursuit of happiness.

REFERENCES

The author would like to remember Bill Collins, spiritual opera companion, and Mary Rafter, whose love of opera inspired me in my undergraduate years.

Adami, Guissepi, ed. *Letters of Giacomo Puccini.* Trans. Ena Makin. Philadelphia: Lippincott, 1931.

Angel, Myron, ed. Thompson and West's *History of Nevada.* 1881. Reprint, Salem, N.H.: Ayer Company, 1973.

Belasco, David. *Gala Days of Piper's Opera House and the California Theatre.* Sparks, Nev.: Falcon Hill Press, 1991.

———. "Girl of the Golden West." Typescript. N.d.

Bellah, Robert, et al. *Habits of the Heart.* Berkeley: University of California Press, 1985.

Carner, Mosco. *Puccini: A Critical Biography.* New York: Holmes and Meier, 1977.

Caughey, John W. *Their Majesties, the Mob.* Chicago: University of Chicago Press, 1960.

Cheney, Fannie. "Our Visit to Lincoln School." Handwritten composition book, 1869–1870. San Francisco: California History Society Library.

Clappe, Louise. *The Shirley Letters.* Reprint of serial publication in the *Pioneer,* January 1854–December 1855. Salt Lake City: Gibbs M. Smith, 1970.

Clendenning, John. *Life and Thought of Josiah Royce.* Madison: University of Wisconsin Press, 1985.

Collins, William, and Bruce Levene. *Black Bart.* Mendocino, Calif.: Pacific Transcriptions, 1992.

Culberson, William C. *Vigilantism.* New York: Greenwood Press, 1990.

DeSantis, Vicent P. *The Shaping of Modern America.* Arlington Heights, Ill.: Forum Press, 1989.

Hine, Robert V. *Community on the American Frontier.* Norman: University of Oklahoma Press, 1980.

Hine, Robert V. *Josiah Royce.* Norman: University of Oklahoma Press, 1992.

Hymowitz, Carol, and Michaele Weissman. *A History of Women in America.* New York: Bantam, 1978.

Kuklik, Bruce. *Josiah Royce: An Intellectual Biography.* Indianapolis: Bobbs Merrill, 1972.

Langley, Henry G., comp. *San Francisco Business Directory*, 1867, 1869, 1874. Published by the author. San Francisco: California Historical Society Library.

Lasch, Christopher. *The True and Only Heaven*. New York: Norton, 1991.

Lincoln Grammar School Association. *The Lincoln Observer* 2, no. 4 (June 1869). San Francisco: California Historical Society Library.

Lincoln Grammar School Association. "A Day at Lincoln School in 1866." Bulletin no. 31. San Francisco: California Historical Society Library.

New York Times, December 11, 1910; December 18, 1910; November 19, 1911.

Paul, Rodman. *California Gold*. 1940. Reprint, Lincoln: University of Nebraska Press, 1965.

Peterson, Richard H. *Manifest Destiny in the Mines*. San Francisco: R and E Research Associates, 1975.

Puccini, Giacomo. *La Fanciulla del West*. Trans. R. H. Elkin. 1910. Reprint, New York: G. Ricordi, 1983.

Riesman, David. *The Lonely Crowd*. 1950. Reprint, New Haven: Yale University Press, 1961.

Royce, Josiah. *California*. 1886. Reprint, New York: Knopf, 1948.

———. *Philosophy of Loyalty*. 1908. Reprint, New York: Macmillan, 1930.

Seligman, Vincent. *Puccini Among Friends*. London: MacMillan and Co. Ltd., 1938.

Shinn, Charles Howard. *Mining Camps*. Reprint of the 1885 edition, New York: Knopf, 1948.

Winter, William. *The Life of David Belasco*. 2 vols. 1918. Reprint, New York: Moffat, Yard and Co., 1930.

From Sensational Dime Novel to Feminist Western
Adapting Genre, Transforming Gender

Writing under the pen name "Dorothy D.," Frances Fuller Victor (journalist, poet, and fiction writer) exclaimed in the San Francisco *Daily Morning Call* in 1875: "Men, as well as women, look down upon a woman-worker. While a man would be commended for industry and money-making . . . a woman's attempt to gain both a competency and a position in society by the same means is frowned down. . . . Every day men grow richer, more selfish, less home-loving. Hence, in a great measure, woman's occupation of ministering to man, the provider, is failing her. She is being left to starve alone by the wayside of life" ("Poor Ladies"). Victor identified women's social and economic condition as a main problem of the mid-nineteenth-century West. In her complex analysis, she indicted men for perpetuating women's social subordination. At the same time, she acknowledged that "we are all of us made what we are by the circumstances that form us as a mould" ("The 'Girl of the Period' "), and she repeatedly challenged women to accept responsibility for their education, for their preparation for economic self-support, and for helping others of their sex. Articulating a need for overhauling society, Victor captured her social vision most vividly in her western fiction.

Although she later denounced the sensationalism of the cheap, ephemeral illustrated weeklies, and indirectly, dime novels, Victor was one of the women writers of early dime-novel westerns before male writers took over the genre in the late 1860s. She herself eventually fused the format and sensationalism of dime-novel westerns with her feminist social concerns in her transformed dime novel, *Judith Miles; or, What Shall be Done with Her?*, which was serialized weekly in the Portland suffragist paper, the *New Northwest*, from December 5, 1873, to May 8, 1874.[1] In this narrative, the sensational dime-novel western metamorphoses into a penetrating critique of gender relations in western society and a vehicle for beginning women's reconstruction of themselves and their social relations. *Judith Miles* includes dramatic but realistic conflicts over land, criminal acts and trials, Indian attacks on emigrant wagon trains, and army outpost adventures, but it focuses on mid-nineteenth-century class and gender constraints on women's education and employment in the West and pleads for women's social and economic independence.

In proposing a remapping of the contours of nineteenth-century western literary history and social history in this essay, I undertake several related tasks. I seek to establish the significance of a little-recognized western public figure, Frances Fuller Victor, and to revise traditional conceptions of a popular western genre, the dime novel. Finally, I argue that a forgotten western novel by Victor deserves acclaim for implementing major changes in literary form and for striving to produce dramatic social change.

More than a Historian:
Westerner, Social Critic, Novelist

Frances Fuller Victor (1826–1902) is most commonly known today (when she is remembered at all) as "the Historian of the Northwest" ("Talented Writer"), the "Mother of Oregon History" (Mills, "Emergence," 300), as a principal writer for the famous Hubert Howe Bancroft western history series, and as an author of prolific historical books and articles treating American expansionism and development in the Far West.[2]

However, her own hard but interesting western experiences fueled the image of the West she portrays in her fiction. Her middle-class, but morally ambiguous, representations of western life are informed by her own two failed marriages in the West. After two years (roughly 1855–1857) on a claim near Omaha, Nebraska, with her first husband, Jackson Barritt, she ended her marriage in divorce on the grounds of her husband's willful absence and gross neglect of his duty toward her (Martin, 9). Her second marriage, to Henry Clay Victor, resulted in a separation after six years when Henry's speculative investments in St. Helens townsites, Santiam gold mines, and coal, iron, and salt mining exhausted the couple's finances. Then at age forty-nine, she was widowed when Henry died in a shipwreck off the Washington coast; he left her an inheritance of legal hassles and debts. Forced to bear these financial burdens alone, Victor, not surprisingly, came to depict women's condition as one of economic degradation, and marriage as a clash of wills and discordant personal and gender visions. Her own experiences drove her to take an active part in the Oregon State Woman Suffrage Association, but she believed that women's social subordination was too pervasive a problem to be easily remedied by suffrage. The need to support herself by her pen positioned Victor to perceive women of her class as a fragmented, subjugated group. Her insights into the social, economic, psychological, and sexual oppression of women dominate her later western short stories, which appeared first in the *Overland Monthly,* the *Lakeside Monthly,* and other western publications, and in her novel serialized in the *New Northwest.*[3]

The Other Dime-Novel Western

To most readers familiar with nineteenth-century popular renditions of the West, the term *dime-novel western* conjures up the wild adventures of Indian fighters, road agents, and flamboyant scouts: Edward S. Ellis's Seth Jones, Edward L. Wheeler's notorious Deadwood Dick, and Prentiss Ingraham's fictional Buffalo Bill—male authors creating male heroes in a predominantly male world of danger, physical trials and combat, capture, rescue, and violence. These figures characterize what the dime-novel western became in the 1870s and 1880s; however, the early history of the dime-novel included a more varied, complicated gender world.

In June of 1860, the New York publishing firm of Beadle and Adams launched one of the most successful publishing ventures of the nineteenth century. It issued dime novels in a continuous series: bimonthly cheap paper-covered novels of about one hundred pages for a fixed price of ten cents. During its first decade, 1860–1870, Beadle and Adams published about two hundred titles in its first series, called simply Dime Novels. They were advertised as stories of "Border Life and Character, Indian Warfare and Frontier Experience, Early Settlement Romance and Fact, Revolutionary Events and Incidents, Sea and Ship Life, &c., &c., &c." (Johannsen, 1:45)—in short, historical adventure tales.

COMPLETE. **BEADLE'S** NUMBER 48.

DIME NOVELS

UNITED STATES OF AMERICA
ONE DIME

THE CHOICEST WORKS OF THE MOST POPULAR AUTHORS

OONOMOO, THE HURON.

BEADLE AND COMPANY.
NEW YORK: 118 WILLIAM ST. LONDON: 44 PATERNOSTER ROW
H. Dexter, Hamilton & Co., 113 Nassau St.

Early dime-novel cover illustration, a Beadle's "Yellow Back."

Not widely known is that eight women authored about a fifth of these early dime novels.[4] Of these early dime novels by women, twenty-five out of thirty-eight feature the frontier as a newly settled community on the edge of the westward-moving country. Edward S. Ellis, the main male writer of early dime-novel westerns, produced nineteen dime novels in the 1860s about Indian warfare, frontier exploration, and first settlement. In some of the women's dime novels about the West, the western setting is only a hazy backdrop; in many, it is an integral part of the action-packed narrative. Thus, women writers did initially compete with their male cohorts in fixing their representations of the "national adventure of moving west" (Jeffrey, 4) in the popular imagination.

What were these women's dime-novel westerns about? A sampling of titles hints at a range of subject matter, geographical settings, and fictional approaches: *Malaeska, the Indian Wife of the White Hunter; Alice Wilde, the Raftsman's Daughter, A Forest Romance; The Backwoods' Bride, A Romance of Squatter Life; Sybil Chase, or, The Valley Ranche; Esther, A Story of the Oregon Trail; The Gold Hunters; The Sagamore of Saco.*[5] In fact, one problem these women's dime-novel westerns pose for literary critics is their diversity, suggesting that women writers brought different ideas to the sensational western adventure tale and did not settle on one working formula that could be easily reproduced. At their weakest, these novels differ little from the frontier romance formula used constantly by male writers: captivity and rescue (often of women characters); fighting "Indians, Mexicans, and outlaws" (Smith, 111). In their most lively, successful versions, women's novels place *women's* experiences and *women* characters as agents and main actors at the center of their exciting, risky western adventures.

If we probe the definitions of the frontier, the concept of wilderness versus civilization, and the issue of sensationalism versus realism, we gain insight into the process by which women's contributions to the genre have been overlooked or dismissed—notably by Henry Nash Smith and Daryl Jones.[6] In *The Dime Novel Western*, Jones defines the "Western" or "Western formula" as "a mode of romance which is set somewhere along the moving frontier at a time when the values of wilderness and civilization are in tension, and which concerns the involvement of a highly stylized protagonist in some form of pursuit. This definition is meant to exclude stories which deal primarily with the agricultural West, and which might more accurately be termed 'regional,' 'local color,' or 'realistic' " (169). One problem with this definition is that it inherently restricts the frontier and the "Western" to the most masculinist and combative representations; women would naturally appear more in stories that feature some developing sense of place and some fixed form of gaining a livelihood. Secondly, the concept of the "values of wilderness and civilization in tension" is actually surprisingly complex in women's representations of western settlements. Focusing on women and women's relations to men leads to a criticizing of the process of settlement and of the whole idea of "civilized" values. For example, women's novels include varieties of *domestic* captivity in rough settlements. Women characters are portrayed as brave and resourceful in meeting the challenges of the hardships of frontier life, but they are threatened by the license that new communities afford supposedly civilized fathers, neighbors, gentlemen. Finally, the critical emphasis on the sensationalism, melodrama, and stylized elements of dime novels overlooks the way women's dime-novel westerns blend sensationalism and realism in entertainment and social critique. In these novels, heroic, spunky, female characters perform daring physical acts to save themselves and others, creating sensational excitement but also embracing the possibilities of expanded roles. When these novels end by converting unconventional girls into brides, wives, and mothers, they reproduce dominant nineteenth-century domestic roles for women, but not without first having questioned and destabilized conservative gender ideals.

Furthermore, in their most successful moments, women's dime-novel westerns refute some of the criticisms directed at the dime-novel western as whole: that this popular, mass-produced genre uncritically celebrated Manifest Destiny and operated as an uninformed generator of illusions and fantasies about the West by distant eastern writers (Tuska and Piekarski, 244–45). For example, the two dime novels by Frances Fuller Victor and a number of those by her sister, Metta Fuller Victor,[7] reflect these women's early lives spent in Ohio in the 1830s, in Michigan in 1840s, and Frances's firsthand knowledge of "the excitement and hardships of pioneer life" in Nebraska (Orville J. Victor, 510). Her two dime novels—*East and West; or, The Beauty of Willard's Mill* and *The Land Claim, A Tale of the Upper Missouri*—set in Nebraska Territory around Council Bluffs, Iowa, and published in 1862—combine sensationalism and realism in their representations of western communities. They broach, and even explore, many of the sordid features of westward expansion: greed for land, water, and economic opportunity; unscrupulous use of force and violence; the cost in lives, particularly of women and children; and even mistreatment of Indians and Mormons.

Beyond Dime-Novel Roots: No Villains, No Heroes

When Victor turned again to novel writing in 1873 at age forty-seven, she had physically and metaphorically traveled far. She had become a far westerner in 1863 by her move to San Francisco with her second husband, and her two disastrous marriages had pushed her beyond conventional feminine roles. On the one hand, her serialized novel, *Judith Miles; or, What Shall be Done with Her?*, reflects her personal knowledge of western landscape and historical western conflicts. The principal action of the novel takes place roughly between 1867 and 1870. Its twenty-three chapters divide into three distinctly different western settings: the San Joaquin Valley of California; the route from California to Texas, including Fort Kellogg, in Arizona Territory; and the San Francisco of the military and professional set. On the other hand, the novel and its place of publication (the *New Northwest*) reveal Victor's ideas of gender equality, illustrating how far her views of women's roles and the social construction of gender had evolved. The story recounts young Judith Miles's struggles toward independent womanhood against numerous, diverse social obstacles.

"To change story signals a dissent from social norms as well as narrative forms," critic Rachel Blau DuPlessis asserts in *Writing Beyond the Ending* (20). Or stated another way, because narratives "create fictional boundaries for experience" (3), the act of changing conventional plots, characters, and endings disrupts readers' expectations. It also reveals where social and literary conventions intersect and suggests striking parallels between questioning narrative form and questioning political and legal forms (ibid., x). In *Judith Miles,* Victor both adapts and undermines the narrative conventions of women's dime-novel westerns, pushing sensational fiction even closer to both serious literary production and revolutionary social statement.[8] *Judith Miles* enacts a double critique of western society in terms of class and gender. Victor examines and criticizes the social construction of men *and* women in both the property-owning, uneducated class *and* in the educated, moneyed class.

The most obvious convention of women's dime-novel westerns that Victor transforms is the heroine's relationship to men. She builds on and complicates the male-female relations by embedding her characters in complex realistic, social circumstances, by extending sympathy to her male characters, and by refusing clear-cut designations of "good" and "bad": there are no villains and no heroes. In the course of the novel, Judith Miles experiences life-changing relationships with her father, with her first mentor-lover, Carl Shultz, and with her guardian-lover, Major Floyd. Each of these men loves and helps Judith, and yet each personally and socially manipulates her and hurts her.

Victor initially establishes that Judith's father, Jack Miles, has real grievances and is engaged in social/economic conflicts that have high stakes. The novel begins in the San Joaquin Valley of Fresno County with a problem meant to be representative of rural California in the late 1860s and early 1870s. Small, independent ranchers—cattle herders like Jack Miles from Texas—are pitted against large landowners. These small ranchers are also being squeezed by the railroad, which demands a right of way through their land that could result in spooked cattle and burnt grazing land. In addition, the big landowners and the increasing number of wheat growers threaten to block the ranchers from their sources of water and to force them to fence their land at great cost. As these pressures build, Jack Miles becomes more convinced of the increasing value of his land and is indignantly unwilling to be frightened into selling it cheaply.

Economic/social and domestic problems intersect in Jack Miles's proud hatred of the schoolmaster, the telegraph, and the railroad; constantly fleeing these advances, he abuses his domestic power. Judith's conflict with her father centers on the issue of will, authority, and his refusal to acknowledge the selfhood of any other family member: "Was he always to keep on going from place to place and dragging those who could not resist him farther away from things desirable?" (chap. 2).[9] She accuses him of causing her mother's death by forcing her weak, pregnant mother to make the overland journey from Texas to California. Judith also blames her father for sending her brother, Boone, to meet his death at the hands of Apaches on the moneymaking venture of a cattle drive to Texas.

Her most intense disagreement with her father revolves around the issue of "things desirable": her aspirations for a different quality of life, one shaped by education and intellectual-cultural advance, versus her father's insistence on maintaining his proud, independent, uncultivated life-style. Judith must hide her secretly acquired novels and volumes of poetry and her drawings from her father.

The crisis in her conflict with her father occurs when he has been arrested for setting fire to the wheat fields belonging to the greedy land baron, Judge Spedden. Judith, as the key witness, must lie to defend him in court. She violates her own sense of integrity and perjures herself to keep her father from going to jail, aware that her only friend, Shultz, knows she is lying. Yet, she affirms her allegiance to her father: "We belong to a class that will not bear to have superiors. Pap has not education but he has pride, and anger—and injustice" (chap. 8). Through Judith, Victor assesses Jack Miles's failings while she elicits sympathy for his provocations.

In *Judith Miles,* Victor appears to employ familiar dime-novel plot devices for treating father figures. Most of the dime-novel westerns by women feature father-daughter conflicts in families where the mother is virtually silenced or dead. At the climax, the father is either redeemed from his misguided economic/social activity by the daughter's heroism and/or suffering or he is shown to be hopelessly hardened and must be killed off. Victor finds the father-daughter conflict in *Judith Miles* so intractable that she exploits the convention of sudden death to remove Jack Miles. In his stubbornness, Jack Miles disregards the warnings about Indian depredations on the route through Arizona Territory. He and all of his party, except Judith, are killed. She possesses the excellent riding skills of all dime-novel heroines and happens to be seated on a fast horse at the time of the Apache attack.

However, as sensational as all these manipulations of plot at first appear, they actually uphold a logic of realism and push the narrative toward innovation. Confronted with her lack of options, Judith perceives the social and personal injustice of her father's selfishness and protests, although futilely, her father's plans for her. The narrator articulates this resistance and proposes that women rethink the cultural prescription of self-abnegation and submission: "How hard a thing it is for women that it so often happens the most cruel blows of destiny are brought upon them by the personal acts of those whom they love or are closely related to. They have . . . to bear the bitterness of subjecting every strongest inclination to a despotic will. . . . I think the new gospel that is demanded in the world of women is the gospel of selfishness" (chap. 4). In this novel, the powerful and very real gender constraints of an inequitable social system compel Judith's capitulation. However, if Miles's death truly operated like a dime-novel stroke of fortune, it would occur at the end of the novel and leave the beautiful daughter free to marry her gentlemanly lover. Instead, he is dispatched as a controlling force and dubious protector early in the narrative, enabling Victor to concentrate on Judith's development as an intellectual and social being.

Victor frustrates and complicates another prominent dime-novel convention by creating a would-be lover who is as realistically flawed as the father figure. In dime-novel fashion, Judith is caught between an educated, cultivated lover who appreciates her beauty and quick mind and an ignorant father. Yet, barriers of class and especially the ambiguous character of the lover obstruct the young couple's love more than the jealous, prejudiced father does. In fact, the narrative asks and refuses to answer directly a troubling question: is Carl Shultz a suitor for Judith's hand at all?

The romance script is marred by a series of increasingly disturbing and morally disillusioning impressions of Shultz. He enters the novel as a handsome, self-assured, twenty-eight-year-old man of the world, a cultivated German who works as the agent for the wealthy Judge Spedden. But the novel early sets in play the notion that Shultz's relationships with women are characterized by an irresponsible exercise of sexual power and a susceptibility to women who are "attractive materially" (chap. 6). When Inez, a pretty Mexican girl, disguised as a vaquero, shoots and wounds Shultz, Judith accepts the truth of the rumors of Shultz's flirtation with Inez. What is more disturbing, in one of their rare meetings, Shultz impulsively seizes Judith and kisses her repeatedly and passionately on the lips. Yet, as they part—she for Texas with her father, he to Germany— he neither explains his behavior nor proposes to her. He offers her only a vague promise of friendship and leaves her with a confusing remark: "Goodbye Judith—beautiful and dear" (chap. 9).

The mystery of Shultz's conduct toward Judith is finally clarified near the end of the novel, but his reappearance disqualifies him permanently as romantic hero. Several years after their separation, Judith encounters Shultz and his pretty German wife at the elegant Cliff House in San Francisco. Judith's lingering dreams of love for him are destroyed by this discovery that he married another: "She had learned . . . that neither culture, nor manner, nor abundant knowledge of any kind, made her ideal man; she had found out that truth and honor do not necessarily reside in colleges; she had discovered the humiliating fact for herself that a *gentleman* may kill time in developing the mind, and gaining the first affections of any single-hearted girl with intellect enough to amuse him, who chances to come his way" (chap. 19). Clearly, men and women do not operate on equal social footing or have the same emotional expectations. Her respect for Shultz suffers its last blow when she meets him again six months later after his wife has been killed in a carriage accident. Once again available, he visits Judith, now attending a girls' school, to explain how he returned to Germany to obey his parents and found himself too weak, despite his love for Judith, to break his earlier betrothal. But she dislikes him for showing no signs of grief for his wife and censures him for excessive self-love: "But *I* call that love which seeks another's happiness and safety. *You* had no regard to either" (chap. 21). Although she thanks him for nurturing her interest in learning and culture, she blames him for stealing her first kiss, an act she considers an emotional and sexual violation. Dashing the image of the romantic hero, the novel illustrates how "good" men—even gentlemen—exploit young women's emotional vulnerability for their own pleasure.

A third relationship with a man, Judith's friendship with her patron-lover, Major Floyd, dramatizes women's social and economic vulnerability. When Judith is rescued by the army after the Indian massacre and taken to Fort Kellogg, Major Floyd, a handsome gentleman in his early thirties, befriends her. Later in San Francisco, he functions as her social mentor and eventually provides the money for her to go to school to become a teacher.

However, once again the novel diverges from conventional paths by debunking another male hero figure. At her coming-out party at eighteen, Judith overhears two women gossiping that the major has passed himself off as an unmarried man. Although after learning how he was tricked into marrying a severe epileptic Judith believes he is a man more abused than guilty, she still declares that his conduct toward her has tampered with friendship and integrity and endangered her social reputation. Her final disillusionment with Major Floyd comes when she realizes that selfish desire has tainted his love and substantial concern for her: "The helplessness which had forced her to accept his patronage he had depended on to bind her to him. Without meaning to be ungenerous, he had exaggerated her helplessness to herself. It is the fashion of society to make women powerless for self-support; and to compel them to exchange their love for the money of men" (chap. 23). Thus, through Major Floyd, as well as Jack Miles and Carl Shultz, Victor unmasks and condemns what she considers the greatest fault of men: a selfish exercise of domestic and social power made possible by a social system that grants men privilege and social dominance.

Oppressed Women as Oppressors

Victor also moves far beyond dime-novel roots in her portrayal of women in *Judith Miles*. Both the physical and social isolation of the beautiful, robust western heroine and her rivals and foils are realistically complicated. Victor herself had been thrust out of "the narrow circle, usually denominated their [woman's] 'sphere,' " into the position of "lone woman" ("Some Thoughts," 1). In response, she developed a view of women that was at once both highly critical and sympathetic. Through her depictions of women characters in *Judith Miles,* Victor conveys her belief that the social construction of gender is intricately entangled in issues of class.[10] Women harm and hinder each other because of their dependence on men and their unresisting subscription to class norms.

The first part of the novel exploits the usual dime-novel ploy of establishing the female protagonist as fit for social success. In one sense, Judith resembles the special motherless dime-novel daughters of squatters, mill-owners, and frontier doctors found in barely settled western regions: "In all her brief life she had never known a dozen persons of her own sex and never a *lady*" (chap. 1). Also like her dime-novel sisters, beautiful, intelligent, strong-minded Judith stands out as an anomaly, inheriting the best qualities of both her parents.

Going beyond these formulas, however, Victor actually explores the class from which Judith comes, depicting its specific oppressiveness to women. The daily physical work, the nomadic life, and the difficulties of childbearing in these rough surroundings inscribe themselves on the bodies of the rancher women in their rapid loss of youth and beauty: the "sun-burnt complexion that might once have been fair and soft, and red, knotty hands that revealed the cause of the slight stoop in the thin shoulders" (chap. 6). The conditions that mark these women's bodies also shape their minds; "they are what their circumstances and education make them" (chap. 2). These women reject and gossip about Judith because she is not interested in their narrow "female" topics of bodily ailments, stock, babies, and "fellers."

If disparity of interests separates Judith from the women of the ranching class, other women's self-interest prevents Judith from establishing nourishing bonds with the wives of the military officers stationed at Fort Kellogg. In her portrayal of Mrs. Stewart, wife of the army surgeon, and Mrs. Kellogg, wife of the colonel, Victor dramatizes how genteel women persistently favor class over gender in their loyalties and social interaction. Although their life in this Arizona outpost is empty and dull, Mrs. Kellogg and Mrs. Stewart must be convinced of Judith's refinement and respectability before they will associate with her. Mrs. Kellogg looks down on "one of the ordinary emigrant class" (chap. 11), Mrs. Stewart comments "how these *movers* dress" (chap. 11), and both are baffled by the conflicting clues to Judith's identity and background: how can a girl carry Browning's *Aurora Leigh* and yet call her father "Pap"?

Mrs. Stewart and Mrs. Kellogg function as Victor's vehicles for examining two kinds of middle-class marriages as well as a means to expose the warped state of bonds between women. The scene that explodes the potential for gender solidarity is the climax of events in which the men of the fort discover and acknowledge Judith's extraordinary beauty. A scandalous incident abruptly introduces Judith to the merciless class and sexual constraints on women and requires Judith's departure from the fort. One day the drunken Colonel Kellogg wanders into Judith's sleeping chamber while she is napping and caresses her feet; Judith wakes up and screams and draws a crowd. Although everyone in the fort knows of the colonel's habits and of Judith's innocence, she is blamed for the colonel's "'aberration' of propriety" (chap. 14). Mrs. Kellogg, miserable in her mismatched marriage, repudiates Judith as an "artful, low-bred creature, and a dangerous person to have in her house— a girl about whose antecedents nothing is known" (ibid.). Even kindly Mrs. Stewart won't quarrel with her husband's commanding officer. The narrator ironically exposes Mrs. Stewart's form of culturally exemplary womanhood as the self-preservation of another group of oppressed women: "Advancing the Doctor's interests was advancing her own without seeming to be thinking of herself, and it obtained for her the reputation from others of being a most devoted and self-abnegating wife" (chap. 10). In this novel as elsewhere in Victor's fiction and journalism, she analyzes how women's dependence on men and on marriage as the only acceptable source of social status prevents women from working together.

From Heroine to Female Hero

It is in Victor's portrayal of her female protagonist, Judith, that she most dramatically alters and supercedes dime-novel—indeed, most nineteenth-century literary—conventions for shaping the lives of women characters. The typical dime-novel heroine is often depicted recovering a social status her family has lost through financial misfortune in the East or the hardships of pioneering in the West. She triumphs through her own heroic physical acts and "earns" her marriage to the worthy hero through her synthesis of frontier virtues and moral superiority and cultivation. DuPlessis illuminates the narrative "rules" involved for women in nineteenth-century fiction at large: "authors went to a good deal of trouble . . . to see to it that *Bildung* [quest, education] and romance could not coexist and be integrated for the heroine at the resolution" (3). Most commonly, the "female hero" who has been engaged in the pursuit of self-development and self-realization must transform herself into a "heroine-wife," subordinating quest to marriage (DuPlessis, 11). However, Judith's personal and social progress does not end in marriage. The novel's conclusion protests, rather than affirms, social norms for women.

As a first point of difference, Judith's self-realization emphasizes intellectual and character development and represents a real change of class, from uneducated nomadic western rancher to cultivated middle-class respectability. The beginning of the novel focuses on Judith's hunger for learning and on her character transformation. Her response to Shultz's paintings and literature, her blossoming critical thinking, and the rapidity of her intellectual progress impress Shultz, particularly as she overcomes her shyness and boldly pronounces her aesthetic judgments. In the massacre that frees her from her father's domination and from her mothering responsibilities to her little sister, and in her long convalescence from brain fever, Judith is literally reborn, signaled by a change in physical appearance and demeanor: she loses her sunburn, a mark of the "mover class," and develops a lily-white complexion, the sign of a lady. Her manner changes, as for the first time in her life others are taking care of her, and her new life and her sorrows render her more thoughtful, dignified, and spiritual. This rebirth allows her to advance up the social hierarchy on her own personal merit.

However, transforming a rancher's daughter into a lady is not Victor's goal but rather a narrative strategy to manifest a social problem she considers equally detrimental to women's self-development. Middle-class gentility brings inequitable, arbitrary social expectations as limiting in their own way as Judith's original class identity. Unable to imagine any other option for Judith, Mrs. Stewart counsels her to use her beauty as her only capital to obtain the protection and status of a rich husband. However, Judith analyzes her own depth of affections and considers the abusive, mismatched, or mediocre marriages she has observed: "She had no knowledge of anything that a woman might live for except love, and to be willing to live for that one sentiment, it must be something more satisfying than any form of it she had ever witnessed" (chap. 13). Already, Judith questions marriage as the sole destiny for women and longs for independence, for the opportunity for self-determination: "Why do I never have anything to say about my own destiny? Do all women, I wonder, have to be buffeted about in this way?" (chap. 14). First, the novel asserts, women need the privilege and power of choice.

In the final third of the novel, Victor places her heroine in conflict with the enormous social and economic obstacles to middle-class women's independence. Judith frankly confronts her social position—without money and without family—and takes responsibility for herself: "she would accept whatever work could be found for her to do that promised independence" (chap. 16). Yet Judith's experiences in San Francisco show that possessing a willingness to work and the courage to resist society's pressures to conform to conventional gender roles are only one part of the battle for women.

In the home of Judge and Mrs. Brazee, Judith is trapped in intricate webs of social expectations and class-determined gender norms. Within Judith's first few days in the city, Mrs. Brazee urges Judith to spend all her money (most of her $200) on an outfit for high society. Most of all, Mrs. Brazee, who is socially embarrassed to associate with a girl who is looking for work, imprisons her in the leisurely existence of middle-class feminine respectability: "But in Mrs. Brazee's house she seemed under a spell. There was no necessity for exertion, almost none for thought, almost every want being anticipated. The conversation was always upon subjects that ignored the common wants of existence, and led the thoughts away from them. Nothing met the eye but elegance; she, herself, had been made elegant" (chap. 16). The gulf between woman as decorative, passive object and practical, active worker grows increasingly unbridgeable for Judith.

At last attempting self-determination, Judith struggles against limited economic opportunities and her complete lack of preparation for self-support. Her frightened but brave efforts to find employment meet with realistic rebuffs. Working in a telegraph office, book bindery, or millinery requires skills or time and money for an apprenticeship. If she could operate a sewing machine and do fine work, she might earn $400 a year, hardly enough to supply the "books, leisure, pleasant surroundings, congenial society" to which she has become accustomed (chap. 18). Her beauty and refinement disqualify her as a servant because she now looks and acts too cultured to be a children's nurse and would be considered a threat as a servant, and her haphazard education prohibits her from teaching even the youngest students. Major Floyd informs her that she could sell her beauty in cigar stores or fashionable photograph galleries, but this alternative approaches prostitution. Ironically, Mrs. Brazee comments, "It is a great pity, is it not, that a girl should have grown up without any sort of useful knowledge?" (chap. 17). The seriousness of her situation pushes Judith increasingly toward despair and thoughts of suicide: "girls better educated, and more accustomed to self-dependence than I, have thought it, and done it" (chap. 18). However, typical of popular fiction, the novel preserves the heroine from this realistic tragic end.

The conclusion of *Judith Miles* partakes of happy dime-novel denouement while it simultaneously upsets the conventions of nineteenth-century women's fiction through a feminist fantasy of open-ended independence. Just when Judith has decided that she must dispense with Major Floyd's illegitimate help and depend on herself, Judge Spedden informs her that by her father's deed of gift to her (he never sold his ranch), she owns two thousand acres of land in the San Joaquin Valley. Addressing both the novel's personal and social/economic conflicts, Victor has Judge Brazee advise Judith to get more for her land than Spedden's offer of $20,000 by selling the land to small farmers and thus preventing the growth of a "landed aristocracy" (chap. 23). In the final chapter, Judith also discovers that her brother is alive. Acquiring money and family in one day at the age of eighteen, Judith feels "unspeakable relief at being at last mistress of her own life, freed from charitable obligations" (ibid.).

Neat and simple as this resolution to Judith's quest for social identity and livelihood appear, it nevertheless resonates with complexity, as it violates the romance script employed in women's dime novels, the conventional marriage ending. *Judith Miles* is remarkable for its time because it concludes with an *initiation* of quest for the female hero and presents that quest in entirely positive terms. Besides voicing the desire to continue her self-realization by developing her artistic talent, Judith also decides to employ her experience and money to break down the barriers between women and between women and society: "When Madam M—— gets through with me, I intend to do some good in the world. I think I should know what to do, after my experience, for other ignorant girls" (ibid.). In effect, Judith chooses to use her newfound agency to begin the remolding of society. She will provide other girls with a practical education to equip them for the harsh struggle for economic survival that she just barely escaped. It is most significant that the novel culminates in Judith's rejection of marriage to Major Floyd sometime in the future and in her repudiation of marriage in general as a means to women's fulfillment and social identity. Concluding the novel, Judith's final words to Major Floyd embrace a pursuit of unfolding potential:

> "Why compel me to say that I do not love you—as you desire; why mention love to me at all? My life is only dawning now. . . . I must take time to know myself and work out my destined career. . . . As to love . . . I know not what it is; nor what its power over me in the future may be. Go away from me; let me be. Come back, if you choose, sometime in the future and observe my progress. I shall at least understand myself better than I do now." (ibid.)

The novel militates against later conventional happy courtship and marriage for Judith; there are no good marriages in this novel, only destructive, unhappy, compromised ones. In accord with the ideas of James Stuart Mill, to whom Victor alludes in chapter one, the conclusion of *Judith Miles* suggests that happy marriage will only be truly possible when marriage becomes one among many viable options for women and when men themselves learn that they no longer wield social, economic, and sexual power over women.

Innovative for its time, this novel also resists the narrative paradigm that presents alternatives to conventional marriage as deprivation and punishment for women; the ending proclaims female independence and vocation. Judith is not socially or morally unfit for marriage, but rather, marriage as it is socially constituted in the nineteenth century is unsuited to a woman of her intellect, personal beauty, and depth of character. The novel traces the heroine's path from cultural impoverishment, to ideal world and love, to worldly disillusionment, and finally to realistic but fortuitous opportunity. In effect, *Judith Miles* inverts dominant narrative patterns: if a heroine is a female protagonist confined within social and literary conventions, then Judith progresses from a heroine to become a female hero.

Beyond Popular Truths

The irrecoverable readers of the San Francisco *Daily Morning Call* and the *New Northwest* cannot attest to the efficacy of Victor's astute social analyses. We can only speculate about the lives she influenced. She herself endorsed a theory of gradual social evolution: "The average mass of men and women always conform to existing circumstances. . . . Thus, in all ages there have been individuals who saw clearly truths that it took ages more to make popular" ("Contrasts Masculine and Feminine Nature"). But she also believed in the power of fiction and education to inaugurate the slow process of reconstructing individual lives and gender roles, as *Judith Miles* exemplifies.

Victor's social and fictional vision become significant at the point where twentieth-century western historiography, cultural criticism, and literary history converge in the search for the untold stories—historical and fictional—of the nineteenth century. Examining the male master narratives of the frontier, historian Richard White explains how Frederick Jackson Turner—with his story of an "advance into an empty continent" (54) and a conquest of nature—and Buffalo Bill's Wild West show—with its story of conquest as retaliation against Native American aggression—"divided up the existing narratives of American frontier mythology" (11) and "erased part of the larger, and more confusing and tangled, cultural story to deliver up a clean, dramatic, and compelling narrative" (ibid.). Among those "erased" stories are women's fictional representations of women in western settlement. These women's narratives refute the idea of women's invisibility and unimportance on the multiple western frontiers and reveal how the lens of gender exposes a different set of social conflicts.

Victor's western fiction should hold a prominent place among rediscovered women's western literature because of its close connection with historical issues and its effort to employ change on the level of narrative to address social problems. Historian Elizabeth Jameson contends that "we need to listen to the many voices of the women who lived the history that they can tell us" (Armitage and Jameson, 161). Literary critic DuPlessis argues that "writing beyond the ending [of the romance plot] begins when authors, or their close surrogates, discover that they are in fact outside the terms of this novel's script, marginal to it" (5). Very much involved in western history, Victor found herself outside conventional gender roles. Speaking for her class of subordinated, powerless women, Victor, through her character Judith Miles, claimed women's right to explore their potential, to discover careers, to make their own progress.

NOTES

1. To my knowledge, *Judith Miles* was never reprinted as a bound novel. Abigail Scott Duniway edited and published the *New Northwest* from 1871 to 1887. According to Jean Mary Guske Ward, "paid subscriptions to the *New Northwest* probably never exceeded about three thousand, but the paper was shared extensively with non-subscribers in Western frontier communities" (8). Duniway herself published eighteen serialized novels in this paper. Like *Judith Miles,* these novels have western settings and focus on the condition of women in the cause of women's rights. Duniway's novels exhibit greater polemic didacticism than Victor's fiction. Duniway employs her characters and plots to expose and fight intemperance, the sexual exploitation of women in marriage, inequitable divorce and property laws,

and restricted economic opportunities for women. Her novels typically end in a happy, equitable marriage.

2. In 1869, Victor published *The River of the West* (San Francisco: R. W. Bliss; Hartford: R. J. Turnbull, 1870), written as a biography of Joe Meeks but also as a documentation of the early fur trade. In 1872, she published *All Over Oregon and Washington* (San Francisco: John H. Carmany). Throughout the 1880s, she anonymously wrote a number of volumes of the Bancroft history series, among them *History of Oregon* (two volumes), *History of Washington,* (two vols.) *Idaho, and Montana,* and *History of Nevada, Colorado, and Wyoming* (two vols.). In frustration, she later remarked, "If I had been able to place my name where it belongs on these six volumes I should have made an international reputation" ("Autobiographical Sketch").

3. Victor gathered ten of her short stories and published them, along with a collection of her poems, in *The New Penelope and Other Stories and Poems* (San Francisco: A. L. Bancroft, 1877). Recently two of her short stories have been reprinted in contemporary western anthologies. Glen Love included "On the Sands" in *The World Begins Here: An Anthology of Oregon Short Fiction* (Corvallis: Oregon State University Press, 1993); Ida Rae Egli anthologized "How Jack Hastings Sold His Mine" in *No Rooms of Their Own: Women Writers of Early California* (Berkeley: Heydey Books, 1992).

4. Metta Fuller Victor (sister of Frances) wrote fourteen early dime novels for the first series, many of them dime-novel westerns; the next two most prolific women writers, Ann Sophia Stephens and Mary Denison, wrote seven each; Mrs. Henry Thomas wrote three; Frances Fuller Barritt Victor, Mrs. Ann Porter, and Mrs. Elizabeth Oakes-Smith each wrote two; and Clara Augusta wrote one. Although most of these women stopped writing dime novels after the 1860s, Beadle and Adams continued to reprint these women's novels for decades, often with different titles.

5. For a complete listing of dime novels and of women authors and their novels with dates of publication and a brief description of their subjects, see Johannsen's *The House of Beadle and Adams.*

6. Even Christine Bold and Jane Tompkins in their studies of western fiction and formulas ignore women's early efforts in the genre of sensational writing about the West and discuss the western as entirely a male phenomenon.

7. Metta and Frances married two brothers, giving the two sisters the same last name. In 1862, Beadle and Adams billed Metta Fuller Victor as one of its main producers of "Frontier and Border Stories," along with Edward S. Ellis. In her novel *The Backwoods' Bride,* Metta, in fact, came the closest of the women writers to generating a lively dime-novel western plot that concentrated on the heroine. However, this heroine hovers precariously on the border between respectable heroism and sensationally disruptive female assertiveness and rebellion. For a variety of reasons, including

her choice of permanent residence in New Jersey, Metta abandoned western material after the 1860s and devoted her attention to writing numerous dime-novel mysteries and society romances.

8. In its themes—its treatment of women's social subordination, sexual vulnerability, and compulsion to marry—as well as in its exploration of the limits society places on women's potential within and outside marriage, *Judith Miles* anticipates both Henry James's *Portrait of a Lady* (1880) and Edith Wharton's *House of Mirth* (1905). Its economic/social conflict over land in central California touches on issues central to Frank Norris's *The Octopus* (1901). Although *Judith Miles*—restricted in part by its length—lacks the narrative density, the extensive, deep psychological probing, and the artistic experimentation with viewpoint that many scholars value in the works of James and Wharton, it nevertheless exhibits substantial ambiguity and realism in its characterization and much poetic description of the California landscape. In his *History of Oregon Literature*, Alfred Powers comments that Victor "had considerable gift for fiction if she could have had time from history to develop it" (307). Powers quotes William Morris's assessment that Victor was "the most versatile figure in Pacific Coast literature" (313).

9. The serialized chapters of *Judith Miles* always appeared on the front page of the *New Northwest*, usually printed in three to six long columns. These chapters appeared weekly, roughly over six months. I have cited quotations by chapter only in parentheses after each quotation.

10. Victor discusses class in complex terms, as a matter of values as well as economic status. Within that large, vague group, the middle class, Victor especially criticizes those who live "a life of ease and indulgence" and do not sympathize with or aid the "industrious women many of whom labor for their own support" (*The Women's War with Whisky,* 12). In her documentation of the 1874 temperance crusade in Portland, she asserts that "all reforms have been begun by, and carried along by, the laboring, self-reliant, middle-class of people" (ibid.). In *Judith Miles* and in her journalism, Victor objects that many genteel values—say, those held by the professional and military sets—negatively influence all "middle-class" women.

R E F E R E N C E S

Armitage, Susan, and Elizabeth Jameson, eds. *The Women's West.* Norman: University of Oklahoma Press, 1987.

Bold, Christine. *Selling the Wild West: Popular Western Fiction, 1860 to 1960.* Bloomington: Indiana University Press, 1987.

DuPlessis, Rachel Blau. *Writing Beyond the Ending: Narrative Strategies of Twentieth-Century Women Writers.* Bloomington: Indiana University Press, 1985.

Jeffrey, Julie Roy. *Frontier Women: The Trans-Mississippi West, 1840–1880.* New York: Hill and Wang, 1979.

Johannsen, Albert. *The House of Beadle and Adams and Its Dime and Nickel Novels: The Story of a Vanished Literature.* 2 vols. Norman: University of Oklahoma Press, 1950.

Jones, Daryl. *The Dime Novel Western.* Bowling Green, Ohio: Bowling Green University Popular Press, 1978.

Martin, Jim. *A Bit of a Blue: The Life and Work of Frances Fuller Victor.* Salem, Ore.: Deep Well, 1992.

Mill, John Stuart. *The Subjection of Women.* 1869. Reprint, New York: Prometheus Books, 1986.

Mills, Hazel Emery. "The Emergence of Frances Fuller Victor—Historian." *Oregon Historical Quarterly* 62 (September 1961): 309–36.

Powers, Alfred. *The History of Oregon Literature.* Portland, Ore.: Metropolitan Press, 1935.

Smith, Henry Nash. *Virgin Land: The American West as Symbol and Myth.* Cambridge: Harvard University Press, 1950.

"Talented Writer Dies in Oregon[:] Frances Fuller Victor, Known as 'The Historian of the Northwest' Passes Away." *San Francisco Chronicle,* November 26, 1902, p. 8.

Tompkins, Jane. *West of Everything: The Inner Life of Westerns.* New York: Oxford University Press, 1992.

Tuska, Jon, and Vicki Piekarski, eds. *The Frontier Experience: A Reader's Guide to the Life and Literature of the American West.* Jefferson, N.C.: McFarland, 1984.

Victor, Frances Fuller. "Autobiographical Sketch." *Daily Oregon Statesman,* June 16, 1895, p. 2.

——— [Dorothy D., pseud.]. "Contrasts Masculine and Feminine Nature." *Daily Morning Call* (San Francisco), August 1, 1875, 5.

———. *East and West; or, The Beauty of Willard's Mill.* Dime Novel #35. New York: Beadle and Adams, February 1, 1862.

——— [Dorothy D., pseud.]. "The 'Girl of the Period.'" *Daily Morning Call* (San Francisco), June 20, 1875, p. 1.

———. *Judith Miles; or, What Shall be Done with Her?* Serialized in *New Northwest* (Portland, Ore.), December 5, 1873–May 8, 1874.

———. *The Land Claim. A Tale of the Upper Missouri.* Dime Novel #39. New York: Beadle and Adams, May 31, 1862.

——— [Dorothy D., pseud.]. "Poor Ladies." *Daily Morning Call* (San Francisco), April 25, 1875, p. 1.

———. "Some Thoughts About Ourselves." *New Northwest* (Portland, Ore.), February 27, 1874, pp. 1–2.

———. *The Women's War with Whisky; or, Crusading in Portland.* Portland: Geo H. Himes, Steam Book and Job Printer, 1874.

Victor, Orville J. "Frances Fuller Barritt." In *Poets and Poetry of the West: with Biographical and Critical Notices,* by William T. Coggeshall. Columbus: Follet, 1860.

Ward, Jean Mary Guske. "Women's Responses to Systems of Male Authority: Communication Strategies in the Novels of Abigail Scott Duniway." Ph.D. diss., University of Oregon, 1989.

White, Richard. "Frederick Jackson Turner and Buffalo Bill." In *The Frontier in American Culture: Essays by Richard White and Patricia Nelson Limerick,* ed. James R. Grossman. Berkeley: University of California Press, 1994.

Rhetoric of a River
Tracing Language and Change

Marc Reisner writes in *Cadillac Desert* that "Nevada is the one western state without any mentionable rivers at all" (478). Reisner is referring to the amount of water Nevada's rivers carry, and within the context of western North America, where such rivers as the Columbia, Sacramento, and Rio Grande exist, Nevada's largest rivers seem little more than streams. Even the infamous Colorado is a Nevada river only briefly, forming a few miles of border with Arizona. In a contest of size, Nevada's rivers aren't worthy of mention.

But in other ways Nevada's rivers are eminently mentionable. Most of Nevada lies within the Great Basin, where rivers drain to desert sinks or to ancient lakes full of minerals and legends. As a result of the rain shadow created by the Sierra Nevada range to the west, the Great Basin is among the driest regions on the continent. In this arid and internal land, Nevada's meager rivers become important for what little water they carry; they deserve mention out of proportion to their size.

Great Basin rivers are ribbons of life. Diverse communities and cultures have depended upon these rivers for sustenance. Human communities develop rhetorics of their rivers, specialized languages and lexicons connecting the people with the water. As individuals grow within their river language, they are persuaded by its very presence, by the rhetoric that both describes and prescribes their relationship with the river. A people's rhetoric will indicate how the people view and value their river, how they connect with the basin its supports, and the nature of their economies within that basin. The rhetoric will simultaneously determine how the river is valued, initiating individuals within this river language and thereby prescribing the terms by which a people relate with their river. Changes in the rhetoric of a river can ripple among these relationships, affecting the people, the river and its basin.

Names

A rhetoric of a river begins with names. The words used to describe what is known today as the Walker River have changed dramatically in the past 165 years. The Walker originates in the central Sierra Nevada and flows north and east to Walker Lake in the high desert of the Great Basin. The east and west forks of the Walker slice across the river basin through a gauntlet of places and names: states called California and Nevada; counties called Mono, Douglas, Lyon; canyons called Walker, Hoye, and Wilson; valleys called Bridgeport, Antelope, Smith, Mason; towns called Bridgeport, Walker, Coleville, Topaz, and Wellington. The two forks join in Mason Valley and continue, past Yerington and Wabuska, into Mineral County, through Schurz, and on to Walker Lake.

Two Northern Paiute reservations exist in the lower reaches of the Walker River Basin. The Yerington Paiute Tribe's Campbell Ranch Reservation lies in northwest Mason Valley, connected to the river with a system of irrigation ditches. A few miles downstream, north of Walker Lake, the river splits the larger Walker River Indian Reservation, home of the Walker River Paiute Tribe. Although the river basin has existed for ages, the current catalog of names used to describe the river and its features has developed only recently. In less than two hundred years, the rhetoric of the river has been transformed. Remnants of an older rhetoric exist in little-used books and in the memories of the Northern Paiute people, the elders who remember a language and a way of life.

Numu

The people known as Northern Paiute called themselves by a different name. They called themselves *Numu*, which means People.

The Numu lived within a rhetoric of the river. They named the river *Agai Hoop*, which means Trout River. The Numu lived with the river, in its same canyons and valleys and at the edges of the lake into which it flowed. They called the lake *Agai Pah*, Trout Lake. There were trout in the lake and river; there were *agai*.

There were many bands of Numu, stretching north and south, and each band of Numu was called by a separate name. The Numu living at the northern edges of Agai Pah, near Schurz and the cur-

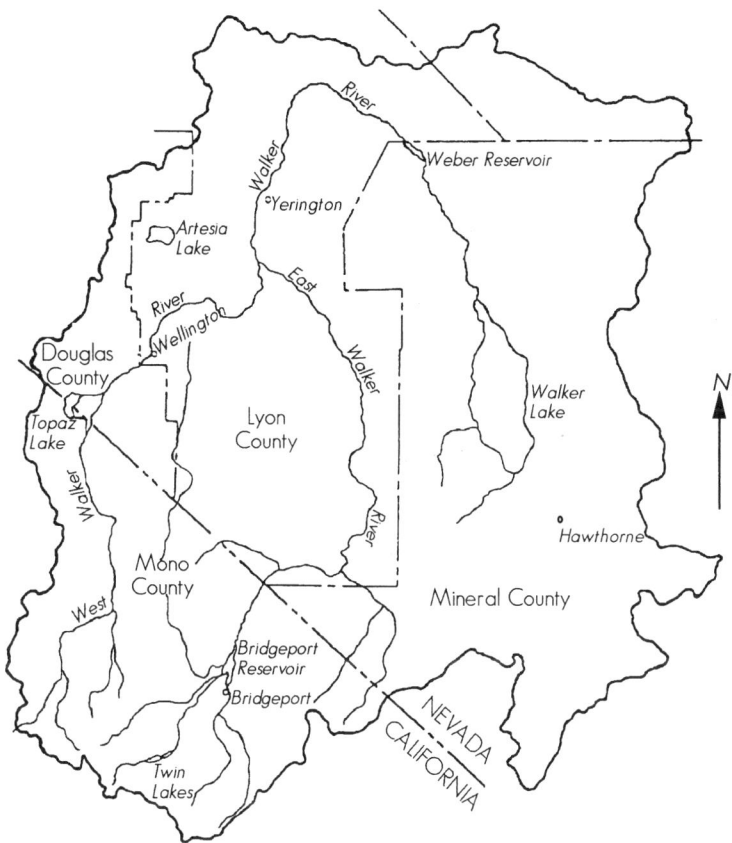

Walker River Subbasin, Central Lahontan Basin. (Adapted from *Water and Related Land Resources, Central Lahontan Basin, Walker River Subbasin,* USDA, 1969)

rent site of the Walker River Indian Reservation, were called *Agai Ticcutta.* Ticcutta means Eaters; the People living near Trout Lake were called Trout Eaters.

The Numu living in the valleys to the west of Agai Pah were called *Tubusi Ticcutta. Tubusi,* or grass bulb, grew in the valleys known today as Smith and Mason, and the Tubusi Ticcutta, the Grass Bulb Eaters, harvested the tubusi in season.

All the Numu bands were called in this manner, according to the foods of their region. To the north lived the *Cu-Yui Ticcutta,* the Cu-yui Eaters, of Pyramid Lake, and the *Toi Ticcutta,* the Tule Eaters, near the Carson Sink. The Fish Eaters, *Pugwi Ticcutta,* lived near the southern end of Agai Pah. Further south lived the *Cozabee Ticcutta,* the Fly Larvae Eaters, of Mono Lake. There were more bands as well, each with a name drawn from its region and surviving on agai, tubusi, cu-yui, and other foods. The Numu hunted and harvested seeds and bulbs, and in the autumn they traveled into the hills to gather piñon nuts. They went into the regions of the other bands and traded. When it was time for the agai to spawn, the Tubusi Ticcutta traveled downstream to help the Agai Ticcutta capture the fish.[1]

The Numu bands were connected in this way, with one another, with the water, with the lands in which they lived. The language of the Numu honored the connections. Their names for the water and the foods they ate were used to build the names of rivers and lakes and features of the land. The Numu named the river Agai Hoop for the agai, the trout. They named the lake and themselves in the same way, a rhetoric of connection. When the people spoke of the water, the plants or the trout, they spoke of their existence and their relationship with the river. The language of the Numu, of the Grass Bulb Eaters and the Trout Eaters, connected the People in their life with the waters and the land.

Walker

In 1833 the connections began to fray. That year a man named Joseph Reddeford Walker arrived in the Agai Hoop basin. Walker led a group of trappers along the Trout River from east to west, and returned the following year from California. During his sweeps through the lands of the Numu, Walker and his men killed nearly sixty of the People.

Soon, more parties of *taivo*, white people, were traveling through the lands of the Numu. In 1843 the man named Joseph Walker led another group of taivo through the area, past Agai Pah and along Agai Hoop. This time Walker's party killed over forty Numu.

In the fall of 1845 the famous explorer Captain John C. Frémont came to the Trout River basin. Frémont had read Joseph Walker's descriptions of Agai Pah and Agai Hoop and expected a bounty of trout. But the agai were hidden deep in the waters of Agai Pah, waiting for the time to spawn. Frémont and his group were disappointed.

Frémont renamed Agai Hoop and Agai Pah, calling them Walker River and Walker Lake. He named the waters for the white man he considered to have discovered them, and the Numu names faded. The People continued calling the waters by the old names, but the connection was broken. New names had been imposed from the outside, commemorating a man who had killed nearly one hundred of the People (Johnson, 21–23).

Frémont's renaming signaled a fundamental change in the rhetoric of the river. The words, the names, no longer carried the connection among the waters and the agai and the People. The name Walker meant death for Agai Hoop and the Numu rhetoric of connection.

Irrigation

The names continued to change, and with the changing language came different uses of the river and relationships with it. More taivo came into the lands of the Numu. In 1859, people of European heritage began to settle the valleys upstream from Walker Lake, the home regions of the Tubusi Ticcutta. Late in the summer of that year, Timothy and Cyrus Smith brought their cattle to the valley now known as Smith Valley. They came across the Sierra in search of good grazing land, which they found in the river bottoms of the Walker. In the fall a man named N. H. A. "Hoc" Mason came into the valley now known as Mason, and settled there the following year (Kersten, 79–80). The valleys of the Tubusi Ticcutta were named for these first taivo settlers, no longer for the grass bulb that grew in the region.

Agriculture steadily increased as more settlers came to the river valleys. For the first time, irrigation became a widespread practice on the Walker River. Ditches and diversion dams were built. More and more water was taken from the river and applied to the land to support the enterprises of the new settlers, their pasture and cropland.

On December 8, 1859, the same year in which the first white people settled in the valleys upstream, the Walker River Reservation was established on lands surrounding Walker Lake, the traditional homelands of the Agai Ticcutta and the Pugwi Ticcutta. From the beginning, the People on the reservation were encouraged to practice agriculture on their lands, to plant, to water the soils, to make them produce. Their earliest efforts consisted of cutting the wild hay in the river bottoms. But the Numu on the reservation, the Agai Ticcutta, had little knowledge of the taivo methods of irrigation (Johnson, 58–59).

Irrigation wasn't unknown to the Numu. Some bands of Numu practiced irrigation prior to the coming of the taivo, but a different kind of irrigation. One of these bands, according to the authors of *Searching Out the Headwaters,* was the Northern Paiutes of California's Owens Valley: "The Owens Valley Paiutes, generally described as hunters and gatherers, also developed irrigated agriculture. They constructed diversion structures in the valley's creeks, as well as regularly spaced ditches lateral to the creeks, each about 40 inches wide, and temporary dams to regulate water flow" (Bates et al., 20). The agriculture and irrigation practiced by the Owens Valley Numu were, according to John Walton, "tightly integrated with the broader patterns of settlement" (ibid.). In other words, the irrigation practices of the Owens Valley People, like the life-styles of the Numu in general, maintained and honored the People's connection with the water and the land.

There is also evidence of Numu irrigation in the Walker River basin, in what is now Smith Valley. In *The Yerington Paiute Tribe: A Numu History,* the earliest taivo settler in the region, Timothy Smith, commented on an irrigation ditch he found off Desert Creek, a Walker River tributary in southern Smith Valley. Smith said the ditch was half a mile long. Some tribal elders recalled the story of the ditch off Desert Creek: "There were two grasses here. One we call 'pozeda,' the other 'mahabeta.' 'Pozeda' is just like clover. We picked it and ate the leaves green. 'Pozeda' grows along Desert Creek. 'Pozeda' was always there but 'mahabeta' was planted by the Old People. They say some Numu from Bridgeport came here to Desert Creek to plant 'mahabeta'" (Hittman, 18). According to the story, not only was there irrigation, but it was used in part to support a crop that had been imported, indicating a regional agricultural economy. The account of how the ditch came to exist indicates the Numu way of life, their rhetoric of connection. The Numu, the Tubusi Ticcutta, claim the ditch was made by two fish native to Desert Creek. One fish wanted to go down out of the creek but couldn't make it, so the other fish "went down there on his belly, you know. That's how the ditch was made" (ibid.). Even when Numu irrigation did occur, the language used to explain it was connected with the environment and creatures of the region.

Numu knowledge and practice of irrigation were integrated with the pulse of the land. The Numu on the Walker River Indian Reservation at Schurz, whether or not they were aware of the irrigation practices of their kindred Numu bands, were ill equipped to begin large-scale irrigation farming. Such irrigation was outside their rhetoric of the river; they needed the new tools and to learn the new ways. It wasn't until 1866, seven years after the reservation had been established, that the Agai Ticcutta built their first irrigation ditch, but that ditch and many thereafter washed out in the spring floods.

The Agai Ticcutta adapted slowly to agriculture and became further disconnected from their language and heritage: "The native economy had been shattered by the invasion of the whites. The People worked their small plots on the reservation then went into Mason and Smith Valleys to work for the whites. Many took the names of the whites they worked for" (Johnson, 61). The Tubusi Ticcutta, who had been granted no reservation land in their traditional valleys, began to work on the taivo farms and ranches as well, in order to survive. They, too, took the names of the people they worked for. Michael Hittman writes, "One of the clearest signs of change from the traditional Numu culture was the acquisition of Taivo names" (21). More and more, the Numu of Agai Hoop were disconnected from their rhetoric and their traditional relationships with the river.

Controlling the Water

Even as the Numu went to work for the white people, the taivo agricultural operations were becoming larger. The replacement of the Numu names and language occurred in conjunction with the rise of agriculture in the basin. Irrigators who best understood the ways of western rivers—the wide variations in flow from season to season and year to year—understood the need to control and have access to a supply of water. Two men with such knowledge established miniature agriculture empires in the Walker River basin. Both men also held land outside the basin and played important roles in the other battles over water in the West, especially in California's early water conflicts and intrigues. Both men understood the evolving relationship between language and irrigation.

One of these men was named Henry Miller. By the 1880s, Hoc

Mason, the first white settler in Mason Valley, had acquired 20,000 acres of land. But drought and severe weather late in the decade left Mason bankrupt, and his holdings reverted to Henry Miller, who had bankrolled Mason's enterprise (Kersten, p. 119). Miller was the head of the famous Miller and Lux ranching operation, which at its height controlled over a million acres of land in the West. Marc Reisner calls Miller "a mythical figure in the history of California land fraud," a man who acquired much of his land in California's San Joaquin Valley through shady interpretations of the Swamp and Overflow Act (44). Miller was adept at using the emerging laws concerning land and water in the West to his advantage.

The other man, Thomas B. Rickey, owned many acres upstream from Miller's Mason Valley holdings, in the Antelope and Bridgeport Valleys of California. Rickey also owned land in the Owens Valley area farther south, land which played a key role in the successful attempt by the city of Los Angeles to control and divert water from the Owens River. At one point, Rickey owned 200,000 acres in California and Nevada (Kersten, 121–22; Reisner, 63–65, 69).

According to Kersten, "Before 1900, the available water supply of the Walker system was undergoing heavy pressure from irrigators along the river" (163). Within only forty years of the first taivo settlement, water supply in the Walker River basin was a major issue. Similar conflicts over water supply were occurring along many western rivers, and the presence of Miller and Rickey directly connected the small and isolated Walker River basin with those conflicts. Both Rickey and Miller knew that it was water that gave their lands value, that they needed a reliable water supply. Perhaps it was inevitable that these men would turn the conflict over Walker River water rights, the rhetoric of the river, into a legal battle.

Among Rickey's land holdings, at the north end of Antelope Valley, was a natural lake bed that occasionally held water. Rickey planned to divert water from the West Walker and store it in this reservoir site. When Miller learned of Rickey's plan, he became concerned about the effect such upstream storage would have on his downstream water rights: "In 1902, Miller and Lux, seeking to protect the water rights of their Mason Valley ranch, filed suit in United States Circuit Court against Thomas B. Rickey and all other water users on the Walker River" (Kersten, 163). The lawsuit, *Miller and Lux v. Thomas B. Rickey et al.*, marked the beginning of another chapter in the rhetoric of the river. The Numu rhetoric had been replaced, including the names for the river and the lake, for the foods, for the people themselves. The changing rhetoric of the river used the names of the recent white explorers and settlers.

For the first time, the rhetoric of the river began to be written down. The rhetoric, which had increasingly been a rhetoric of irrigation, became in 1902 a rhetoric of litigation. Less than seventy years after Joseph Walker's first visit to the Agai Hoop basin, the Walker River ran into a court of law.

Litigation

Miller and Lux v. Thomas B. Rickey et al. involved almost all of the water users along the river. The suit, finally settled in 1919, determined the legal water rights for those water users who had participated in the process and codified their rights in a document called Decree 731.

Decree 731 established Walker River water rights according to the doctrine of prior appropriation. The *Water Words Dictionary,* in defining the "prior appropriation doctrine," states that "the first person to take a quantity of water and put it to *Beneficial Use* has a higher priority of right than a subsequent user. Under drought conditions, higher priority users are satisfied before junior users receive water" (206). The prior appropriation doctrine had developed during the taivo settlement of the West as a method of securing and assigning water rights. The most common beneficial use for water, throughout the West and especially on the Walker River, was irrigated agriculture.

In creating Decree 731, the task of the federal court was to determine which lands had been irrigated beneficially, as well as to determine the year in which the beneficial use had begun. Through various sorts of evidence and testimony, the court established rights to Walker River water reaching back to 1860, when the first white settlers began irrigating. The rights were expressed as a certain amount of water, in cubic feet per second, to be applied to a certain acreage according to a certain priority date (Kersten, 164).

After 1902, and especially after 1919, newcomers to the Walker River basin, whether immigrants or born into the region, lived within a very different kind of rhetoric of the river, one that spelled out the very details of water use. Prior to Decree 731 there was no legal system for distributing the river water among the various users. After the decree such a method was written into law. Decree 731 established water rights and priority dates for most of the water users in the basin. But there were still holes in the decree. What Decree 731 did not do was address the possibility of water storage in the river basin or satisfy the United States government and the Walker River Paiute Tribe.

The issue of water storage was addressed in 1919, the same year the decree went into effect. That year, the Walker River Irrigation District was organized by farmers and ranchers in Smith and Mason Valleys to store water for irrigation. By 1924 the district had constructed two reservoirs—Topaz Lake on the West Walker, at the site of Thomas Rickey's planned reservoir, and Bridgeport Reservoir on the East Walker. For the first time, significant water storage possibilities existed in the Walker River basin, and irrigators could hope to have water available later in the growing season. In both rhetoric and physical appearance, the way of the river resembled less and less the old river called Agai Hoop.

Bridgeport Reservoir Dam was completed in 1924. In that same year, the United States government, on behalf of the Walker River Indian Reservation, sued the Walker River Irrigation District and all other water users in the river basin. The government and the Walker River Paiute Tribe were unhappy with the water rights granted to the reservation by Decree 731. Under the decree, the reservation's water rights were determined by the same method used to determine the rights of any water user. In order for a right to exist, water must have been diverted from the river and used to irrigate an amount of land beginning in a certain year. According to the court's determination in the decree, the reservation's earliest water right was for 4.7 cubic feet of water per second on 385.95 acres with a priority date of 1869, a decent right but not among the best in the system. Some priorities on the river were dated as early as 1860.

In arguing for an amended water right, the government and the tribe depended in part upon a 1908 U.S. Supreme Court case called *Winters v. United States.* According to the *Water Words Dictionary,* "In *Winters,* the Court held that when reservations were established, Indian tribes and the United States implicitly reserved, along with the land, sufficient water to fulfill the purposes of the reservations" (319). The *Winters* precedent seemed to apply to the Numu on the Walker River Indian Reservation, for they had been encouraged to practice agriculture since the establishment of the reservation in 1859. The tribe hoped that a favorable ruling based on Winters would greatly improve the reservation's water right.

On March 21, 1936, the federal District Court ruled in the case of *United States v. Walker River Irrigation District et al.*, creating Decree C-125. The new decree superseded Decree 731, and improved upon it in as well, comprehensively detailing water rights for almost every user throughout the river basin. The decree also addressed the issue of water storage rights, especially for the Walker River Irrigation District reservoirs. The decree noted which individual members of WRID had storage rights and in what quantities (Jones, 59).

The initial ruling, however, was not favorable to the Walker River Indian Reservation. Decree C-125 granted the tribe water rights totaling 22.93 cubic feet of water per second on 1905.55 acres under five separate priority dates (United States, Decree C-125, 10). Only minor details differed from the water right in the previous decree; for example, the earliest priority date was changed from 1869 to 1868.

In making his ruling, District Judge St. Sure made the following statement:

> Briefly, the facts . . . show that . . . commencing in 1860 the whites acquired title from the United States to land above the Indian Reservation, bordering on and adjacent to the Walker river and its tributaries; that they also acquired water by prior appropriation for a beneficial use, and actually irrigated and reclaimed such lands; that they have enjoyed undisputed and undisturbed possession of such lands and such water rights for more than 50 years; that to dispossess them now would bring ruin to long-established settlers, and return to waste the lands which they, by their industry and with the acquiescence of the government, reclaimed from the desert.
>
> Under such facts and circumstances this court is not moved to give a decree destroying the rights of the white pioneers. (United States, 14 Federal Supplement 11)

The government and the Walker River Paiute Tribe had been hoping for an 1859 priority date on their water rights. The judge, however, completely discounted *Winters* and ignored the changes that had occurred in the Numu way of life and their rhetoric of connection. His statement was a clear endorsement for the newer rhetoric of the river, for irrigation by the "white pioneers." Under the latest document in the rhetoric of the river, the Walker River Indian Reservation remained a fairly junior water-right holder.

On the basis of the *Winters* precedent, the government and the tribe immediately appealed the ruling on the reservation's water right to the Ninth Circuit Court of Appeals. The court ruled on the appeal on June 5, 1939: "The decree is reversed with directions to enter a decree adjudging the United States to be entitled to the continuous flow of 26.25 cubic feet of water per second, to be diverted from Walker River upon or above Walker River Indian Reservation . . . for the irrigation of two thousand one hundred acres of land on the reservation . . . with a priority of 1859" (United States, 104 Federal Reporter 340). Decree C-125 had been amended, granting the reservation more water on more acreage with the earliest priority date on the river system. With the amended water right and its early priority date, with a reliable water supply and the corresponding ability to irrigate effectively, the Numu of the Walker River Reservation, the old Agai Ticcutta, became full participants in the rhetoric of irrigation and an agricultural economy.

Howard Rogers

The litigation process that resulted in Decree C-125 had begun in 1902, when Henry Miller sued Thomas Rickey. That was also the year in which Howard Rogers was born, in Smith Valley, to a Numu mother and a taivo father. The life of Howard Rogers was the intersection of the evolving rhetorics of the river.

In an interview near the end of his life, Howard and his wife, Lena, recalled the details of nearly a century of life in Smith and Mason Valleys (October 15, 1994). Howard lived his early years with his mother's Numu band, remnants of the Tubusi Ticcutta, as they ranged along the Walker River in search of survival. Some of the People in Howard's band still spoke the Numu language and knew the older ways. Howard learned these things as he grew, the Numu language and all that it carried. He learned the ways of gathering piñon nuts and other Numu foods. He learned the traditions and rituals, the sacred places. He learned the stories of the People, how the world came to be the way it was.

Howard learned the old story of the two fish in Desert Creek who made the Numu ditch, the story that explained how pozeda and mahabeta were irrigated:

Atsa paggwe [little fish], you know, he's going to make that ditch. So he started out. Just like a ditcher. But when he got down there and look back, no water. So he just stood down there at the bottom and said, "*Paaia ya-ya!* No water coming behind."

That other fish is little. But he's got a big head and a little horn on his big head. He's only about six inches long. And he was over there, layin' down, pickin' a little rock up, throwin' pebbles down, makin' a small hole with his pebbles. Then he went down there. He heard his partner callin' for water, and so he belly-whopped down there. Ploughed that ditch. Then the water came right behind him. (Hittman, 19)

In the stories and names he learned, Howard carried the remnants of the Numu rhetoric of the river, the language connected with the seasons and the trout and the grasses.

But Howard Rogers was immersed in a mixed rhetoric. His Numu band still camped along the river and moved with the seasons, but now the moves were often tied to the rhythms of irrigation, of planting and harvest, not to the spawning of the agai or gathering tubusi. Many of the Numu worked the farms and ranches, and when Howard was old enough, he did so as well. He learned the ways of farming and ranching and taivo irrigation. He learned to negotiate the rhetorics of the river.

Campbell Ranch

The Numu of Smith and Mason Valleys had never been granted a reservation of their own, only a small colony on the outskirts of Yerington. While the Walker River Paiute Tribe was in the midst of a legal fight to improve their reservation's water rights, the old Tubusi Ticcutta had nothing to fight for at all.

In 1936, the same year in which Decree c-125 went into effect, the federal government purchased a ranch and water rights in Mason Valley for the Yerington Paiute Tribe, the approximately 1,100-acre Campbell Ranch. The Campbell Ranch lands had been through several owners during the time of irrigation on the Walker River and were originally a part of the Miller and Lux holdings in Mason Valley (ibid., 41). Although several miles from the river, the ranch was connected with the system through the Campbell ditch and other irrigation ditches.

In 1936, Howard and Lena Rogers brought their children from Smith Valley to Mason Valley and the Campbell Ranch. They were among the original assignees to the new reservation and were granted the use of approximately thirty acres of land. A total of twelve such assignments were created on Campbell Ranch. Howard and Lena Rogers named their assignment the R7 Ranch and began to run stock and plant and irrigate.

The new residents of Campbell Ranch had a hard time surviving on the fruits of their thirty acres alone, and Howard continued to work outside the reservation. Michael Hittman writes that "Howard Rogers broke horses in Smith and Mason Valley" (43). He continued to range over the lands of the Tubusi Ticcutta, to irrigate in the taivo way, to gather piñon nuts in the fall. Howard continued to exist in the mixture of his rhetorics.

Campbell Ranch itself existed in a mixture of rhetorics. A new reservation on old Miller and Lux land, Campbell Ranch existed in the shadow of Decree c-125 and of the rhetoric of irrigation and litigation embodied in that document. Campbell Ranch had water rights determined under prior appropriation, 8.5777 cubic feet of water per second over 715 acres of land with priority dates ranging from 1864 to 1905. Campbell Ranch was a member of the Walker River Irrigation District and had the right to 552 acre feet of the water stored in Topaz Reservoir and 253 acre feet of the water stored in Bridgeport Reservoir. Campbell Ranch and its water rights were the product of the development of irrigation in the Walker River basin. Campbell Ranch was the home of Howard Rogers, of the People, of what remained of the Tubusi Ticcutta. From its inception, Campbell Ranch existed as the combination of these contradictory forces.

Beneficial Use

When Decree c-125 came into effect in 1936, it immediately became the most important document in the rhetoric of the Walker River. Decree c-125 was the result of more than thirty years of water rights litigation, and more than forty years of increasing irrigation pressure on the river system prior to that. At the time of its ruling, the court made sure that the decree would remain important: "The Court retains jurisdiction of this cause for the purpose of . . . correcting or modifying this decree" (Decree c-125, 72–73). In the following years there were some revisions to the decree. Most significant, the priority date and amount of water for the Walker River Indian Reservation's water right were adjusted as a result of the government's appeal. But the integrity of the decree as a governing document remained intact. When Howard Rogers died in December of 1994, Decree c-125 was still the most important document in the rhetoric of the Walker River.

Decree c-125 articulates the rights to water use for virtually the entire river basin, listing in detail the owner of the right, the amount of water, the amount and position of the land, and the priority date. Among those entities appearing in these listings are the remnants of the Agai Ticcutta and the Tubusi Ticcutta. The decree also accounts for the Walker River Irrigation District's right to store water in its reservoirs. And it even addresses the rights to the occasional flood waters, water that occurs when all the water rights in the system have been satisfied.

The text of the decree declares that "the owners of the use of the several amounts of water from the several streams . . . are entitled to divert and use such waters of Walker River and/or its tributaries as the case may be, for the beneficial purposes specified, subject to and in accord with the priorities above set forth" (Decree c-125, 70). This is essentially a restatement of the prior appropriation doctrine, which is the guiding principle behind the decree. A water-right holder has the right to divert the amount of water for its beneficial use, assuming all water-rights holders with earlier priority dates have been satisfied.

Essentially, Decree c-125 is a document concerning the right to irrigate in the Walker River basin. Almost invariably, irrigation is the "beneficial purpose specified" in the particular listings of the decree. Any water rights granted for a beneficial purpose other than irrigation are so insignificant as to be meaningless. And in order for irrigation to take place, water must be diverted from the river.

Agai Pah

Within the dominant rhetoric, the rhetoric of irrigation, the lake once known as Agai Pah is dying. The altitude of Walker Lake's surface is estimated to have been 4,083 feet in 1882, a figure that remained fairly stable until about 1920 (Rush); in 1990 the altitude of the lake's surface had dropped below 3,960 feet above sea level (Jones, 33). In a little over 100 years the lake level has dropped more than 100 feet, and most of this loss has occurred in the last 70 years. According to the Nevada Division of Water Resources, "Walker Lake has been receding since the turn of the century as a result of upstream water diversions coincident with long-term climatic changes" (32). Roger Bezayiff, who as federal water master for the Walker River basin is charged with distributing water according to Decree C-125, stated in an interview (December 1, 1989) that the water of the Walker River is allocated at 135 percent of its average annual flow and storage. In other words, in an average year, 35 percent of water rights go unfulfilled. Only in exceptional years such as the winter and spring of 1995 does water reach Walker Lake, and this is not enough to reverse the decline.

While irrigation has certainly played some part in the lake's loss in elevation, it has played a more significant role in the loss of the native cutthroat trout fishery. According to the *Walker River Atlas*, "Before upstream agricultural water development, cutthroats from Walker Lake are reported to have migrated as far upstream as Robinson Creek, above Bridgeport Valley" (Jones, 85). The cutthroat had lived within Agai Pah and Agai Hoop as a total system, not just within the lake or the river. Irrigation disrupted that dynamic: "Before the intruders came there were many fish. But the whites in Mason and Smith Valleys built irrigation dams. If the fish succeeded in getting over the dams their offspring often ended up in some rancher's field" (Johnson, 95). Less than 100 years after the arrival of Timothy Smith in 1859, the cutthroat trout native to Agai Pah were essentially gone. Ironically, the end of the trout's ability to spawn was the dam that created Weber Reservoir, built on the Walker River Indian Reservation in the 1930s to store the reservation's water right (Jones, 85). Within the rhetoric of irrigation, the Agai Ticcutta participated in the demise of the thing for which they had once been named.

A hatchery program was created to replace the native cutthroat trout fishery, but now even that is imperiled: "The concentrations of dissolved minerals and salts are getting so high that the lake is in danger of losing its fishery" (Bremner). Irrigation contributed to the death of the native strain of agai, and it continues to contribute to the dying of a lake.

Evolving Rhetoric

When Howard Rogers died, a little of the memory of the older rhetoric of the river died with him. Howard had spoken the Numu language, had known the Numu names, the Numu stories, the Numu ways. But the Numu rhetoric began to be replaced in 1833, when Joseph Walker arrived, or in 1845, when Frémont named the river after Walker. The rhetoric of irrigation superseded the prior rhetoric of the river, and that has thrown Walker River basin out of balance.

A return to the Numu rhetoric of connection would not be feasible. The agai and the Agai Ticcutta are dead. Under the present system and despite an exceptional water year in 1995 (ibid.), the demise of Walker Lake as a life-supporting body of water is likely imminent. The water in the system is appropriated at 135 percent of its average annual storage and direct flow, which means that only in rare years will significant amounts of water reach the lake.

The lake called Agai Pah is already gone, dead with the agai it was named for. The people living with the river have changed, and the language has changed as well. The rhetoric can continue to evolve, to come back into balance. In the evolving rhetoric, irrigated agriculture might continue to exist. Enough water might flow into Walker Lake to sustain its viability. Enough water might remain in the river to support the fisheries upstream. But in order for that balance to be achieved, room must be made for these things in the rhetoric. A document like Decree c-125 must open up and recognize rights beyond irrigation, or some other rhetorical vehicle must be found.

The Walker River is in the Great Basin, the driest region in the nation. There is pressure on the Walker River system, competition among water users, conflict among the various interests. The Numu rhetoric of connection has been replaced. But perhaps enough of the memory of that rhetoric remains to provide the model for a new rhetoric of connection, a way to negotiate among the interests and users. Perhaps language can help shape a new balance.

NOTES

1. The details on the Northern Paiute language and way of life are from *The Yerington Paiute Tribe: A Numu History,* 3; *Walker River Paiutes: A Tribal History,* 7–9; and *Paiute-English, English-Paiute Dictionary.* These texts represent both the Yerington and Walker River Paiute Tribes, and there are minor differences in the spellings for some words. For ease of discussion I have consolidated the spellings, drawing from both tribes. For example, I have used *Numu* from the Yerington sources, but the Walker River text spells it *Numa.* The Yerington spelling for *Agai Pah* is *agi baa'a.* For *Agai Hoop* it is *agi-witu hooopu.*

REFERENCES

Agricultural Experiment Station, University of Nevada. *Economic Study of the Walker River Irrigation District.* Reno: The Agricultural Experiment Station, 1933.

Bates, Sarah F., David H. Getches, Lawrence J. Macdonnell, and Charles F. Wilkinson. *Searching Out the Headwaters: Change and Rediscovery in Western Water Policy.* Washington, D.C.: Island Press, 1993.

Bezayiff, Roger. Interview by author. November 11, 1994. Telephone interviews by author. December 1, 1994, December 5, 1994.

Bremner, Faith. "First Good Shot of Water Since the Drought Began." *Reno Gazette Journal,* April 28, 1995, final edition, sec. A, p. 1.

Giron, Bernie. Interview by author. November 17, 1994.

Hittman, Michael. *The Yerington Paiute Tribe: A Numu History.* Yerington, Nev.: Yerington Paiute Tribe, 1984.

Howard, Tony. Interview by author. November 17, 1994.

Johnson, Edward Charles. *Walker River Paiutes: A Tribal History.* Schurz, Nev.: Walker River Paiute Tribe, 1975.

Jones, Jeanine. *Walker River Atlas.* Sacramento: State of California, Resources Agency, Department of Water Resources, 1992.

Kersten, Earl William, Jr. "Settlements and Economic Life in the Walker River Country of Nevada and California." Ph.D. diss., University of Nebraska, 1961.

Nevada Division of Water Resources. *Alternative Plans for Water Resource Use.* Vol. 1. Carson City: Nevada Division of Water Resources, 1974.

Poldevaart, Arie. *Paiute-English, English-Paiute Dictionary.* Yerington, Nev.: Yerington Paiute Tribe, 1987.

Reisner, Marc. *Cadillac Desert.* Rev. ed. New York: Penguin, 1993.

Rogers, Howard. Interview by author. October 15, 1994.

Rogers, Lena. Interview by author. October 15, 1994.

Rogers, Sandy. Interview by author. October 14, 1994.

Rush, Eugene F. *Hydrologic Regimen of Walker Lake, Mineral County, Nevada.* Washington, D.C.: U.S. Geological Survey, 1970.

USDA Nevada River Basin Survey Staff. *Water and Related Land Resources, Central Lahontan Basin, Walker River Subbasin.* Carson City: U.S. Department of Agriculture, 1969.

U.S. District Court for the State of Nevada. Decree c-125. Reno: U.S. District Court, April 14, 1936.

———. *United States vs. Walker River Irrigation District.* March 21, 1936. 14 Federal Supplement 11.

U.S. Ninth Circuit Court of Appeals. *United States vs. Walker River Irrigation District.* June 5, 1939. 104 Federal Reporter, 2d Ser.

Walker River Irrigation District. *By-Laws and Rules and Regulations.* Yerington, Nev.: Walker River Irrigation District, n.d.

Hydraulic Cities
The Urbanization of the Mid-Columbia Plateau

In the late 1800s scores of Euroamericans traveled west to cultivate land in the arid West.[1] The river bottoms were settled first, leaving the higher, drier parcels for later homesteaders. By the 1890s, it became obvious that most of the region was unsuited for agriculture without the aid of irrigation. Boosters, settlers, and politicians extolled the region's potential—with reclamation, they promised, the West could "blossom like the rose." No one questioned the agrarian ideal: whether the myth of the yeoman farmer was unrealistic in such a dry and fragile environment. Instead, the area would be populated by agriculturalists in a development closely resembling lands east of the Mississippi River.

The federal Reclamation Act of 1902 provided much of the technology, expertise, and means to water millions of acres in the West. To secure passage of the legislation, supporters used the argument of sustaining America's homestead tradition. Thus, the western landscape was perceived or "read" in agricultural terms—the numerous valleys lying between mountain ranges or the almost desert strips were seen as potential breadbaskets. The only obstacles were technological or economic in nature. An American culture imbued with notions of the agrarian ideal dictated this response.

But today, western populations are changing again. In contrast to the earlier pastoral image, many western locales, once settled by agriculturalists and sustained by federal reclamation projects, are being transformed into "Western cityscapes."[2] Thus the subject of a transformed, urbanized West is a familiar one, considered by journalists, economists, historians, political scientists, and geographers, to name a few. Cities such as Las Vegas, Phoenix, and Albuquerque expand as newcomers arrive in search of a particular quality of life with a western backdrop. Scholars, alarmed over a diminishing water resource base to support the burgeoning population, explore the effects of urbanization. Libraries contain numerous books examining the loss of agricultural land to urban use and the subsequent impact this transition will have on water supplies. Some scholars applaud the transformation, believing that urban users consume less than agricultural users and that the delivery system for residential use is usually more efficient. Still others, most notably Helen Ingram, lament the shift to urbanization as she views the impact on rural communities and the loss of a rural life-style. To Ingram, the losers are the rural poor, including Native American and Hispanic water users (Ingram 1990, 1987).

Yet economists Terry L. Anderson and Donald R. Leal see the transition as an opportunity to employ market incentives to water resources. They advocate a western economy that would include water market transfers, reasoning that by transferring and attaching a market value to water resources, water will possess a real value. Further, an enlightened self-interest will guide the use of water supplies, resulting in a more efficient use of the resource (Anderson and Leal 1991). Others view these events in light of who is controlling the resource, and many reach the same conclusion—whether urban or agricultural use, water supplies are controlled by a few (Gottlieb 1988; McCool 1987; Worster 1985, 1994).

My case study of the Mid-Columbia Plateau, with particular emphasis on the southern Yakima Valley where the city of Kennewick, one of the Tri-Cities with Richland and Pasco, is located and irrigated by the Kennewick Irrigation District, is intended to add to these insights. From the late 1960s up to the present, in an economy increasingly dependent on the Hanford Nuclear Reservation, members of the Kennewick Irrigation District and its environs witnessed an urban transformation as subdivisions replaced orchards and other agricultural enterprises. Once portrayed as an agricultural mecca, the Tri-Cities is now often depicted as an urban oasis with its residents living in quiet, suburban bedroom communities— a shift affecting the inhabitants and environment in several ways.

In the nineteenth century, developers and settlers perceived the land in agricultural terms, envisioning fertile, thriving farms with the aid of irrigation. Now, developers and residents project a landscape dotted with industrial parks, commercial and professional sites, and residential dwellings surrounded by green, manicured lawns, all with the aid of irrigation. Further, this change in perception has reenforced another belief that existed before urbanization, namely, the potential of technology to change the desert. The agricultural paradise that settlers first predicted for the area could only be realized through twentieth-century technology, and the same holds true today. If the area is to be urbanized with more residential water users, then new engineering techniques need to be applied to provide the crucial resource of water. As a result, by altering the current water delivery system, the habitat that it supports will also be affected. But physical surroundings (or rather, the limitations of the Mid-Columbia Plateau to sustain a growing population) are no more considered now than they were in the late 1800s. Instead, it is believed that technological innovations will accommodate growing settlement. The dominant culture of capitalism and industrialization remains intact, as Tri-Cities' residents view progress and technology as solutions in and of themselves. Ironically, the appeal to many of the residents of the Mid-Columbia Plateau is the same landscape they wish to alter.

But urbanization has had other consequences. In the Yakima Valley, irrigators, environmentalists, the Yakima Indian Nation, and recreational and commercial interests all compete for water in the face of a diminishing salmon population; urbanization adds one more dimension to the conflict. Finally, western institutions such as the Kennewick Irrigation District have evolved in response to urbanization. Initially, irrigation district officials appeared as unsophisticated, struggling farmers. The image changed, however, as the district grew, and by the 1990s, the district could boast of a sophisticated administrative machinery, employing a large staff, assessing more than 14,000 water users, publishing a newsletter, hiring a resource manager to market district property, and maintaining memberships in regional and national water associations. Accompanying the evolution is an increase in wealth and power. Despite the far-reaching implications of urbanization, the residential water user seems less aware of, or at the least indifferent to, the scarcity of the resource than was his agricultural predecessor. Thus the manipulation of water in the West—this time through PVC-lined ditches and underground pressurized pipelines, instead of dams, reservoirs, and hydropower facilities—continues to characterize and transform the area.

Located in southern Washington, the Mid-Columbia Plateau surprises the first-time visitor with its sharp contrasts: a desert land-

scape, yet a riverine environment with its many tributaries empty-
ing into the Columbia River. The predominant image is that of a vast
expanse of blowing tumbleweed, rabbit brush, cheatgrass, and sagebrush. A unique terrain, the arid plateau is a flat plain interrupted
by basalt terraces or plateaus that rise out of the river canyons and
dry coulees. Along the river bottoms grow cottonwood and willow
trees, and in the canyons above live the rattlesnakes, chukar par-
tridge, and other wildlife.

Rainfall is minimal, with annual precipitation ranging from seven
to nine inches, and the climate varies from high, desertlike tem-
peratures in the summer to cool winters. The area is classified as
"arid steppe" vegetation, which supported early inhabitants with
the camas root and bitterroot, various berries, large quantities of
salmon, and deer, elk, and sharp-tailed grouse. The Columbia River
is the major river to cut through this landscape, draining the Yakima,
Snake, Spokane, Flathead, Kootenai, Okanogan, and Clark Fork
Rivers.

The early inhabitants of the Mid-Columbia were the ancestors
of several Native American tribes: the Yakima, Nez Perce, Paluse,
and Klickitat. All seminomadic cultures, they subsisted on a diet
of roots, especially the camas root, berries, fish, and game. In this
riverine environment, water played an important role in their mythology. In their cosmology, "the sun (*an*) is Father; water (*cuus*),
the first sacred food." The tribes lived next to the rivers and relied
extensively on salmon. The spring chinook salmon runs were an integral part of a 12,000-year-old culture (Hunn, 91).

By 1855, however, the first indication of change occurred with
the Stevens Treaty, forcing most of the area tribes to cede land to
the United States that would later be parts of Washington, Oregon, and Idaho. The signature tribes were provided land that would
eventually be reduced to contemporary reservations, including the
Yakima Indian Reservation, where many of the descendents of the
Mid-Columbia Indians live. Washington territorial governor Issac
Stevens pursued the treaty, hoping to free up the land and attract
settlers to the interior. However, it would take the arrival of the
Northern Pacific Railroad in 1883 for settlement to ensue.

Yet even with the railroad, early settlers—envisioning an agricultural economy—expressed disappointment when they first encountered the region. In the area surrounding Kennewick, in the
southern end of the Yakima Valley, located nearby the conjunction

of the Yakima and Columbia Rivers, newcomers described the area as "nothing but hot winds, and dust and sagebrush," a "bunchgrass waste." Later, the townsite of Kennewick was depicted as "one of long waiting and hope deferred" (U.S. Public Works Administration 1936; *An Illustrated History*, 227).[3] The only way to transform what these settlers believed to be a barren, useless land was through irrigation. After private developers started work on an irrigation project to reclaim up to 50,000 acres, one local newspaper reported in 1893 that "two years ago if a man had settled on a piece of that land he would have been advised to emigrate to Steilacoom or Medical Lake [area mental institutions]. Water makes all the difference. The people residing in the district bounded by the canal are putting in the crops, some setting out orchards, others seeding their land to alfalfa, potatoes or oats" (*Yakima Herald*, May 25, 1893). The phrase "water makes all the difference" underscored the history of Euroamerican settlement in the arid West.

From that point on, the history of the Mid-Columbia Plateau and perhaps its most valuable resource, water, would be radically different from the preceding 12,000 years. Throughout the region, private developers, followed by state and federal agencies, embarked on a series of irrigation enterprises—tapping water supplies in the Yakima and Columbia Rivers—that still shape the political, social, and economic well-being of the area. After forming the Kennewick Irrigation District in 1917 (an area comprising 38,000 acres and later 55,000 acres), water users sought for the next forty years to secure federal financing of the project. A maturation process took place as district officials evolved from naïve, Babbitt-type boosters, constantly frustrated in their attempts to deal with the United States Bureau of Reclamation (USBR), to the present-day sophisticated, image-conscious agribusiness and community leaders. Further, the gap between the Washington-based USBR and the rural irrigation district closed as their goals paralleled each other, and the political power that was once solely in the hands of the federal agency devolved to the local elites.[4]

In 1917, however, none of these events was foreseen as the Kennewick Irrigation District began its quest for federal funding. Local boosters extolled the fertility of area farms: the county agriculturalist stated that "there is no other body of land in the Northwest where the per acre yield of those food products so much needed at this time, would be as great as here." The local media portrayed the Kennewick Highlands, a 4,000-acre tract within the irrigation district, as a Garden of Eden, with unlimited potential. But in ten years these perceptions would be drastically altered. Farmers were forced to plant different crops and federal financing was still not attained (*Kennewick Courier-Reporter,* December 6, 1917).

By the 1920s, federal officials received alarming reports from area farmers in the Kennewick Highlands that if the USBR did not offer the settler hope, his only option would be abandonment. One supporter of the Kennewick project said he hoped his project would be chosen next by the USBR "as hope is everything when confronted by a hard situation" (Rudkin to Jones, Jones Papers). Other reports described the condition of area families as "pitiable" without an adequate water supply (Moulton to Jones, November 20, 1926, Jones Papers). Further, when the USBR did survey the district to determine whether to award federal monies, the engineers concluded: "The unimproved land on the upper part of the division is rough and broken. A relatively long canal will have to be constructed for a narrow fringe of land until it reaches the main body of better land in the vicinity of Kennewick. The land is quite sandy and will require a large amount of water to grow crops under irrigation. This land is not regarded as having the fertility or the water holding capacity of much of the land of the Yakima-Benton Division" (Commissioner to Chief Engineer, August 1, 1923, in National Archives). Despite the disparaging comments, Kennewick boosters persisted in their efforts with a "never-say-die" attitude. Thus, the persistence of a cultural perception of the land, regardless of conflicting evidence, has a long history (*Yakima Daily Republic,* February 13, 1930).

Bad luck plagued the district during the 1930s, prompting one area resident to remark that in the Kennewick area, "they have three different classes of people, one here, one coming, and one going" (Denhoff to President Roosevelt, April 12, 1935, in National Archives). Many of those leaving, however, left behind large tracts of land, and the district assumed ownership. With urbanization, the abandoned land became valuable commercial and residential real estate. But in the 1930s, owners considered the land too worthless to even pay taxes on it.

But Kennewick's destiny was to change with the advent of a global war and the subsequent establishment of the nearby Hanford Nuclear Reservation, which appropriated 6,000 to 7,000 acres of irrigated agricultural holdings. Construction of the Kennewick division

meant replacing the lost agricultural land, and federal officials reasoned that the division would provide homesites for returning vet-
erans and jobs for displaced wartime construction workers. Finally,
boosters reminded federal officials that the area had "the earliest
producing season in the Pacific Northwest" (U.S. Dept. of Interior
1947:19; Fyfe to Crownover, June 20, 1945, in Kennewick Irrigation District Archives). In 1948, the district received congressional
authorization for the reclamation project.[5] Underlying the entire report recommending authorization was the assumption that land developed in the Kennewick division would be used for agricultural
purposes. Although a small portion of the lands that had been previously farmed were being converted into residential lots, the USBR
planned for the newly irrigated land in the district to be divided
into full-time farms or acreages large enough to sustain a family at
"an adequate level of living" (U.S. Dept. of Interior 1947:1,19). Experts provided estimates of incomes from farming operations on
various soil classifications, demonstrating that families could earn
a livelihood through cultivation of the designated 160-acre tracts.
All of this pointed to a continued belief in the agrarian myth of the
yeoman farmer (ibid.:116–17). Despite the misfortunes suffered by
many Kennewick agriculturalists in the 1920s and 1930s, the conviction persisted that Kennewick land could, and should, support
primarily a farming community.[6]

Residents in the community shared these sentiments, perceiving
an agricultural landscape. The only obstacle to realizing the landscape had been technological, which was now being corrected. Thus
it was with great pride that one observer remarked that "engineering history is being made" and that the construction firms were
"staging a pitched battle with nature, matching engineering skill
against a rampaging river and solid basalt rock to win more than
19,000 acres of raw, arid land over to peaceful usefulness" (*Tri-City
Herald,* March 7, 1954).

The federal agency also provided agents as part of a settler assistance program. Thus, settlers were helped in establishing themselves and bringing new land, completing homestead entries, under
irrigation. Federal officials hoped the reclaimed land would be devoted to the raising of high-income crops like mint, tree fruits,
and asparagus. To ensure that the newcomers would be farmers,
the potential settlers applied for the homesteads and had to have
worked in agriculture for at least two years. Further, the applicant

was to submit five recommendation letters, of which four had to be from fellow farmers. Once chosen, the USBR assured homesteaders of help with soil classification and crops. By 1957, the new irrigation and power works were in place, ready to serve a predominantly agricultural population.[7]

Despite these intentions, the area began to urbanize in the late 1960s, spurred by the sparkplug of the Tri-Cities' economy—the Hanford nuclear works. Urbanization first occurred with an increased number of subdivisions, resulting in one of the first problems the district encountered, namely, delivering water to residential lots that had once been agricultural land. Thus in the area that was once touted as a "Garden of Eden" and promised the highest per-acre yield in the Pacific Northwest district, ditchriders were unable to deliver an adequate amount of water because of the increased number of residential water users. When the Bureau of Reclamation planned the irrigation works, the procedure for water service was for the ditchriders to deliver water to the high point on each forty-acre parcel (Kennewick Irrigation District Minutes, May 5, 1970). Also, the demand for water by agricultural users followed a certain pattern, which ditchriders could predict. When lands were sold and broken into subdivisions, the district staff was obligated to supply water to each forty-acre tract and made arrangements to accommodate this type of delivery. Thus, the Kennewick district was not prepared to deal with the growing number of suburban users, all tied into the one main hookup, which had earlier served the forty-acre parcel.

These changes precipitated a second problem. Not only did the ditchriders have to contend with an increased number of irrigators for each forty-acre tract, but the type of water user also changed, from one with agricultural needs to one with suburban requirements. Where the agriculturalist irrigated so many acres at a certain time and notified the ditchrider of his schedule, the urban user applied water to the lawn at different peak hours with no advance warning. Instead, the demand of the residential client was instantaneous, making it difficult for the ditchrider to determine how much to turn into the canal. Further, many residential water users who lived near the canal placed pumps that were too large in the ditch and were taking out more than their share of water and not leaving enough for others. In short, the ditchrider had to contend with unregulated water and unanticipated flows. The establishment of local improvement districts (LIDs) resolved part of this problem but also presented new difficulties.[8]

Local improvement districts create a system of pressurized underground pipes that can provide water directly to the individual homeowner. Praised for their efficiency, the LIDs do cut down on water loss through seepage and evaporation and offer the water user a more conservation-oriented structure. But at the same time, without the open canal and the seepage that results, groundwater levels in the surrounding areas are affected, and in areas where LIDs have replaced an open ditch, springs have dried up. Further, with an earthen-lined canal, the seepage that results helps to dilute the nitrate level, a product of pesticides used for crops, in the surrounding agricultural fields. Also, any plant or wildlife supported by the canals is eliminated, although one could argue that this habitat was only introduced through irrigation and was not part of the "natural order."

Still another problem exists regarding residential water use and the establishment of LIDs. When discussing the shift to urbanization, many scholars note that residential water users consume less water than agricultural users do. In the case of the Kennewick district, however, this is a flawed argument, since some residential users consume as much (if not more) water as the farmers and in some instances are billed for excess water. Whether this is a result of the low rates the district can offer (district assessments for residential water users are approximately $70 a season) or just a disregard for the resource, or both, requires further examination, but urban users in this area do not view water as a scarcity, not when they are pumping 4 gallons of water per acre, or applying 3½ acre feet of water per acre for a 198-day season. In contrast, residential users living outside Kennewick Irrigation District boundaries and relying upon city water pay an estimated $2,500 a season based on pumping 4 gallons of water per acre. The irrigation district can offer such low rates because of revenue generated from the sale of prime commercial real estate, specifically the land that settlers abandoned in the 1930s. Because of these circumstances, district personnel contend that residential users are the least conservation-minded, even though the technology exists for a more efficient water supply system (Volk interview).

Illustrating this indifference or arrogance regarding the area's resources were comments made at a public hearing on water shortages during the summer of 1994, when the Yakima Valley was ex-periencing its third successive drought year. The drought, of course, had caused water shortages, but the Bureau of Reclamation deter-mined to retain 64,500 gallons of water per minute in the Yakima River to sustain the anadromous fish population, which is in a sharp, alarming decline. Displeased over a reduced water supply, one residential water user remarked, "Dead grass makes people very unhappy," while other water users grumbled about "dry flower beds and yellow grass withering in the desert heat." To someone unaccustomed to the marvels of modern-day irrigation technology, "yellow grass and desert heat" are compatible images, not flower beds, green grass, and desert heat (*Tri-City Herald,* July 26, 1994).

The argument to preserve the salmon population is a compelling one, based on statistics that estimate the salmon and steelhead re-turning runs are down by over 80 percent from the mid-1980s. In the spring of 1994, biologists expected 6,200 spring chinook salmon to return to their spawning grounds; instead, only 600 were counted. Residential users, however, were not the only ones critical of the bu-reau's decision, later sanctioned by the courts, to release reservoir water to act as flushing flows and insure the outmigration of the chinook salmon and steelhead populations. Irrigators throughout the Yakima Valley expressed dissatisfaction and doubt concerning whether a pulse of water would succeed in protecting the fish. But no one can deny that the salmon and steelhead population are dis-appearing fast from the Columbia basin, and if a viable population is to be sustained, a redistribution of water will undoubtedly have to occur.[9]

Despite conflicting images and probable future disagreements over the water supply, the Kennewick Irrigation District is increas-ingly becoming an urban district. Further, the district is engaged in promoting the transition. In a recent public relations news-letter published by the district, headlines proclaimed "Irrigation: A Bargain for Everyone" and "KID Looks to the Future: Expansion Projects Under Study." Under the first headline were photos of up-scale suburban homes surrounded by immaculate green lawns; a brief paragraph touted the use of inexpensive irrigation water for residential dwellings. Currently, the district serves more than 14,000 residential users and almost 600 agricultural users. Ironically, one of the reasons irrigation water is considered a "bargain," in addition to its low cost, is its environmental advantages. By using district water,

Suburban home lots using irrigation water. (From *Farm & Community Canal,*
Kennewick Irrigation District. Reprinted by permission.)

"energy, chemicals, storage facilities, normal components of treated domestic water are avoided" (*Farm and Community Canal*, 1991).

Under the second headline, "KID Looks to the Future," was a discussion of the Tri-Cities' population growth and how the district is facilitating that growth by providing water to newly developed residential areas. In guaranteeing growth "at a sustained rate" (ibid.), the district perceived its role as a utility furnishing a service, similar to the power or phone company. Thus, not only have district lands been urbanized, but the resource, water, has also undergone a process of urbanization. And with the new technology in the form of LIDs, which makes water deliveries less conspicuous—no more open canals and drainage ditches—public awareness of the scarcity of that resource is diminished. Compounding the situation are the low rates that users pay for irrigation water, further fostering an ignorance of its worth. (Unlike the new resource economists, I do not agree that applying market incentives is the answer, since that still does not recognize the intrinsic value of the resource.)

In that same article appeared photos of a residential area being developed in a classic Mid-Columbia landscape—dry, broken land with sagebrush the only visible ground cover. The author describes the landscape, remarking that "water is the basic unit from which the success of the Tri-Cities is built upon. One need but look at the sage covered slopes of the Horse Heaven hills to realize that without water the Tri-Cities would be a dreary, unproductive setting." The district may soon be servicing these new areas, as feasibility studies are being conducted to determine whether to construct new LIDs.

Sprinkled throughout the newsletter are pictures of engineering feats—new pump stations, canal linings, drum screens—all necessary for the district's increasingly urban complexion and a testimony to the experts' confidence in facilitating the transition. More than one hundred years have passed since the first settlers arrived in the Yakima Valley, and although the economy has changed, cultural perceptions regarding the landscape and the efficacy of technology persist. Nowhere is the belief in technology's potential more evident than in area efforts to "enhance" the basin's water supply. Anticipating future water shortages in the mid-1980s, federal, state, and local officials formed the Yakima River Basin Enhancement Project. The purpose of the organization was to increase the river's water supply, and most of its members sought to do so by raising "the level of dams, construct[ing] short-term storage facilities, and instituting conservation measures" (*Spokane Spokesman-Review,* September 28, 1986).

The move to increase storage facilities began in the late 1960s when federal officials proposed the Bumping Lake Enlargement, which would have supplemented the summer water supply. While nothing came of the proposal, the water supply for Yakima basin residents became an explosive issue because of an earlier drought in 1977. At that time, the Yakima Indian Nation, alarmed about the effects a drought and an overappropriated river would have on the anadromous fish population, filed for 1,390,000 acre feet from the stream and requested that water be kept in the river at key points for fish propagation. Not surprisingly, these actions were opposed by irrigators, and in order to address all of the competing claims, the Washington Department of Ecology in 1977 filed a suit, *Washington v. Acquavella et al.* Still not settled and unlikely to be for many years, the suit has 5,000 defendants representing wildlife, environmental, recreational, agricultural, residential, and Indian interests.[10]

Meanwhile, as the suit progressed, the Yakima River Basin Enhancement Project reached an impasse because of irreconcilable differences between the water users (Chasco interviews, April 4, 1987, August 21, 1991). Still, enhancement studies continued; and finally, in October 1994, a $100 million to $120 million Yakima River basin water-enhancement bill passed the Senate, although funding had to be secured in the next fiscal year. The bill is aimed specifically at finding a compromise between the needs of irrigators, principally agriculturalists, and the protection of the salmon. Thus, new and improved conservation measures would be enacted, such as lining the canals and increasing the storage capacity of Lake Cle Elum, one of the Yakima River reservoirs. Storage capacity would be augmented by raising the reservoir by three feet. These steps would save water that could be returned to the Yakima River and subsequently increase the in-stream flow (*Yakima Herald-Republic,* October 6, 1994). According to one report, the legislation is just "an interim step toward building new irrigation storage that will provide more water for a variety of needs" (*Yakima Herald-Republic,* October 20, 1994). Once again, technology will resolve the problems of a "limited" environment.

Yet a finite water supply is not the only obstacle the Kennewick division is encountering in its transition to an increasingly urban district. Booster newsletters fail to describe the problems caused by the development of subdivisions in an area that still services agricultural lands. While the Kennewick district provides water to more than 14,000 residential users in 140 local improvement districts (and that number keeps growing), 60 percent of district land remains agricultural. Thus, open, earthen-lined canals still wind their way throughout the division. Most irrigation canals experience breaks, whether through the work of burrowing rodents, excessive rains, or soil composition, and the Kennewick project is no exception. In the late 1950s, when the district had suffered numerous ditch breaks, the losses that were sustained had been minimal, since the washouts only affected farmland.

As the number of subdivisions multiplied, however, district officials worried about the location of new subdivisions. Often real estate developers platted subdivisions in a potentially dangerous area, such as below an irrigation canal. If the ditch broke at that particular point, considerable personal and property damage could occur. A canal failure could jeopardize the lives of hundreds of urban users. In 1979, a disastrous break did occur: forty feet of the main canal gave way, and 164,000 gallons of water a minute raced down the embankment and derailed an Amtrak train, injuring sixty-five passengers (*Tri-City Herald*, May 7, 1979). But even if another washout does not occur, many residents will have to contend with canal seepage.

Because of the changes, the board decided that district officials should work with the Benton County engineer and planning commission regarding the approval of such developments within district boundaries. Despite precautions, developers still located subdivisions below the canals. The district would place a caveat on the plats for these subdivisions to warn potential buyers of the possibility of washouts. This seemed the only step that it could take. As a result, the district inserted numerous warnings in filed surveys at the county courthouse (Kennewick Irrigation District Minutes, March 2, 1971, October 12, 1978).[11]

Still the problem persists, and as land becomes more valuable, developers seem less mindful than ever of the risks involved. In the end, the district will probably assume more responsibility and replace open canals with piping, which, as mentioned earlier, affects area resources in other ways. Water-table levels will be affected and any habitat supported by the canal system will be eliminated.

The response of irrigation district officials to these new problems reveals another aspect of the impact of urbanization. The Kennewick Irrigation District board, consisting of five members, has evolved from politically naïve, impoverished farmers into image-conscious, financially adept managers. Ironically, although the residential users have the votes to control the board, representation is still primarily agricultural and the decisions of board members reflect district urbanization. Successes include the sale of district property, resulting in subsidies for water assessments, a public relations campaign, and the development of commercial lands. Evincing a managerial style worthy of the largest corporations, the district hires consultants, attorneys, and engineers to maximize district revenue, secure water rights, supply as many users as possible, and constantly rehabilitate the system.

One of its first forays into this new arena was in 1977 when the directors decided to advertise for proposals on the planning and development of district holdings. Not limiting themselves to the immediate vicinity, the board published the advertisement in the *Tri-City Herald*, *Daily Journal of Commerce* in Seattle and Portland, and *Forbes*. The announcement was written in broad terms and called for proposals in the "planning, developing and leasing [of] approximately 3,500 acres of land . . . for commercial, residential, industrial and farming purposes" (*Tri-City Herald*, June 15, 1977). By September 1977, the directors chose an outside consultant, Robert W. Young from San Francisco, to handle the development of district land. Relations between the board and Young eventually soured, but not before he had negotiated contracts that earned the district more than $5,000,000 in gross sales revenue. The tracts that Young leased were located in the vicinity of a shopping mall and would be home to commercial developments.[12]

By 1985, the board pledged to supervise the district's land itself, replacing Young, and to use the revenue "for the best long-term benefit for all the patrons of the District." The directors planned to accomplish this "through retention of the capital as an investment and utilization of interest revenues to hold down assessments" (*Farm and Community Canal* 1985). In the past, the board had applied the proceeds from land sales to district operation and maintenance expenses, which in 1985 amounted to $7.51 per subsidy (*Tri-City Herald*, May 26, 1985). By applying the subsidy, particularly with the residential users who just paid a flat fee, there were no economic incentives to encourage conservation.

By 1990, the Tri-Cities was in the midst of another boom, with district land increasing in value. In response, the district hired a full-time resource manager to lease, sell, and plan residential development by setting up subdivisions. The resource manager does not oversee actual construction but does set up the infrastructure of the designated subdivision. Again, profits will go toward a reduction in assessments for district water users, and with district property holdings representing a fair market value of $15,000,000, water users should enjoy lesser assessment costs (Macon interview; Chasco interview, August 21, 1991).

In addition to these activities, the district board has also become concerned with its community standing, particularly as it takes more of a role in developing real estate. Thus, an annual newsletter provides updates on district activities, and future promotional plans include a videotape of the district. With these endeavors and the hiring of a professional to develop and market its land, the district has demonstrated an awareness of its place in the community and the potential for growth. The board has assured community agencies that district lands will not be developed haphazardly but will follow a master plan, one that should enhance the community as well as benefit district water users. Again, these tasks reflect not only area urbanization but the board's participation in the transformation.

Despite the trend toward urbanization, district board and staff continue to emphasize that the district still serves a large agricultural population. Further, the remaining orchard and farming interests are productive and successful. But the statistics favor the residential user. In terms of dollars and cents, the residential user returned more of a profit to the district. In a recent preliminary study, residential users were found to pay 70 percent of the collected assessments while they accounted for 66 percent of the costs. There was also a trickle-down effect: as a district gains more urban users, the demand for water increases. In 1994, urban users made up 14,137 accounts, or 96 percent, of the accounts, while there were 560 agricultural accounts, or 4 percent (Chasco interview, April 15, 1986; Garner interview). This growing demand, in turn, could cause such a rise in assessments (when subsidies from real estate are curtailed) that agricultural use of the water would be impractical. The Central Arizona Project illustrated this possibility when the urban clients increased to the point that the farmers went out of business.[13]

State legislative changes have also favored the residential users. In 1985, voting procedures were revised so that within "irrigation districts under 200,000 acres, there will be two votes for each five acres of assessable land or fraction thereof." Before the ruling, in order to run for office in the district, a candidate had to own at least five acres (*Tri-City Herald*, October 16, 1985). Now a lot owner would be eligible to sit on the board, and if the residential users joined forces, they could control the outcome of an election. But with voting turnouts of only 2,000 in the last board election—and of those, only 25 percent were residential users—a power struggle between farmers and urbanites does not appear likely (Garner interview).

Yet despite who is shaping policy, the district is becoming increasingly urbanized. Today a Wal-Mart, Aamco Transmission, assorted motels, and subdivisions replace a vista that was once farms and dryland. This growth shows no signs of declining, despite recurring droughts and impending adjudication of the Yakima River.

Clearly, precedents were established with the first irrigation enterprises in the nineteenth century, namely that Euroamericans did not have to come to terms with an arid environment. Technology accommodated settlement and still does. But in our time there are differences. With urbanization, the water user is more removed from the resource base. Underground, pressurized pipelines providing water almost deny the reality of living in an arid environment. In the case of the Kennewick district, the infrastructure required to live in an urban oasis is increasingly complex, illumined by an expanding bureaucratic and technological edifice and resulting in a greater web of dependency. Despite these problems, district officials, engineers, resource managers, and residents are more confident than ever about their ability to modify landscapes and the need to do so. Paralleling the growing infrastructure is an increase in power and wealth, and at present all of the irrigation districts in the Yakima Valley are employing their wealth and power to insure continued use of the Yakima River. Urbanization has had far-reaching and varied consequences. Perhaps the most significant is the persistence of a culture to replace "hot winds, dust and sagebrush" (U.S. Public Works Administration 1936) with Wal-Marts, Aamcos, and Holiday Inns.

NOTES

1. I would like to thank Donald Worster and the participants of the environmental colloquium in the Rockefeller Program on Nature, Culture, and Technology, where an earlier draft of this paper was presented. I benefited greatly from their comments and discussion. Errors and omissions are my own. This paper also was presented at the Environmental History Conference in Las Vegas, Nevada, March 9, 1995.

2. John Findlay in his work *Magic Lands: Western Cityscapes and American Culture After 1940* (Berkeley: University of California Press, 1992) offers one of the best studies of urbanization in the West, demonstrating not only how long urban centers have been a part of the American West, but their impact on a national culture.

3. For a general history of the Pacific Northwest, consult the following works: D. W. Meinig, *The Great Columbia Plain: A Historical Geography, 1805–1910* (Seattle: University of Washington Press, 1968); Carlos A. Schwantes, *The Pacific Northwest: An Interpretive History* (Lincoln: University of Nebraska Press, 1989).

4. Many of the facts relating to the early history of Kennewick and the Yakima Valley came from the Northern Pacific Records, Minnesota Historical Society, Minneapolis.

5. For legislation authorizing the Kennewick project, see Senate, *Authorizing the Construction, Operation, and Maintenance, Under Federal Reclamation Laws, of the Kennewick Division of the Yakima Project, Washington,* 80th Cong., 2d sess., S. Rep. 1404.

6. In the Bureau of Reclamation's *Definite Plan* (n.d.):1–9, government officials were more adamant about the primacy of agriculture and cautioned against a local economy without a firm agricultural base.

7. Numerous sources detailed the process for settling the reclaimed areas and guaranteeing agricultural use, including the following: Kennewick Irrigation District Minutes, June 15, 1954; Settler Assistance file; Public Notice No. 1, February 23, 1956, USBR Correspondence Files pre-1958; Kennewick Irrigation District Minutes, October 25, 1954; W. L. Karrer to Van E. Nutley, September 12, 1956, in USBR Correspondence Files pre-1958, all in Kennewick Irrigation District Records, Kennewick Irrigation District Archives, Kennewick, Wash.

8. These problems are discussed at length in an interview with Paul Chasco, Kennewick Irrigation District project manager, April 15, 1986. And in a study commissioned by the Kennewick district, the Century West Engineering Corporation concluded that the canals for the old lands were "designed to deliver at a constant flow, typical of a farm's demand for water," but with the residential users the engineers found "considerable fluctua-

tions" and "operation difficulties reflected in the daily guessing-game of es-
timating user demand, weather conditions and delivery lagtime." Century
West Engineering Corporation, "Urban Canal Fluctuations—Kennewick,
WA" (1982), in Kennewick Irrigation District Archives.

9. Several newspaper articles discussed the dwindling salmon popula-
tion. See, for example, *Yakima Herald-Republic*, December 29, 1994; *Tri-City
Herald*, June 3, 1994, August 5, 1994; *Yakima Herald-Republic*, May 5, 1994. For
a brief history and legal discussion of the salmon problem, see Charles F.
Wilkinson, *Crossing the Next Meridian: Land, Water, and the Future of the West*
(Washington, D.C.: Island Press, 1992).

10. A discussion of the drought and the various responses to it are in-
cluded in the following documents: Kennewick Irrigation District Minutes,
January 2, 1968, March 1, 1977, May 18, 1977, September 9, 1982; *Tri-City
Herald*, July 22, 1986; *Spokane Spokesman-Review*, September 28, 1986.

11. For some specific examples of the location of subdivisions, refer to
the board's reaction to a new platted area in the Meadow Springs vicinity,
the land between Division Four and the Highland Feeder. See Kennewick
Irrigation District Minutes, February 6, 1973, June 3, 1975.

12. For a discussion of Young's accomplishments and transactions with
the board, see the following: *Tri-City Herald*, September 6, 1977; Chasco
interview, April 4, 1987; *Tri-City Herald*, May 26, 1985; Kennewick Irrigation
District Minutes, 1978–79, April 10, 1980, March 9, 1983; *Tri-City Herald*,
April 15, 1983.

13. Additional support for the economic advantages in serving urban
users can be found in Leonard J. Arrington and Thomas G. Alexander, *Water
for Urban Reclamation: The Provo River Project* (Logan: Utah Agricultural Experiment Station, Utah State University, 1966), which examines the Provo
River Project, where a major share of the water goes for city and industrial use. The authors concluded that "if reclamation projects such as this
[Provo River Project] are to be viewed on a purely dollars-and-cents basis,
increasing consideration is apt to be given to proposals to turn over a large
share of the water to urban and industrial use."

REFERENCES

Anderson, Terry L., and Donald R. Leal. *Free Market Environmentalism.* Boulder: Westview Press, 1991.
Arrington, Leonard J., and Thomas G. Alexander. *Water for Urban Reclamation: The Provo River Project.* Logan: Utah Agricultural Experiment Station, Utah State University, 1966.
Chasco, Paul. Interviews by author. Kennewick, Wash. April 15, 1986,
April 4, 1987, August 21, 1991.

Findlay, John. *Magic Lands: Western Cityscapes and American Culture After 1940.* Berkeley: University of California Press, 1992.

Garner, Charles. Telephone interview by author. January 19, 1995.

Gottlieb, Robert. *A Life of Its Own: The Politics and Power of Water.* San Diego: Harcourt Brace Jovanovich, 1988.

Hunn, Eugene S., with James Selam and family. *Nch'i-Wana, "The Big River:" Mid-Columbia Indians and Their Land.* Seattle: University of Washington Press, 1990.

An Illustrated History of Klickitat, Yakima and Kittitas Counties. N.p., 1904.

Ingram, Helen. *Water and Poverty in the Southwest.* Tucson: University of Arizona Press, 1987.

———. *Water Politics: Continuity and Change.* Albuquerque: University of New Mexico Press, 1990.

Jones, Wesley L. Papers in the University of Washington Archives, Seattle.

Kennewick (Wash.) Courier-Reporter.

Kennewick Irrigation District. *Farm and Community Canal.* Kennewick: Kennewick Irrigation District.

Kennewick Irrigation District Archives, Kennewick, Washington. Kennewick Irrigation District Records.

Macon, Michael. Telephone interview by author. August 20, 1991.

McCool, Daniel. *Command of the Waters: Iron Triangles, Federal Water Development and Indian Water.* Berkeley: University of California Press, 1987.

Meinig, D. W. *The Great Columbia Plain: A Historical Geography, 1805–1910.* Seattle: University of Washington Press, 1968.

Minnesota State Historical Society, Minneapolis. Northern Pacific Records.

National Archives, Washington, D.C. Record Group 115: Records of the Bureau of Reclamation.

Schwantes, Carlos A. *The Pacific Northwest: An Interpretive History.* Lincoln: University of Nebraska Press, 1989.

Spokane Spokesman-Review.

Tri-City Herald (Kennewick, Wash.).

U.S. Congress. Senate. *Authorizing the Construction, Operation, and Maintenance, Under Federal Reclamation Laws, of the Kennewick Division of the Yakima Project, Washington.* 80th Cong., 2d sess. S. Rept. 1404.

United States Department of Interior, Bureau of Reclamation. *Appendix Report of the Kennewick Division, Yakima Project, Washington.* Boise, USDE, 1947.

United States Public Works Administration. Federal Writers Project, Washington Pioneers Project (1937–38). *As Told by the Pioneers.* W. F. Sonderman interview by Augusta Eastland. Washington, D.C., 1936.

Volk, Ben. Telephone interview by author. February 6, 1995.

Wilkinson, Charles F. *Crossing the Next Meridian: Land, Water, and the Future of the West.* Washington, D.C.: Island Press, 1992.

Worster, Donald. *Rivers of Empire: Water, Aridity, and Growth of the American West.* New York: Pantheon Books, 1985.

———. *An Unsettled Country: Changing Landscapes of the American West.* Albuquerque: University of New Mexico Press, 1994.

Yakima (Wash.) Daily Republic.

Yakima (Wash.) Herald.

Yakima (Wash.) Herald-Republic.

Wisecracking Glen Canyon Dam
Revisioning Environmentalist Mythology[1]

*The canyonlands did have a heart, a living heart, and that heart was
Glen Canyon and the wild Colorado.*
—Edward Abbey

*The unregulated Colorado was a son of a bitch. It was either in flood
or in trickle. It wasn't any good.*
—Floyd Dominy

In Leslie Marmon Silko's *Almanac of the Dead* (1991), Arizona's Glen
Canyon Dam splits apart amidst six disguised eco-warriors as they
scale dynamite down its front. The eco-warriors become lost in a
haze of rubble and dust, their requiem a rush of water as the Colorado River bursts from its concrete prison. In this scene the giving
of human life restores nonhuman life and nature regains its primacy
in a cycle of sacrifice and renewal. Although only a short part of a
long novel, Silko's fictional destruction of Glen Canyon Dam brings
to the fore issues of wilderness protection and human agency. It is
an essential part of her longer almanac, which tells an even larger
story of the restoration of power to the land and its people. Leslie
Marmon Silko's novel is far too complex to summarize succinctly.
However, its primary themes include the self-destruction of what
we call "America" (through drugs, domestic terrorism, and other
forms of self-inflicted violence) and the rise of indigenous groups,
the poor, and other marginalized peoples from north and south of
the Mexican-American border.

Equally important, her six-page chapter takes on one of the most
powerful myths of the contemporary environmental movement by
reconfiguring Edward Abbey's entire novel, *The Monkey Wrench
Gang* (1975), the "real" 1981 protest by Earth First! at Glen Canyon,
and the resulting nine-minute videotape, *The Cracking of the Damn*
(1982). For the purposes of this essay, whether the examined text is

Photo of Glen Canyon Dam courtesy of the U.S. Department of the Interior, Bureau of Reclamation.

"fictional" (Abbey's or Silko's novel) or "factual" (the Earth First! protest) is unimportant. All three texts can be read as representations of a particular fantasized action (the destruction of Glen Canyon Dam) that has resonance and significance in and out of an environmental movement largely based in the southwestern United States.

Together, the texts of Abbey, Earth First!, and Silko provide a brief history of the environmental myth of the cracking of the dam. While a crucial component of the individual tellings of the myth is that they borrow from and build on one another, these recitations of the destruction of Glen Canyon Dam often describe worlds (and futures) that are radically different from one another. Close readings of these texts reveal the ways in which their authors construct environmental movements, prospects for societal change, and the shifts within a movement that has been challenged by the environmental justice movement, among others, to address issues of race, class, and gender. Thus, the Glen Canyon myth and its retellings are important in that they are used to theorize strategies within the environmental movement(s), strategies that are inclusive or exclusive, radical or mainstream. By changing the myth, one can change the environmental movement itself.

While these texts falls into a chronological order (with Abbey's novel appearing before the Earth First! action and Silko's novel most recently), all three texts undermine linear time as their intertextuality constructs a space in which they act upon and are acted on by the others. It is Abbey who warns his readers that his book, "though fictional in form, is based strictly on historical fact. Everything in it is real and actually happened. And it all began just one year from today" (Abbey 1975). Silko also conflates past with present and future in an almanac that recounts mythologies of journeys that appear to be repeating themselves with various characters, mythologies that simultaneously teach of the past and predict the future. The strength of these texts is in their "timelessness," their cyclical action and activism that, in one instance, is embodied in a loop of videotape.

The dialogues among these incarnations are critical, for it is only through these dialogues that each narration has deeper meaning. Therefore, what is important is not so much the myth of the dam itself (even when it is a kind of origin myth, as it is in the case of Earth First!) but the ways in which various people reconfigure the myth and how those reconfigurations reveal the perceived audience of the myth and strategies for environmental defense. Abbey and, to a lesser extent, Earth First! tell the Glen Canyon myth as though it were aimed at a primarily white, male "American" audience, and the strategies for that audience, while in a sense revolutionary, in the end are limited and narrow because they do not actively seek to unite people across borders of race or gender. (In light of Silko's novel, much of which forces the U.S. reader to acknowledge those millions of "Americans" who live south of Arizona, New Mexico, California, and Texas, my use of *American* here is somewhat problematic. My use of the term mirrors the narrow use of it by Abbey and Earth First! when I am writing about them, the wider implications of it when I am writing of Silko.)

In contrast, Silko offers up a version of the myth that transgresses national borders and boundaries between groups that exist as a result of differences in race, gender, or sexual orientation. Consequently, her strategies are meant to unite a variety of people within the dynamics of environmental activism.

Myth and *mythology* are illusive terms; they are applied equally to origin stories, sacred texts, and popular legends, and have been devalued: considered somewhat less truthful than "fact." In terms of semiotics, though, myth is a relatively simple concept. According to Roland Barthes, mythology is a "system of communications" that has a historical foundation in that it borrows exclusively from what has already been communicated. In other words, the "raw materials" of myth must already be operating within the society at which the myth is aimed; thus "myth is speech stolen and restored," or re-presented to the community. The "raw materials" in the myth examined here include the dam itself, and American beliefs about wilderness, deserts, water, and the importance of the American West as a mythical place of freedom and individuality (Barthes 1972).

The materials for the myth of the destruction of Glen Canyon Dam were in popular use by 1963, the year the dam was completed. The canyon was scouted as a dam site as early as 1916, and the eventual dam was simply one in a series of dams on the Colorado River, the first being Hoover Dam in 1931. The dams were meant to control the river, to reign in its power for irrigation and electricity in an era in which wilderness had little value. Additionally, Glen Canyon Dam was to end long-standing water disputes between the states that shared the Colorado basin. And it was the last "great" dam of the Bureau of Reclamation, a final hurrah before wild rivers, preservation, and recreation became meaningful issues (Martin 1989).

Because it actively subverts older, more mainstream myths of progress and Manifest Destiny, the eco-warrior myth examined here might be better termed a counter-myth. Underlying the destruction and restoration of it is the belief that Glen Canyon was lost unnecessarily, that a more adamantly protectionist environmental movement could have saved the canyon. In a compromise with the federal government that inspired people like Abbey and Dave Foreman, cofounder of Earth First!, to call for no compromise in the defense of nature, David Brower, executive director of the Sierra Club, and its board agreed to abandon their struggle to save Glen Canyon in order to assure the preservation of Echo Park in Dinosaur National Monument. Thus, the Glen Canyon myth runs counter to American myths of progress and faith in technology as it simultaneously runs counter to environmental strategies of working within the system (Scarce 1990).

Edward Abbey and a Ghost River Bound

Many people who have written about Edward Abbey have taken it for granted that he is above all an environmental or nature writer, while others, like Scott Slovic, emphasize his leanings toward anarchy. While scholars debate whether Abbey was an environmentalist or anarchist, a novelist or nature writer, there is certainly a strong affinity between the more radical wings of the environmental movement in the United States and the man who, in the 1960s, fell in love with the southwestern deserts. For many who have battled to protect the canyons and mesas of Arizona, Utah, and New Mexico, Abbey provides a poetical and political voice to their struggles. An avid river rafter, he felt a profound loss as he floated down Glen Canyon just before its dam was completed in 1963. In one of the many essays he wrote about Glen Canyon and Lake Powell, the 180-mile-long storage reservoir created by the dam, Abbey describes the Colorado as a "ghost river still bound," claiming that "a part of my heart lies buried beneath that enormous pond" of the artificial lake (Abbey 1978).

Abbey wrote about the destruction of Glen Canyon Dam in a number of novels, short stories, and essays and was the first to fully articulate the Glen Canyon myth in print. Perhaps best known of his works is *The Monkey Wrench Gang*. This novel follows four pro-environmentalist vandals through a number of adventures around the Utah-Arizona state line. Although his monkeywrenchers do not attempt to obliterate the dam within the confines of the novel, the desire to do so, and the verbalization of that desire, holds something like a catalog of eco-"terrorism" events together. The destruction of the dam stands out as an ultimate act of restoration of both the wildness of the Colorado River and the wildness of the human soul. The release of the river by eco-warriors could reinstate a freedom of humanity and wilderness as both are wrested away from the dehumanizing, imposing, and controlling formation of the concrete dam and the corporate/governmental world the dam represents. At the same time, according to *Ecodefense: A Field Guide to Monkeywrenching*, "monkeywrenching is non-violent resistance to the destruction of natural diversity and wilderness." It is individual, ethical, deliberate, and is not revolutionary.

Although Glen Canyon Dam is not destroyed by Hayduke and the gang in the novel, an examination of a similar act of eco-"terrorism," the collapsing of Glen Canyon Bridge in the Epilogue of *The Monkey Wrench Gang* (which begins the novel), illuminates what the cracking of the dam might look like as authored by Abbey. In this short chapter, Abbey focuses on speech and the rituals that surround speech.

Sound is everything as cars line up for miles to witness the official opening of Glen Canyon Bridge. The sound is indecipherable for most of the onlookers who endure the ritual of State speech from the sticky vinyl seats of their cars. Amplifiers crackle and screech in the desert heat while "the speech goes on, many round mouths, one speech, and hardly a word intelligible" (Abbey 1975). The content of the (State) speech is not important to the ritual. The ritual is one that conjures up "Americanism," a misplaced patriotism whose core is no more substantial than the red paper bows that flank the bridge or the large gilded scissors that will be used to cut those bows.

George Washington Hayduke, Abbey's anti-hero hero, wears "a yellow hard hat decorated with the emblematic decals of his class— American flag, skull and crossbones, the Iron Cross." On the back of his coveralls, "in vivid lettering, is stitched the legend AMERICA: LOVE IT OR LEAVE IT ALONE." His uniform is loud, another form of speech proclaiming identification with a particular class with a particular creed. The word *America* appears twice in this short description, each time evoking a mythical place, as the "America" that Hayduke continually risks his life for is one that is truly left alone. His uniform evokes and subverts the patriotism that the ritual of State speech evokes. The signs—flags, mottoes—are the same, but what they signify is vastly different; "America: Love it or leave it (alone)" takes on a new, environmentally radical connotation.

Abbey constructs a scene in which Hayduke becomes visible for a moment, identifiable as an individual in a crowd of politicians as he makes some adjustments to what appears to be a ribbon and then melts back into the masses, retiring "quickly back into the obscurity of the crowd where he belongs." Throughout his novel Abbey offsets his very individualistic Hayduke with crowds or masses, those who follow policy, who do not struggle for their vision of "America." Even the informal group of monkeywrenchers who often work together cannot undermine the importance of the individual in Abbey's text as Hayduke periodically escapes to undertake singlehandedly some of the best adventures of the novel. The destruction of the bridge is one of these adventures.

It starts off with a scattering of fireworks that most people immediately accept as part of the official ritual. The sounds of explosion are muffled by the pops and bangs of firecrackers, the subversion hidden under what looks like part of the sanctioned protocol. For many, the sounds from the amps are more a part of their surroundings than the collapse of the bridge. Most people present at the site cannot be witnesses. Here the act of witnessing is passive, one more of confusion than of clarity or revelation. Abbey's witnesses expect to watch an official opening of a massive structure; and although they watch it "live," most cannot see what occurs but can only hear the explosion. The destruction is within "poor view" for all "but the Indians on the hillside." In Abbey's narration, there is nothing that allows the throngs of people in their cars or the Indians any kind of agency. They passively wait; they passively watch the bridge collapse into the canyon. Hayduke becomes the authentic hero, an individual in dress and action who rises above the inauthentic, corrupted masses of politicians, citizens, and Native Americans.

The Indians on the hillside are, according to Abbey and Hayduke, inauthentic Indians, corrupted by generations of governmental dependence and life on the reservation. For much of the novel the wild and independent Hayduke is defined against modern Native Americans who are inactive because of drink or who act as tribal policemen in a malignant form of the United States' power on the reservation. In this period of American Indian Movement (AIM) activism, Abbey assumes that tribal police work in consort with the federal government. Near the end of the disintegration of the bridge, "a solitary smoke signal . . . like one huge inaudible and astonishing exclamation point signifying surprise" rises from the canyon, and the first of many co-optations of an "authentic," older Indian tradition occurs. As the novel proceeds, Hayduke and his gang cover their tracks with hints at a radical "enemy Indian," at Red Cloud and the American Indian Movement. Hayduke seemingly makes a better Indian even than his "noble red brethren" who are reduced, in Abbey's estimation, to "men and women drink[ing] Tokay, the swarms of children Pepsi-Cola, all munching on mayonnaise and Kleenex sandwiches of Wonder, Rainbo and Holsum Bread."

Throughout his novel, Abbey wrestles with the authentic and inauthentic, and with borders. Eventually all of his characters must measure up to Hayduke, a hairy, bawdy, independent loner. Unlike everyone else in the novel, Hayduke is not pulled from his allegiance to wilderness by family, career, or other desires. He is as likely to act on his own in the cool desert night as he is to join with a loose-knit group of friends for monkeywrenching revelry. Hayduke is Abbey's authentic hero: dedicated, resourceful, immortal. However, his authenticity is only claimed relationally, as Hayduke and the inauthentic Indians and other villains are interlocked in definition of one another.

Significantly, Abbey does not write of the demolition of a dam and the freeing of a river, but rather writes of destroying a bridge between two states. By sabotaging Glen Canyon Bridge, Abbey simply terminates the flow of people between Arizona and Utah, halting the temporary migration of people across the desert. The land is left to the vultures that lazily swoop the sky, looking for carrion. While the monkey wrench gang assumes that both structures—dam and bridge—equally represent corporate and governmental disregard for the land on which we live, in this border-conscious region a bridge also represents a freedom of access, the possibility of connections, union.

Earth First!'s Crack in the Dam(n)

Earth First! embraced Abbey's myth and, in part, enacted the "bridge scene" upon the dam itself. In the many stories of the genesis of Earth First!, Abbey is credited with being the "tribe's" inspiration. (The word *tribe* is commonly used in the literature about Earth First!. It seems to be the term preferred by the group itself.) Environmentalists Dave Foreman, Howie Wolke, Bart Koehler, and Ron Kezar and former Yippie Mike Roselle started the loose-knit organization in 1980 as an "informal group of Earth radicals who believe in militant actions and courageous positions in defense of Earth and Her diversity of wilderness life" (*Earth First! Newsletter*, 1981). In part a reaction to RARE II, the Roadless Area Review and Evaluation project in which less than one-quarter of the land reviewed was set aside as protected wilderness, in part a reaction to the Reagan administration, Secretary of the Interior James Watt, and the Sagebrush Rebellion, Earth First! was to be a loosely organized network of regional activists who would utilize guerilla theater and wisecrack antics to place committed preservationist views back on the table. As indicated in Foreman's complaint that the Reagan administration called the Sierra Club a radical organization, an Earth First! priority was to re-center "mainstream" environmental organizations so that they could reclaim a moderate position within the political system.

Earth First!'s initial action took place in 1981 during the spring equinox. Earth Image Films made a nine-minute videotape of the action that begins with aerial shots of the dam set to the music of Johnny Sagebrush (Bart Koehler): "Were you there when they built Glen Canyon Dam?/Were you there when they killed this river dead?" (McLeod 1982). Interestingly, it is Abbey who is first introduced to viewers rather than any of the founders of Earth First!. He advocates sabotage when political means fail and claims no kinship or sympathy with the dam heard humming in the background. Thus, it is Abbey who becomes the voice for the Earth First! platform.

Throughout the short film, scenes of the river, the canyon, or the dam are spliced between shots of five or six Earth First!ers preparing a 300-foot roll of black plastic sheeting as about 75 onlookers with signs watch and mill about. In a voice-over, Dave Foreman gives a brief position statement for Earth First!. The viewer watches aerial footage of five people as they walk across the dam and stop in the middle to unfurl the plastic. It rolls down the side of the massive dam, appearing like a small fissure, the beginning of the end. Abbey reads from a speech he prepared: "Surely no manmade structure in modern American history has been hated so much for so long by so many with such good reason as Glen Canyon Dam" (McLeod 1982). Park rangers arrive and question Foreman, who is outfitted in a red, white, and blue jacket that has the letters *USA* on the back, reminiscent of Hayduke's "uniform." In the film's last footage are shots of freely running water, the power structure that transports the electricity generated from the dam to cities in the Southwest, and a drawing of three Native Americans: a woman seated on a horse, a man beside her, and a child next to his dog. In this last frame, the presumed family is in traditional dress as they look down on the dam (and presumably the Earth First! action) from an orange plateau.

Foreman, dressed as a kind of Hayduke, and the Indians on the hillside/plateau remind the viewer of the origin of the performance. The Earth First! action and the tape of it mirror Abbey's choice of audience and key elements of his description. However, instead of referring to images of modern Indians, the Earth First!ers harkened back to an earlier time by imagining and imaging them in traditional dress. These Indians seem to represent the Earth First!ers, who describe themselves as a "tribe" and borrow organizational strategies from their understanding of tribal politics.

In early Earth First! newsletters the action at Glen Canyon Dam is referred to frequently and becomes a unifying theme. In one article, volunteers to get signatures for the Glen Canyon Dam petitions are asked for, as are slides and photographs of the prank and magazine and newspaper articles about it in another. The newsletter offers photos of Abbey at the dam or of the crack for sale as a fund-raising effort, and at least one editorial from a regional newspaper (against the action) was reprinted. The film as well as the action itself becomes an organizing tool, at once illustrating the destruction of a fragile ecosystem and the strategies of the "tribe." In 1982 the newsletter publicized the film as "a great organizing program for local EF! (or other groups') meetings. This movie is a hell of a tool and we should use it to the maximum extent possible" (*Earth First! Newsletter*, February 2, 1982).

The action and the film are effective as organizing and unifying tools because they draw from existing myth. Abbey found a large portion of his audience among environmentalists, desert rats, and river rafters, many of whom were sympathetic to Earth First!. Drawing on a common belief that Glen Canyon represents an especially painful loss to the environmental movement, Earth First! activists took that loss and the myth surrounding it and turned it into theater or performance art, a piece that would signify a new direction in the environmental movement, the promise of renewal and restoration. Abbey's imprint, and the fact that the action was "performance" rather than an actual attack on the structure of the dam, conflate environmental reality with the comic-book qualities of Abbey's novel.

Revisioning the Myth for Radical Change

In a more recent formation of the myth, Silko writes about an actual "hit" on Glen Canyon Dam in her lengthy novel, *Almanac of the Dead*. In an earlier essay, "Landscape, History, and the Pueblo Imagination," Silko illustrates how communities interact with stories to form complex cosmologies. The stories illustrate and illuminate a particular culture through the interaction of the tellers and the listeners (who are often the same) and through reinterpretation. According to Silko, "the ancient people perceived the world and themselves within that world as part of an ancient continuous story composed of innumerable bundles of other stories" (Silko 1987). Traditionally, telling those stories was a communal event in which all participated not only through listening but by contributing segments of the story as well. In *Almanac of the Dead* Silko reinvents and invokes that "ancient continuous story" within the bundles that become interrelated chapters.[2] A conference forms the community, and six eco-warriors on videotape enact the myth first cultivated by Abbey.

Not only does Silko destroy the dam but she makes the destruction part of a cooperative effort to return power to the powerless, which includes not only the Colorado River but humans as well. Eco-"terrorism" becomes just one event in a long litany of revolutionary actions. She does not devote much time to it, and the bombing was done by a character who is introduced while some of Silko's primary characters watch a video of the event, in which he was killed. In contrast to Abbey's focus on the strength of the individual, in Silko's narrative the individual does not survive. The clan, in this case Green Vengeance, does.

Silko introduces Green Vengeance, a group suggestive of Earth First!, at a healers convention attended by Lecha, a seer, Zeta, her sister who runs weapons across the Mexican-American border, and Awa Gee, a computer junkie. The eco-warriors arrive "just when Zeta was beginning to think the holistic medicine convention was a bust," infusing the convention with vitality and action in the action-less world of talk. With a videotape of the dynamiting of Glen Canyon Dam, the warriors offer their act of reestablishing wilderness, which, in turn, has a restorative effect on the people at the convention.

The two warriors hide their identities behind "identical camouflage jumpsuits" and ski masks. That they represent Green Vengeance is more important than their individual persons; the group subsumes the individual. The Hopi, an influential healer, introduces the videotape: "You have all heard the state and federal authorities blame 'structural failure' for the collapse of Glen Canyon Dam. Now you are about to see the videotape footage never before made public by our allies in the struggle." The two warriors who share the stage with the Hopi and the television remain silent.

In marked contrast to Abbey's world of speech and even the multiple sounds of water, music, the hum of the dam, and short speeches in Earth First!'s video, the tape in Silko's story continues both the silence and the unidentifying characteristics of the two Green Vengeance representatives. Ski masks and camouflage clothing create a uniform that unites the warriors into a group whose parts are indistinguishable. Anyone could be in the motel rooms that the camera leads the viewer into, collapsing the difference between the viewer of the videotape (or the reader of the text) and the warriors.

With the security of the group in mind, "the sound track and any voices had been removed." Action supplants sound: the interior of motel rooms and of a vehicle join the "brilliant burnt reds and oranges of the sandstone formations and the dark green juniper bushes flashing past" in a whirl of movement. From the start, the video suggests action and direct agency. The viewer watches bombs being assembled while the camera focuses on "hands carefully arranging black boxes in nests of foam rubber." The sense of motion is enforced by the drive to the dam and then, through the climax of the video, the demolition of the dam. The camera compels silence by "avoid[ing] the masked faces," the location of speech, in favor of the active hands.

Prior to the finale, the camera closes in on the sign for Glen Canyon Dam. The sign fills the screen; then the camera darts to the actual dam upon which "spiders on a vast concrete wall" appear to be dangling. The individuals seem infinitesimal in comparison to the immense structure in place to hold back a river. But together, the six "spiders" can gather a force that will release the river. In the face of these spiders, the dam is powerless.

The spiders become human and represent what humans are capable of. Suspended in front of the dam, the warriors become part of nature, first as it has been imprisoned by a modern society and then as part of its restoration in what Silko offers up as amodern communities. Their actions usher in an alternative environment that is as much old as it is new. Only after the videotape is over do any of the Green Vengeance members identify themselves. The two who have delivered the videotape are revealed as a man and a woman, but even more important, one of the "spiders" is identified. Silko reveals one of the warriors in the interest of myth. One is offered up as Hero and becomes fodder for the new Glen Canyon myth already in the making. Under one ski mask is revealed a gay rights activist dying of AIDS.

The gay hero acts in opposition to the defensively macho male hero that Abbey develops in George Washington Hayduke. In a single stroke, Silko undermines the categories of gender and sexuality that Abbey enforces by writing Hayduke against Bonnie, the only female in Abbey's group of eco-warriors. Scott Slovic writes of Bonnie as an eco-warrior whose "witty feminism and splendid sexuality become her trademarks" (Slovic 1992). However, this reader found her no more "real" than a heroine in a James Bond movie. In contrast, Hayduke is twenty-five-years old, "a short, broad burly fellow, well-muscled built like a wrestler" whose "face is hairy, very hairy." Hayduke is not only a man's man, he is a white man's man. Although he may sport some Shawnee blood (as he speculates), he has no compassion for the hundreds of drunk and lazy Native Americans who filter through Abbey's prose and are the antithesis of the active Hayduke.

In *Borderlands/La Frontera: The New Mestiza,* Gloria Anzaldúa posits a theory that uses the border between the United States and Mexico as a metaphor for the various "borders" that divide people internally and externally. According to her, "the Borderlands are physically present wherever two or more cultures edge each other, where people of different races occupy the same territory, where under, lower, middle and upper classes touch, where the space between two individuals shrinks with intimacy" (Anzaldúa 1987). Anzaldúa calls for a "mestiza consciousness" that will "break down the subject-object duality" that divides our world into gay/straight, black/white, rich/poor, powerful/powerless. The mestiza is able to occupy and work from multiple positionings in much the same way that Silko's gay eco-warrior can.

In her Borderlands theory, of which *Almanac of the Dead* represents a fictional description, Anzaldúa positions homosexuals as bridges between marginalized groups of people because they have "strong bonds with the queer white, Black, Asian, Native American, Latino, and with the queer in Italy, Australia and the rest of the planet." Unlike straight men who define the specifics of culture in terms of what it is not and thus are exclusionary, gay men provide access between cultures by forcing inclusion; their "role is to link people with each other. . . . It is to transfer ideas and information from one culture to another." For example, Silko's hero bridges the gap between gay activists and environmental activists as he becomes both in death. Additionally, as a homosexual, Silko's hero links environmental groups (usually bastions of the white, male middle-class) with the supposed Others at the conference.

As with Earth First!, the technology of the videotape at the conference creates a nearly instant myth. The videotaped image collapses time and space, the spirit world and the physical world. The viewers watch as some things living cease to live; the spiders are a part of the conference but only as images, spirits that are among the viewers but at the same time also apart from them. The metaphysical and the physical are locked in a loop of technology that can be repeated over and over again.

Although Lecha and Zeta interact to a limited extent with the storytelling, Awa Gee contributes significantly to the Glen Canyon myth by revealing the hero in more detail to both the reader and the sisters. In his trailer home, crowded with computers, he intercepted an electronic message that the activist left. Electronically, much like the videotape, the message will be disseminated and repeated, an artifact of myth, proof of the hero. Along with proof of the individual hero, however, the message is a call to action, an awakening of hero figures within the group:

Dear lovers, brothers, mothers, and sisters!
Go out in glory!
Go out with dignity!
Go out while you're still feeling and looking good!
Avenge gay genocide by the U.S. government!
Die to save the earth.
Mold long underwear out of plastic explosives and stroll past the U.S. Supreme Court building while justices are hearing arguments. Bolt in the exit door and flick the switch! Turn out the lights on the High Court of the police state!

Awa Gee saves the "computer readout of the eco-warrior's message although he knew it was risky to keep such evidence" and implicates himself not only in the retelling of the story but in its action as well, as he "decided he would help the eco-warriors turn out the lights" across the United States through computerized sabotage, although they might never even know Awa Gee's contribution. Heroism creates more heroism.

The last sentence in Silko's chapter predicts revolutionary change:

"but if the plan worked, if the lights went out all over all at once, then the United States would never be the same again." Revolutionary change becomes the center from which all events are enacted and toward which all myths lead. Like Silko's gay hero, there are many bridges between cultures in *Almanac of the Dead*. The destruction of Glen Canyon Dam represents a single battle, the restoration of wilderness only part of the larger strategy.

Environmentalism in the Borderlands

All three texts—*The Monkey Wrench Gang, The Cracking of the Damn*, and *Almanac of the Dead*—address what it means to be an authentic hero in an "American" setting. In contrast to Earth First! and Edward Abbey however, Silko blurs ethnic, gender, and sexual preference lines, making it difficult to pigeonhole the characters who people her novel. Categorical borders are erased and the reader is left with a single geographical border, the divide between Mexico and the United States, that in itself is made to appear deeply inauthentic. While Abbey and Earth First! call primarily for a change within the predominant political and social structure, Silko's strategy allows her to create (or reveal) a world that is undergoing a cultural reconfiguration that will soon develop into a political upheaval. The governments of the Americas are dependent on inauthentic borders and categories. By subverting those categories Silko is able to conceptualize the subversion of the geographical border and the governments that defend it.

For example, Lecha and Zeta cross the Mexican-American border with impunity, and it is clear throughout the novel that for many characters the imaginary border is a temporary aberration forced upon a landscape of continuity. Near the beginning of her novel Silko declares, "There was not, and there never has been, a legal government by Europeans anywhere in the Americas. Not by any definition, not even by the European's own definitions and laws. Because no legal government could be established on stolen land." One important key to understanding the borderland world that Silko creates is the assertion that the borderlands are a result of thievery. Silko does not let that thievery appear to be something vaguely of the past, a result of policies set by politicians long dead. Through the character of a real estate agent, Silko forces the reader to acknowledge a continuous act of theft as the plans for a water city, Venice, Arizona, are dubiously carried out. Therefore, any act that carries a character from one side of the border to the next works to undermine the enforcement of that thievery and becomes an act to restore unity to the landscape, a unity that is ironically destroyed with the bridge in Abbey's novel.

More than any of the characters in any of the texts, Silko's gay activist is a conduit between genders, racial groups, and even the physical and spiritual worlds. It is hard to imagine Silko creating her hero without Hayduke in mind. Her nameless hero illuminates the extent to which the Glen Canyon myth has been revisioned; the hero does not separate himself from the group and is willing to sacrifice his own life as a member of a movement that has often defined itself in narrowly masculine terms.

Thus, the queer hero becomes pivotal, a supreme undermining of the borders, within the movement itself and the political borders between states and countries, that Abbey, and to a lesser extent Earth First!, did not tackle in their earlier mythologies. For Abbey the emphasis on individual freedom ultimately meant that he could not advocate a network of activists and activism that would subsume a Hayduke. Abbey defends the western American male hero and thus the boundaries constructed between male and female, white and other, homosexual and heterosexual that accompany him. Silko presents a reconfiguration of those boundaries that sustains the homeland and clan in a world of renewed dependence. Silko's characters implement a change that encompasses more than the small world of individual agency, while Hayduke's monkey-wrenching ultimately results in futility, a mere bandage on a gash of capitalism and exploitation. Finally, because it reenacted Abbey's mythology, Earth First! has had to live with a legacy that is very male, white, and heterosexually oriented, a reputation that has kept it from strengthening ties between other activist organizations, that has left it open to criticism from environmental justice groups and others, and that has become an issue within Earth First! itself.[3]

NOTES

1. I would like to express my thanks to Dr. Leroy Ashby's History 525 class, spring 1995, at Washington State University, for the careful readings

and honest feedback. I am also indebted to Rik Scarce and Paul Hirt for the time they spent discussing with me Earth First!, the action at Glen Canyon Dam, and the importance of Edward Abbey to Earth First!.

2. The "continuous story" is also evoked in the string of tellings by Abbey, Earth First!, and Silko. The myth is shared and malleable, changing shape to meet the needs of the author/storyteller and audience even after it has been written down. Barthes argued that this is one of the functions of myth, that it must be flexible in order to survive.

3. It should be noted that issues of sexism and racism are being actively addressed within the various groups that presently make up Earth First!.

REFERENCES

Abbey, Edward. *The Monkey Wrench Gang.* New York: Avon, 1975.
———. *One Life at a Time, Please.* New York: Holt, 1978.
Anzaldúa, Gloria. *Borderlands/La Frontera: The New Mestiza.* San Francisco: Aunt Lute, 1987.
Barthes, Roland. *Mythologies.* Trans. Annette Lavers. New York: Noonday, 1972.
Earth First! Newsletter. Earth First!.
Foreman, Dave, and Bill Haywood, eds. *Ecodefense: A Field Guide to Monkey-wrenching.* 2d ed. Tucson: Ned Ludd, 1987.
Martin, Russell. *A Story that Stands Like a Dam: Glen Canyon and the Struggle for the Soul of the West.* New York: Holt, 1989.
The Cracking of Glen Canyon Damn. Produced by Toby McLeod. 9 min. Earth Image Films, 1982. Videocassette.
Scarce, Rik. *Eco-Warriors: Understanding the Radical Environmental Movement.* Chicago: Noble, 1990.
Silko, Leslie Marmon. *Almanac of the Dead.* New York: Penguin, 1991.
———. "Landscape, History, and the Pueblo Imagination from a High Arid Plateau in New Mexico." In *On Nature: Nature, Landscape, and Natural History,* ed. Daniel Halpern. San Francisco: North Point, 1987.
Slovic, Scott. *Seeking Awareness in American Nature Writing: Henry Thoreau, Annie Dillard, Edward Abbey, Wendell Berry, Barry Lopez.* Salt Lake City: University of Utah Press, 1992.

What We Do with It Now

The town of Watauga lies just a couple miles south of the North Dakota border, and about eighty miles west of the Missouri River. Watauga originated when the Milwaukee Railroad built the line through in 1906. Like most Dakota towns established around the turn of the century, Watauga boomed during the first few years of its existence. My grandmother claimed that at one time the town could boast of two banks, two grocery stores, and no fewer than four lumberyards among its many businesses. The town even had a doctor. Today, the nearest clinic is thirty miles away; it is sixty-seven miles to the nearest hospital. Most of the businesses closed long ago. The last official population count I have heard is thirty-two.

Watauga as I first remember it in the early 1960s was dying, but a few businesses still opened their doors on Main Street, which in typical western fashion runs perpendicular to the highway. An elevator and a set of shipping pens occupied the space between the Milwaukee Railroad tracks and Highway 12, which run parallel. The shipping pens and the elevator were still in use in the early sixties. When I was in the second or third grade, a rancher from the Black Horse country fifty or sixty miles southwest of us shipped a couple hundred head of cattle up from Texas by train and unloaded them in Watauga. He trailed them home in the time-honored manner, with a chuck wagon providing food. The rancher had his own men, but cowhands from all the little ranches along the way joined in for a few miles or so wherever the herd passed by their ranches. I remember that Dad and my older brother Mike rode along for a few miles, and Mom and the rest of us watched from a nearby hill.

But the drive was an exercise in nostalgia; papers in two counties billed it as "the last trail drive" and used the occasion to mention all the livestock that had streamed through the shipping pens at Watauga in the more prosperous past. As any student of western history knows, the volatile center of the cattle business shifted with the advancement of railroads and the availability of lease-land. Many towns in the West claimed a moment as the premier cow town in the region before they dwindled or even disappeared. Isabel, forty miles southeast of Watauga, names its annual summer celebration "The Days of 1910," as though the rest of its history were a footnote to that one year. Like Isabel, Watauga had her fifteen minutes of fame. In fact, in the competitive boosterism of western Dakota towns during the 'teens and twenties, Watauga outpaced her nearest rivals, McIntosh to the east, and Morristown to the west, although Watauga is the smallest of the three now.

The Milwaukee Railroad no longer sends trains through Watauga. When I was eight or nine, I helped Dad trail a small bunch of yearling sheep from our ranch five miles south of town into Watauga. Already the wild sunflowers and Koshia weed had choked the shipping pens, and those opportunistic plants have long since been crowded out by native grasses. The pens themselves are falling down. Even before the railroad went, the elevator closed. The offices burned down in 1963. The elevator tower still stands, but now it functions only as a rite of passage: by the age of nine or ten, many kids around Watauga have climbed to the top of the elevator.

As Donald Worster suggests in his book *The Dust Bowl*, we in the Great Plains have developed no architecture of our own. We have, however, done the next best thing in Watauga. Scarce materials and scarce money have forced us to adopt as our maxim the adage to "recycle, use it up, wear it out" where buildings are concerned. One still sees tar-paper claim shacks serving as shops, chicken coops, pigpens, or tool sheds. The larger buildings along Main underwent larger mutations.

Wolff's Grocery Store stood on the west side of Main across Highway 12 from the elevator. One of the last major businesses to close, it folded, like others in Watauga, not because the proprietors couldn't scratch together at least a scanty living, but because they grew too old to continue. The building sat empty for several years; then, members of a country-western band bought it. They remodeled it into a steakhouse, complete with a dance floor and a bandstand. For a while business boomed, gathering people from great distances on Saturday nights. But the cost of the remodeling couldn't be recouped, and the band declared bankruptcy and went back out on the road. My parents bought the steakhouse and ran it for a year and a half before selling it to some business people from

Old Railroad depot in Watauga. (Photo by Joe Draper)

out of town. Had the building not burned down, it's hard telling what it would be now.

The Watauga Hotel stood next door. My grandmother worked there for a time in her (and the century's) early teens, one of the many jobs she held in Watauga before she married. She used to help out in the kitchen, baking pies and peeling potatoes. By my time, the hotel housed a large Catholic family, which ran a small liquor store in what was once the vestibule of the hotel. When I was in fourth grade, the proprietress taught me catechism. She held class around her huge kitchen table, and I remember pausing in the midst of our moral instruction so that our teacher could go sell someone a pint of Old Crow.

My parents sold the ranch when I was fourteen and moved away. Later, they moved back to Watauga and bought the old hotel. They lived in it for a few years, then tore it down. In fact, my father did much of the recycling of buildings in town. He first tore down the one bank that still remained, and he used the lumber from the bank and a couple other buildings to build himself a horse barn and a round training barn. He left the vault standing to store feed. For the next ten years or so he supported our family by training horses between stints of construction and destruction.

A vacant lot on which a grocery store once stood lay between the hotel and the next building, the town hall. Until the late seventies, the hall still functioned in the community. Occasionally, local couples held their wedding dances there, especially before the steakhouse burned. The whole community turned out for a wedding dance; people came from as far away as fifty miles, even if they barely knew the couple. Usually the McGregors played for wedding dances; their repertoire suited us well. They played slow country "belt-buckle polishing" songs for the opening ceremonial set of dances; then they played polkas, waltzes, and jitterbugs until most of the older people quit dancing; and they ended the evening with fifties and sixties rock and roll.

Even children went to wedding dances. Three- and four-year-olds took the floor, sometimes with a parent or sibling, sometimes with a neighbor kid. Clots of junior high kids horsed around in front of the open hall doors, and older teens sat in cars, drinking beer and smoking cigarettes, or stood behind the hall for a little privacy. Young couples often concluded the evening up at the graveyard or out at Mallard Dam, two favorite parking spots. Older people took rest breaks in the steakhouse, often settling there permanently once the band started playing rock.

Besides wedding dances, the main secular social event in Watauga was the school Christmas program, also held at the town hall. The two Watauga teachers coordinated it, and after we quit holding a separate celebration at our country school, Prairie View, our teacher helped. Every child made at least two or three stage appearances, and the majority of us weren't talented. I remember a particularly awful production: a junk-band rendition of "Deck the Halls" capped the evening. Still, the whole community turned out for school programs, maybe out of small-town boredom. Or maybe the refreshments served afterward drew people. Every woman in the community brought her specialty, even those whose children and grandchildren had graduated and gone.

The program started at seven o'clock; about eight, Santa Claus came; and the hall rarely cleared until after eleven, as people lingered late talking. About ten o'clock, the teachers and some of the other ladies of the community, those workhorses without whom nothing ever gets done, began to straighten up, shaming some of the men into stacking chairs and sweeping. And finally everyone departed, each woman parceling out whatever remained of the food that she had brought. "Here," she'd say, "I know Bob likes this kind of fudge," or, "Take some of these cookies home for your kids. We'll never eat them all."

After both Prairie View and Watauga school closed and the bar burned down, there didn't seem to be much use for a town hall. It got sold to a man who used it as a mechanic shop, and when he left town, one of my cousins bought it as a feed warehouse.

Next to the town hall lies another vacant lot, then the post office. Around 1920, my grandmother had worked as postmistress there. A large woman, her face showed more strength than softness, and her twenty-four years marked her as a spinster. She didn't plan to marry, although she had kept company with my grandfather for some time. She told me years later that he used to come into the post office, jump over the counter, and propose to her. Then in 1921 the flu epidemic left Watauga full of orphans. The parish priest told Grandma that it was her Christian duty to marry and provide a home for the orphans. She did. The couple started married life with six children, although all but one went to other relatives within a few months. In those days married women didn't work outside the home, so Grandma reluctantly gave up her job at the post office. Grandma used to have to meet the train twice a day, and sorting the huge bags of mail while tending to customers' needs kept her busy all day. Now the post office is only open till noon, and the postmistress almost always has time to chat.

The post office sits on a corner. Main Street for that first block is wide—so wide that even before the steakhouse closed, and people parked their seventies-model cars and pickups head-in up and down that first block, two cars could still meet with room to spare; so wide that when no one was parked on Main Street, usually the case, young hot bloods could cut cookies right on Main Street and laugh at the responsible citizens who came out to shake a fist at their taillights. Even now, the gravel of Main Street is usually marked with cookie tracks, although no one shakes a fist anymore.

After that first block, the road narrows so that cars meeting have to move over. The road goes past a vacant lot and a house, then curves to the right, passes a couple more houses. Then, on the left, is Watauga School. By Watauga standards it's a modest building; no false front, just a long white frame building with a low-pitched roof—two school rooms opening on a long hallway that runs between two bathrooms. My grandmother went to school here, and so did I after Prairie View closed.

In the "little room," where one teacher taught the first three grades, different groups got called up for reading classes, and the teacher directed what the various grades should be doing at any given time—phonics, or language, or social studies, or whatever. The teacher worked hard to get students to be able to read, because as soon as they could, she could just say, "Do page 125," and her students could do it. Those that had trouble could ask her, or more likely, one of the other students, for help.

The "big room" teacher had five grades together. She never held lessons. She wrote assignments on the board, and when school started in the morning, we did them. Students who had difficulty with an assignment would go up for help. If no one needed her attention, she graded papers or else read. As long as we were quiet, we could do as we pleased once we finished our assignments. I usually read, but if there weren't any books around I hadn't read, which happened fairly often since the bookmobile only stopped once every two weeks, I messed around with my Elmer's Glue. I had a notion that if I got the right combination of additives and drying conditions, I could make diamonds.

But the bathrooms provided the best entertainment. Both had wall-sized storage closets. True to the ancient dichotomy, the boys' had the sports equipment, which consisted of a softball with the seams beginning to fray, one baseball glove, two bats (one broken), and a flat volleyball—no net. The girls' bathroom had considerably more plunder. It contained the leavings of about twenty years of art projects: bits of Styrofoam, scraps of cloth, dried out clay, odd-shaped pieces of faded construction paper, and paints of various kinds and stages of dryness. We girls also had the school band: two plastic flutes. Actually, there were three of them, but one had the mouthpiece broken off.

You could sit on the toilet with your knees hugged to your chest, barely breathing into one of the flutes, fingering the notes shown in the one surviving manual. What could be sweeter than those unheard melodies? If music palled—and it usually did, once you blew a bit too hard and the flute sounded, arousing the fear of discovery—you could explore the rest of the cabinet. Sometimes half an hour elapsed before the teacher remembered you were gone and sent someone to knock on the door and say, "Teacher says you're supposed to come back." Then you'd jump, because you'd been expecting it. Nothing startles a person more than having something they expected to happen happen when they were deep in thought about something else.

Cutting grass in Watauga with the school and Protestant church in background. (Photo by Joe Draper)

Watauga School got consolidated well over ten years ago. I remember the fight against consolidation beginning in our country school even before I started first grade. During the sixties, my parents recognized three great evils: Communism, drugs, and school consolidation. There seemed to be no way to close with the first two enemies, so they spent their energy fighting the last. Perhaps they were impractical and those who said that a bigger school offered better education for less money were right. But when our country school closed, and again when Watauga School closed, a big part of the community went with them.

For a while the school stood vacant and got used only for elections. My mother always sat on the election board, since she was the only registered Republican in a community that usually votes conservative. I don't know where elections are held in Watauga now, because about a few years ago a young man from north of Watauga bought the schoolhouse. He'd studied photography somewhere and opened up a studio there. He does well, I hear.

Past the schoolhouse, the road narrows to a dirt track over a little hill, and on the far side of that little hill lies the graveyard. It's big, and empty enough to be lonelier than most. The Catholic section is fullest; family plots are scattered here and there along the path that leads to the big cross on the hill, with plenty of space left for relatives who'll most likely be buried somewhere else. Some names one reads on the tombstones have otherwise vanished from the area completely.

If you take the road back toward town, you pass a little subsistence farm, and then kitty-corner from the school is Saint Michael's Catholic Church. Easily the most imposing structure in town, it's a brick building built along scaled-down Gothic lines with a tall bell tower and stained-glass windows depicting the Stations of the Cross. A spacious churchyard boasts the tallest trees in town. Elsewhere in Watauga people planted Chinese elms, and even those that survive spread half-bare branches. But pine and cottonwood trees grow in the churchyard, and in the summer, the rustling of the cottonwood leaves accompanied the sermon. A concrete slab about the size of a large dance floor fronts the church. In the old days, when the parish priest lived in Watauga in the rectory next door to the church, we had mass at eight on Sunday morning. People used to talk, long after church let out, in all but the bitterest weather. Then in the late sixties, the priest serving our church and the one in Morristown had the church in McIntosh added to his duties, and the priest said mass in Watauga on Saturday night. People still stayed after church to visit, but not quite as long as they had before. Last year the parish lost its priest, and the community only has mass once a month when the priest from Lemmon comes.

A huge empty lot occupies the whole block next to Saint Michael's, except for an old Protestant church on the inside of the curve where the street becomes Main Street proper. I'm not sure what denomination: Baptist, I think. It's been vacant as long as I can remember. I've heard off and on that some people have "plans" for it, perhaps to turn it into a residence, or maybe to move it and use it as a barn. But nobody has, perhaps out of fear of desecrating a church.

Then Main Street widens. On the corner across from the post office stands the old Catholic parish hall. Probably ten years ago, the church built a new hall, much smaller, with a modern kitchen and indoor bathrooms. It has vinyl siding, and they say it's very nice, although I've never been in it.

The old hall extends back a long way from its false front on Main. The front room had one corner divided off with a low wall, and that corner contained the huge old black stove, an equally ancient refrigerator, and sinks, as well as a miniscule amount of counter space. Three or four long tables occupied the rest of the room. The back of the hall was open, although tables were often set up there as well.

The Altar Society put on potluck dinners there three or four times a year, and any major church ritual had its reciprocal feast in the parish hall. Catholic couples who married at Saint Michael's often had a reception in the parish hall before their dance in the town hall. Baptisms, first communions, and confirmations all called for at least rolls and coffee and more likely a full-scale brunch, and no Catholic in the parish, no matter how sporadic his or her church participation, ever was buried without a funeral dinner for the survivors. The Altar Society held its annual bazaar there (although they used to have their bake sales in the basement of one of the bank buildings in Lemmon, since sales there were higher). We held Christmas parties there, and sometimes in January, Father ran a series of bingo games Saturday evenings after mass. Father called the numbers. The hall didn't have a loudspeaker system, and his was the most practiced voice.

When they built the new church hall, Nick Nehl, a distant cousin of mine, bought the old one. He had been to saddle-making school, and he opened up a boot repair and saddle shop in the kitchen portion of the old hall. In the winter months after local ranchers finished winter chores, they often stopped in at the saddle shop. Nick always had the coffeepot on, and a deck of cards whiled away long afternoons. Many of the card players eventually rode saddles that Nick built. He liked to rope and he built a roping arena on the northeast edge of town. At least two evenings a week during the summer he holds team roping practice, and Nick competes at a rodeo or a jackpot roping nearly every weekend in summer. Later he added a feed dealership, and the saddle-making became a sideline. Eventually Nick opened another feed store in Lemmon, where his wife worked. It might have made sense to move there, but he chose to stay in Watauga.

Nick's brother, Pat Nehl, uses the back part of the hall as a shop for his trucking firm. Some of the men who drive for him are small ranchers who need some extra income. Others are young men who grew up on the surrounding ranches and work for Pat a season or two before they leave town. Young people who grow up in the area often yo-yo back and forth between Watauga and other places before finally establishing roots somewhere else. It's hard to leave Watauga, and equally hard to stay there.

Next to the hall is an empty lot, and next to that used to be Ostwinkle's Barber Shop. I can only remember the Ostwinkles as very old, both of them stooped and thin. Heinie gave haircuts in the back of the shop while Lucy guarded the front. She didn't like children much; whenever we were in the shop, she watched us suspiciously and tried to hurry us through the agonizing process of spending our weekly candy nickel. I would have preferred spending my allowance at the grocery store, but Dad made us patronize the Ostwinkles, claiming that they needed the money. But I don't think that the twenty-five or thirty cents a week that our family spent there made much difference to them. Heinie and Lucy both died in the late 1960s, and the building was empty for a while. I don't know who tore it down.

For a while, people threw garbage in the hole where the basement of the candy store had been, then someone 'dozed dirt into it. Eventually, grass grew there again. Dad put up a woven-wire fence and kept a horse or two on the lot.

There was another empty lot, and then the last building before the highway was the old hardware store. Not many buildings in town had a second story behind the false front, but the hardware store did. I can, I think, dimly remember when the business was open, but it's a vague memory, and I may actually be remembering another hardware store in another town. I couldn't have been more than three or four when it closed. Then, as the history of most buildings in Watauga seems to go, the hardware store stood empty for a few years, and the weeds grew tall around it.

The seventies came. South Dakota, especially western South Dakota, lags at least a decade behind the coasts. So during the sixties people in Watauga worried about drugs, and during the seventies some of the younger people took them. During the mid-seventies a story went around that Johnny Carson had said that Lemmon, South Dakota, had the highest per capita drug consumption in the United States. Whether or not the story is true, that many people believed and repeated it shows how widespread people perceived drug use to be in our area. When I was a freshman in high school in 1971, some kids from my class went to Rapid City to learn to be peer counselors. When they got back, they pulled each person in our class aside and questioned us about our involvement with drugs. Mine was pretty limited—the occasional aspirin and coffee; nevertheless, my peer warned me about my caffeine consumption. Years later, I learned that my counselor had been stoned during a good part of his trip to Rapid City. I think he's quit smoking pot, though, and I still drink way too much coffee.

The hardware store had an apartment above it, and during the mid-seventies it served as a crash pad for, as I remember hearing them called, "those hippies from south of town." Like nearly everybody else in town, some of them were distant relatives of mine. None of them had steady jobs, and the consensus was that they sold dope. Cars from the surrounding towns visited the store more frequently than mere sociability would warrant. They lived there for a couple years, and then they were gone—some said to prison, some said to California. Once again, the building stood empty.

My parents bought it in the early 1980s. True to form, Dad tore it down, exposing a huge concrete slab. He saved everything, down to the nails and the wiring, and used it all to build a house on the slab. Then he tore down the hotel and sold the lumber. My parents lived in that house until they moved to Nevada several years ago. A couple more families lived in it, off and on, and then somebody hauled it out of town. Only the slab remains.

Highway 12 runs east and west. If you turn west off Main Street, you pass a billboard advertising the saddle shop–feed store, and then you're out of town. But if you turn east, you go past a couple small tar-paper buildings, old claim shacks moved into town for sheds, then past an abandoned stucco gas station. Another vacant lot, and then a two-story frame house sits back from the highway. In the early eighties an old man either bought it, inherited it, or squatted in it—I'm not sure which. Like several other old abandoned houses in town, this one had no indoor plumbing or running water.

As soon as the old man moved in, he started fixing things up. He painted the house sky blue with red and white trim and put a sign above the front door that read "Uncle Sam's Blue Palace." He constructed two outhouses and painted each of them white with a band of blue stars around the top to complement the half-moons on the doors. He even carpeted them. When Wataugans talk about the meticulous labor he put into his place, they invariably dwell on those carpeted outhouses.

After he finished the outhouses, the old man ornamented his

Joe's Place in Watauga. (Photo by Joe Draper)

yard. He built a couple of birdhouses, which I do not recall birds ever using, a wishing well, and a couple of flower planters. He built convex bridges across the deep but narrow ditch that bounded his property on two sides. All of these he painted white with occasional flourishes of dark blue or red. Then, apparently annoyed by the advice of his more respectable brother, he sunk a post at the edge of the yard and topped it with a book stand. He painted "David's Preaching Post" on it. And after that, he didn't allow his brother any farther onto his property than that.

He kept the yard watered and neatly clipped, trimming the grass around the wooden structures and the flower beds with the same precision that marked all his work. Although he had a couple lilac bushes (many of the old houses in Watauga had a lilac bush or two) and I think maybe even some rosebushes, he grew humble flowers, some marigolds and bachelor buttons, but mostly moss roses. These he grew in kidney-shaped beds edged with stones he'd painted white.

Reclusive by nature, the old man's rare forays to the local cafe caused more comment than even the advent of a tourist whose car bore New York license plates. Yet with that social generosity that even recluses sometimes have, he put up a sign designating his yard as "Whitestone Park," adding "Visitors Welcome." And travelers on the highway did stop there sometimes to eat their picnic lunches and to use the carpeted outhouses. Several years ago, the old man died, and the house is empty again. The little structures have all disappeared, and the paint on the house has faded. The flower beds have been planted back to grass and the stones hauled away. No sign welcomes visitors anymore, but someone does keep the yard mowed.

The last building on the east edge of town is the one remaining gas station and cafe, Joe's Place, usually referred to as either "Buzzy's" or "Janice's." The place underwent at least three separate phases of construction. Originally, there was only a service bay and a small cafe. A room behind the service bay held supplies needed in the shop, a couple of freezers and coolers. When Buzzy and Janice bought the place over twenty years ago, they added a pool table and foosball table so the kids in town would have something to do.

The café originally seated four on stools at a counter and another four or five at the one round table. When the present owners bought the place, they added room for three more tables and put in indoor bathrooms. As the world expanded and Watauga shrunk, Joe's Place bridged the gap between Watauga and the world. When the liquor store closed, the cafe added a locked cabinet stocked with Jim Beam, Windsor, Old Crow, and other favorites. After the store closed, they stocked donuts, bread, milk, and ice cream—those staples that wouldn't last between expeditions to stores in Lemmon or McIntosh. When videos became popular, Buzzy added movie rentals to the business, and even before that, the box of put-and-take books (mostly westerns and thick romance novels, the kind with sex scenes) saw constant use.

A walking plow that has stood in front of the cafe for years attests to Buzzy's ruling passion. For years he's gone to nearly every estate sale within driving distance. Buzzy houses the antiques he's spent a lifetime gathering in the "Watauga Museum," as they named the final addition to the cafe. In it Buzzy has old harnesses, saddles, bits and bridles of all kinds, spurs, old dishes, cast iron stoves, rocking chairs, bedsteads, crockery, iron skillets, hoes, lanterns, all that and more, piled in long furrows leading back to the past.

Writing Our Story

When we only spoke our story,
forests breathed deep and listened,
branches held, leaves quivered
with the understanding of owls.
Our story caught the push of wind,
reached upward with giant pines,
echoed deep in all roots to bedrock.
Our voice moved to the quick hooves of deer,
stretched with coyote's call to a clouded moon.
But now we write our separate stories,
and forests shiver, split and groan,
ground to pulp for treatises,
novels, Sunday supplements
and poems like this.

Flooding the Boundaries of Form
Terry Tempest Williams's Ecofeminist
Unnatural History

By subtitling *Refuge* "an *Un*natural History of Family and Place," Terry Tempest Williams at once alludes to the literary tradition of natural-history writing and announces her departure from the form. At first glance, *Refuge* appears to be conventional natural history. The book's cover design, for example, features an unpeopled natural scene of a bird flying over a lake rimmed by distant mountains. The short biographical note about Williams at the front of the book states that she is naturalist-in-residence at the Utah Museum of Natural History, immediately establishing her authority to write about nature.

Both the prefatory map of the Great Salt Lake and the table of contents, in which chapters are named for different bird species, bespeak familiar literary terrain, territory opened up by the pioneers of American natural history, men like William Bartram, Alexander Wilson, John James Audubon, Henry Thoreau, and John Burroughs. Appearing at the back of the book is a typical list of rare and regular bird species of the Great Salt Lake, arranged phylogenetically and including their Latin scientific names.

From cover to cover, then, *Refuge* initially conforms to our expectations about natural-history writing. Indeed, the text itself follows the nature writing path in many ways, including close observation and detailed description of birds and their habitat, scientific explanations of avian ecology, and the presentation of quantitative data like rainfall and lake level, all enclosed in a first-person, nonfictional form.

What, then, is "unnatural" about *Refuge*? How does it depart from the traditional genre? Setting is one difference, for Williams describes not only natural areas but also populated urban areas and indoor settings, places such as downtown Salt Lake City, New

York City, Bloomingdale's, Nordstrom's, hospital corridors, and the rooms of her family's house. Subject matter is another difference, for the book is about people as much as it is about nature. Williams writes about her family, especially about the strong bonds among generations of women—her grandmother Mimi, her mother, Diane, and herself. Extending her sense of family, Williams probes into Mormon history and culture, unearths information on the ancient Fremont peoples, and visits Mexico to participate in the rituals of the Day of the Dead.

Yet another departure from traditional natural history may be described as the gendered stance of *Refuge.* Where writers like Bartram, Muir, and Leopold, and even Annie Dillard and Ann Zwinger do not thematize their sex, Williams wears her gender on her sleeve and remains ever-conscious of how being a woman colors every aspect of her experience. Further distinguishing *Refuge* from natural histories of an earlier century are "unnatural" developments in the world, for Williams comes to believe that the cancer killing the women of her family may have been caused by exposure to radiation during above-ground atomic testing that took place between 1951 and 1962. Although she learns to accept death as "natural," the knowledge that her mother may have died prematurely—an unsuspecting victim of Cold War militarism—causes Williams to commit civil disobedience, protesting further "unnatural" abuse of what she calls the "Motherbody," "Mother Earth."

The most striking formal feature of *Refuge,* further distancing it from mainstream natural-history writing, is its conflation of natural history with personal, familial history. *Refuge* splices together two stories, the story of the catastrophic flooding of the Bear River Migratory Bird Refuge and the story of Diane Tempest's spreading cancer. Although purists might insist that the two narratives are logically distinct and that their marriage in one book is arbitrary and "unnatural," nonetheless, emotionally the two are as intertwined as the strands of a rope. As Williams remarks, "I could not separate the Bird Refuge from my family. Devastation respects no boundaries" (40). Just as the rising Great Salt Lake laps over protective dikes, *Refuge* breaches the conventional boundaries of natural history's subject and form.

Many other traditional boundaries also dissolve; in fact, I argue that this book's mission is to contest boundaries of all sorts. The separation between person and place collapses in statements such as "I am desert. I am mountains. I am Great Salt Lake" (29). Observer and observed likewise fuse as Williams recalls of her mother, "I began breathing with her. . . . Mother and I became one. One breathing organism" (230). No longer is there a clear delineation between pleasure and pain or between health and sickness. Even life and death intergrade as Williams refers to birth as our first death and describes death as becoming fully born.

Inside and outside are paradoxically the same when Williams quotes the gnostics, who teach that "what is inside of you is what is outside of you and the one who fashions you on the outside is the one who shaped the inside of you. And what you see outside of you, you see inside of you" (267). Similarly, matter is imbued with spirit, and dreams infuse reality. The closed doors between private and public are thrown open as Williams describes intimate family prayer meetings, reprints her mother's private letters, and publishes her own personal journal entries. Likewise the personal and the political merge as Williams questions patriarchal practices of Mormon home life and as the personal tragedy of cancer in her family prompts Williams to join a political march against nuclear testing.

On a formal level, Williams makes ambiguous the difference between nonfiction and fiction. Birds, for example, are portrayed not just literally, as objects of a naturalist's close observation, but also lyrically and symbolically, as elements contributing to the beauty and meaning of a narrative. Thus, white-faced glossy ibises literally "eat worms" (18), lyrically flash "iridescences of pink, purple, and green" (17), and symbolically "are the companions of the gods" (18), associated both with death and with birth. In her description of birds and also of landscapes, Williams maintains the scientific accuracy of a nonfiction writer while she deepens the symbolic resonance of the work, using the techniques of a novelist.

The structure of *Refuge* may appear to lack premeditated design, seeming to simply follow the chronological entries in a nonfiction journal. In actuality, Williams has carefully shaped and paced the material to resemble the plot of a novel and to reproduce a novel's emotional impact. It is this strong sense of plot that makes *Refuge* so much more moving and even cathartic than much of the dry natural-history writing of the past.

One clue to *Refuge*'s novelistic construction can be discovered in the precise measurements of the level of the Great Salt Lake, accu-

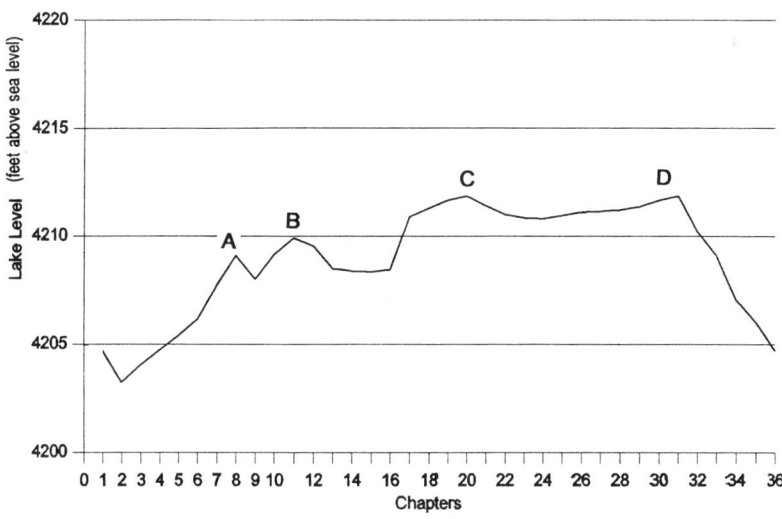

Changing levels of the Great Salt Lake in *Refuge*. Maximum lake levels correspond to climaxes in the story's plot. A. "Mother began her radiation treatment this morning." (77) B. Terry Tempest Williams has a small cyst removed from her breast: "Nothing is familiar to me anymore." (97) C. Mother "embraces" her cancer; Terry lies beside her mother, strokes her hair, breathes with her "within the secrecy of sisterhood." (158) D. Mother dies; funeral is held; Terry rebels against Mormon dogma and decides to accept the "Motherbody as a spiritual counterpoint to the Godhead." (241)

rate to the nearest one-hundredth of a foot, that Williams prints after each chapter title. Of what possible relevance are lake-level statistics to the story? If one uses these statistics to construct a graph (see fig. 1) with chapter numbers on the horizontal axis and lake elevations on the vertical axis, one will find that the resulting curve resembles the plot structure of a traditional novel, with rising action, climaxes, falling action, and denouement. With the skill of a fiction writer, Williams has arranged her factual material so that the highest lake levels correspond to turning points and personal transformations in the family narrative.

In this light, a closer scrutiny of the cover of the book reveals the same fiction/nonfiction fusion. We see a realistic, sharply focussed, full-color photograph of a peregrine falcon superimposed over a dreamlike, blurred-focus, monochromatic photograph of the Bonneville Salt Flats. Are the flats covered with water, or is that seeming lake really a mirage? We cannot tell. Recalling Marianne Moore's definition of poetry as "imaginary gardens with real toads in them," here we have an imaginary landscape with a real bird in it. As *Refuge* implies, poetic truth is always a blend of fact and figment.

I believe that what is "unnatural" about *Refuge*—particularly its gendered stance and its contesting of boundaries—can be attributed to Williams' ecofeminist aesthetic. In *Refuge*, Williams invents a literary art form consonant with ecofeminist philosophy.

Before pursuing the connection between Williams's artistry and ecofeminist philosophy, a brief review of the latter may be in order. Ecofeminism, as a philosophical discourse and social critique, calls attention to the links between the treatment of women and the treatment of nature.[1]

Ecofeminists believe that patriarchy is responsible for the world's social and environmental ills and that these ills cannot be cured through technology or piecemeal legislation or local clean-up days, but only through a total revolution in thought and action such that the patriarchal social order itself is overturned. Ecofeminists have drafted a Declaration of Interdependence, which reads in part, "It is our belief that man's dominion over nature parallels the subjugation of women in many societies, denying them sovereignty over their lives and bodies. Until all societies truly value women and the environment, their joint degradation will continue."[2]

Most ecofeminists agree that the patriarchal system rests upon a dualistic and hierarchical way of describing reality. For example, take the dualistic pair mind and body. Ever since Descartes we have tended to downplay the continuities between mind and body and instead have emphasized their differences, even defining them as opposites. Furthermore, not only do we enforce the separation between mind and body, we hierarchically rank them, such that mind is more highly valued than body. Similarly, ever since the Greeks, we regard spirit or idea as separate from and of greater worth than matter. Such dualistic pairs abound in the Western way of viewing the world. A partial list looks like this:

mind	body
spirit	matter
reason	emotion
humanity	nature
men	women

For each of the pairs, the term in the first column is regarded as valuable in and of itself, while the term in the second column is considered a resource, valuable only insofar as it serves the interests of the first. Furthermore, all the terms in a given column are associated with one another. Thus, men are regarded as fully human, possessing the uniquely human attributes of mind, spirit, and reason, whereas women are viewed as closer to nature, and are relegated to the sphere of the body, matter, and emotion.

An ecofeminist response to this situation differs from a feminist response in that many feminists, following Simone de Beauvoir's lead, argue that it is time to regard women as fully human and grant them the same status, privilege, and power that men enjoy. In contrast, ecofeminists argue that such a change, while improving the plight of women, still elevates the human over the nonhuman, keeping the other dualisms and the attendant domination in place. These ecofeminists would like to see the entire dualistic structure dismantled and replaced by a holistic view that sees all things as parts of one system and emphasizes the similarities, continuities, and connections among them.

In a nutshell, the ecofeminist argument is that men dominate and exploit both nature and women. Other culpable verbs in the ecofeminist critique include *oppress, master, violate, subjugate, rape, abuse, control,* and *conquer.* Ecofeminism calls for a new paradigm that assigns all things equal value and replaces attitudes of domination and competition with those of respect and cooperation. Ecofeminist thinking values the community over the rugged individual, and, rather than asserting independence, acknowledges our dependence on all elements of the ecosystem. Ecofeminism celebrates diversity, respecting difference while recognizing the universal kinship of all life forms. Both ecofeminist philosophy and the aesthetic experiments of *Refuge* deconstruct dualisms such as humanity/nature, self/other, mind/body, and intellect/emotion, replacing them with a holistic vision of connectedness and interdependence.

The majority of ecofeminist work has analyzed social, economic, and political structures. Williams is one of the first thinkers to bring an ecofeminist perspective to bear on aesthetics. The ecofeminist aesthetic informing *Refuge* reveals itself in the contrasting descriptions of two desert sculptures. The first is a nine-story steel-and-concrete structure by Karl Momen entitled "Metaphor" but jokingly referred to by locals as "The Tree of Utah." As Williams writes,

"Its brightly colored spheres (leaves?) resembled enormous tennis *balls,* thirteen feet in diameter, poised on top of an eighty-three-foot lightning *rod*" (127; emphasis mine). The plaque below the towering sculpture explains that Momen, a European architect, saw the West Desert as " 'a large canvas with nothing on it' " (ibid.) and that "Metaphor" is his attempt " 'to put something out there to break the monotony' " (ibid.). Williams points out that "the man-made tree rose from the salt flats like a small phallus" and that its shadow resembled "a mushroom cloud" (ibid.). "The Tree of Utah" represents what might be called masculinist art. The "tree"—vertical and linear—is an imposition, an arrogant, insensitive, narcissistic, and even aggressive act committed by a foreigner who has never taken the time to learn to appreciate the land on its own terms. The sculpture works against the land rather than with it. Williams' mother dismisses the tree as " 'another roadside attraction' " (ibid.) and they drive on.

Williams spends much more time experiencing and discussing Nancy Holt's sculpture entitled "Sun Tunnels," to which Williams and her grandmother Mimi make a pilgrimage. "Sun Tunnels" is a configuration of four large concrete tunnels laid out on the desert in the shape of an open X. In the top half of the tunnels are cut sets of different-sized holes that correspond to four different constellations. " 'During the day, the sun shines through the holes, casting a changing pattern of pointed ellipses and circles of light' " (268). The eight-foot-high interior diameter of the tunnels invites the viewer to come inside, and the thick walls ensure that the temperature is fifteen to twenty degrees cooler inside than outside. Holt notes that " 'there is also a considerable echo in the tunnels' " (ibid.).

To Mimi, the sculpture looks like four pieces of conduit pipe lying on the job site of a construction firm, but as she will discover, this sculpture is not meant to be gazed upon as an object but to be entered into and experienced. The sculpture does not call attention to itself but redirects attention outward to the natural surroundings. As Williams writes, "The Great Basin landscape is framed within circles and we remember the shape of our planet, the shape of our eyes, our mouth in song and in prayer" (269). In an article excerpted in *Refuge,* Nancy Holt writes that she was personally transformed while conceiving this art. After several days of camping at the site, Holt "located a particular sound within the land and began to chant. This song became her connection to the Great Salt Lake desert"

(268). In an interview, Holt describes her experience to Williams, " 'I became like the ebb and flow of light inside the tunnels' " (269).

The contrast between "Metaphor" and "Sun Tunnels" could hardly be more gender-marked: the one is an erection; the other a conception. For Momen the man, the landscape is mute, a blank canvas upon which to project his own fantasy. For Holt the woman, the landscape has a voice, and art becomes a way of harmonizing with the land, of echoing its sound. The first act of the artist is not to speak but to listen humbly to the land. Connection rather than alienation results. At peace, Williams falls asleep inside one of the tunnels and wakes to find her grandmother standing at the center of the four tunnels, "turning slowly, looking outward in each direction" (270).

In *Refuge*, Williams creates a literary analog to the kind of art represented by "Sun Tunnels." As the pioneer of a new ecofeminist style of nature writing, Williams expands the boundaries of the nature-writing genre to encompass matters of gender, breaking the ground for natural-history writing to open itself to new methods and concerns.

Yet even as the book breaches conventional boundaries of subject and form, there is one boundary that not only remains intact but is actually reinforced: that is the division between the sexes. In characterizing *Refuge* as an ecofeminist work, I intend this criticism to apply more broadly to the ecofeminist project itself.

Throughout *Refuge* Williams highlights, not the similarities, but the differences between men and women, privileging the special bonds that exist among women. With the exception of her male family members and friends, Williams depicts men as rather dense creatures who need to feel in control and whose motto is "dollars-and-cents." Men satirized in this book include not only the "beergut-over-beltbuckled men" of the Canadian Goose Gun Club (12), but also Mormon leaders, government officials, civil engineers, military officers, and some medical doctors. Even among her loved ones, Williams characterizes individual differences as sex-linked. Thus, Brooke of the "analytic mind" offers a rational, scientific explanation of a mirage, while Terry prefers to think of it as a symbol of hope on a hot day, and Brooke thinks about the genetic information of a species and the embryology of a curlew, while Terry says a silent prayer for the bird and remembers a special bond that she formed with one (86). While Diane's impending death causes her husband, John Tempest, to withdraw or burst into fits of rage, daughter Terry enters ever more intimately into what she calls "the secrecy of sisterhood," "the privacy of women" (158).

In *Refuge* Williams explores what it means to be " 'a woman connected to other women' " (51). The book's final dream-vision is one of worldwide sisterhood, with women from all over the globe dancing wildly around a blazing fire in the desert, preparing themselves to reclaim the earth, presumably from its male captors. Williams writes, "A contract had been made and broken between human beings and the land. A new contract was being drawn by the women, who understood the fate of the earth as their own" (288).

Williams is right to open up natural history to gender issues. But I wish that invoking gender were done in the spirit of bridging differences rather than exaggerating them. I hope that in *Refuge: The Next Generation* the men of the world will also be invited to dance around that blazing fire.

NOTES

1. For helpful introductions to ecofeminism, see Diamond and Orenstein, Gaard, Gray, *Hypatia* 6, no. 1, Plant, and Plumwood.
2. Reprinted in the *Ecofeminist Newsletter,* a publication of the NWSA Ecofeminist Task Force (1989).

REFERENCES

Diamond, Irene, and Gloria Feman Orenstein, eds. *Reweaving the World: The Emergence of Ecofeminism.* San Francisco: Sierra Club Books, 1990.

Ecofeminist Newsletter. A publication of the NWSA Ecofeminist Task Force (1989). Middletown, Conn.: Center for the Humanities, Wesleyan University.

Gaard, Greta, ed. *Ecofeminism: Women, Animals, Nature.* Philadelphia: Temple University Press, 1993.

Gray, Elizabeth Dodson. *Green Paradise Lost.* Wellesley, Mass.: Roundtable Press, 1979.

Hypatia 6, no. 1 (spring 1991). Special issue on ecological feminism, edited by Karen J. Warren.

Plant, Judith, ed. *Healing the Wounds: The Promise of Ecofeminism.* Philadelphia: New Society, 1989.

Plumwood, Val. "Ecofeminism: An Overview and Discussion of Positions and Arguments." *Women and Philosophy,* ed. Janna L. Thompson. A special supplement to *Australasian Journal of Philosophy* 64 (June 1986): 120–38.

Williams, Terry Tempest. *Refuge: An Unnatural History of Family and Place.* New York: Vintage, 1991.

Nevada in Bloom

I. Nevada

I wish I knew your hills,
browning in early summer suns. I feel
jarring growths
silvered plains, I see trees bursting
from barren ground. You exist
an anomaly, a well-worn rock
cascading from distant skies.
Your healing flesh continually cleaved
by men and money, chaotic growth,
and a certain need to know.
And yet, just as the sage does bloom
there are still the cottonwoods
in June.

II. The Cottonwoods in June

White hair dripping off you
old man, bathed
in ember light, dying rays
bursting through boughs
broken, now unbroken, catching
a falling wisp. Lakes that men made smothered
in early summer snow, your locks sheared
like a woman's hair, drifting and dying
on a blue linoleum floor.
Fowl glide past
and through their mottled reflection,
while mounds like drifts blown
obscure my gray gravelled path
glowing like the hair on your arms

old man, bristling
in the evening wind.

III. In the Evening Wind

Cool air blowing, raising evening blues
over tangerine crests, never dying
till the growing heat of dawn. Two months past
our first forsythia, a grayed landscape
yellowing with promise.
Now coreopis suns burst
through forget-me-not skies, waiting
for the ripeness of plums.
The gray-green tendrils of rabbit brush bud,
then withhold their gold from June
but the cool air blowing past my window tonight
is permeated with sage
in bloom.

IV. Permeated with Sage in Bloom

Stars like candles burn
through vague neon light
beacons for the bowlers, for the game.
I hold hope like a caterpillar
in hand, watch it crawl
up the inside of my wrist.
A snippet of sage lies hidden
inside my satin-lined pocket.
Rubbing the leaves between thumb and forefinger
I am reminded of the outside world.
But these Nevada winds stir,
blow softly in my ear
there is always a chance—
you will win.
Tomorrow I pack and pay bills
because the Greyhound leaves
at noon, but for now I sit

in this well-lit room
pulling slots, rubbing green, and waiting
for the current
of change.

V. Waiting for the Current of Change

We sit, you and I
reading words on white pages, blinking
less than we should. Fifty years
of molecular tests, buildings and bombs
outside our backyard. At one point
they didn't know.
Afterward, those pictures of people
in black glasses watching
golden blossoms of nuclear suns explode
over our desert sands, those pictures
evolved into melting pigs, goats braying
in wooden boxes, charred faces
in foreign towns. Like a toy boat
consumed by the Truckee in May
we were overcome
by the current
of change. Steel signs
and red symbols now mark our maps
into touchable and untouchable zones.
Those big bombs booming under unmovable crusts
were silenced in the peace of one June.
Like the five petals of a desert dogwood
I held hope
for the arrival of spring.
I sit here now, blinking less
than I should, knowing change
always comes in bloom.

Meditations in Stone
Words and photographs

Southern Utah, where the sun is brother to the lizard and both remember the beginnings—when the great seas came and went, lay-
ing down their burdens grain by grain, layer by layer, time's accre-
tion written in stone, revised by tectonic collisions, crustean shrugs,
mountain-thrusts, foldings and explosions, wind and water, leaving
us now with a library whose wrinkles and shadings memorialize
the ages beyond poor human imagining.

Park-like hollow along the Escalante, North Escalante Canyons Wilderness
Study Area. (All photos in this essay by T. H. Watkins. Reprinted by permission)

Escalante Arch, North Escalante Canyons Wilderness Study Area.

And what is our obligation to this great articulation? That we honor it, protect it, embrace its meaning and its hope. We have done precious little to satisfy that cosmic debt: an overused and over-developed national park here, a timber-stripped and cow-bombed national forest there. For most of the rest, nothing, leaving it to the mercy of human articulations that would use it, then use it up.

A rude taking, when there is so much grace to be given.

I found this place of sun and stone and space nearly ten years ago. Like most such encounters, it was a solitary discovery, and never mind that I was not alone at the moment or how many explorers had tramped here before me. Standing at a river bottom and look-ing straight up at a bright ribbon of impossibly blue sky trapped between red slickrock walls that rose five hundred feet from river's edge to eternity, I felt something open in me and take it all in—sky and stone, river and wind. This now was mine: the home of my heart.

Clouds over Harris Wash, proposed Henry Mountains Wilderness in the distance.

Once, I lay on my back in my sleeping bag and watched the stars wink on one by one in the sky above me. My friend and I had spent the previous two days discovering canyon bottoms and mesa tops, and this night we had camped on a wide ledge just below the rim of a place called the Dirty Devil River Canyon. Lying there now, the smell of our dying cook-fire mixing with that of dust and distance, weakly resisting the gentle tug of sleep, I stared up at the diamond-scattered blackness and felt myself drifting into its space. The sky, I said just before closing my eyes. The sky has no lid on it.

In the morning there was snow.

Strangely, in this place of bare stone and unpredictable skies, I re-member the river-bottom trees as much as any other form—the oaks and poplars and willows and cottonwoods, especially the cotton-woods, some of them so fat and old that they remember as much as lizards, their summer-green leaves trembling information like semaphors in the breeze. Sometimes there have been other trees,

(*top*) Phipps, Death Hollow Wilderness Study Area, Escalante River Canyons. (*bottom*) Cottonwood in North Escalante Canyons Wilderness Study Area.

Moonrise over Comb Ridge, Comb Wash Wilderness Study Area.

Moonset over Factory Butte in the proposed San Rafael Wilderness.

too: walking the Escalante River, I explored a narrow canyon just off the main river until I came upon a single, ecologically unlikely ponderosa pine that rose maybe a hundred feet above me. Grown from a cone washed down from the mountains half a century ago, it thrust up like an enormous old sentinel amid a shadowy tangle of willows and box elders and other vegetation crammed into the tiny space, as removed from its own kind here as I was, solitary.

The only real silence here is human, for the land is full of conversation—the rustle of cottonwood leaves, the keening cry of an eagle, the tumbling-down notes of a canyon wren's song, the squawk of magpies, the chuckling discourse of the rivers. And other sounds. Another night, alone now in the depths of the Dirty Devil River Canyon, I doused my fire and watched the moon edge over the rim-rock like the bright eye of God, spilling a silver wash of light over the abstract curves and angles of the suddenly ghostly landscape. Then the coyotes started their yipping, first one, then another, and

Trail in North Escalante Canyons Wilderness Study Area.

Rock spire in Arch Canyon, San Juan-Anasazi Proposed Wilderness.

Desiccated tree in Arch Canyon, in the proposed San Juan-Anasazi Wilderness.

another, until a chorus was being sent up into the night. I joined them for a while—they did not seem to mind—until the unmistakable cries of a mountain lion, its voice crooning the range from the whimpering of a sobbing child to the screams of a tormented woman, stunned us all into silence.

A final memory: Once I climbed the sides of a big hollow in the Escalante Canyons, toiling through patches of prickly pear cactus and pygmy forests of juniper and piñon, brushing past the furry green plumes of Mormon tea and groves of head-high mountain sage so aromatic that my senses swam with the smell of it. When the vertical reach of canyon wall stopped my ascent, I turned and looked back down on the scene—a huge natural park, its floor pale with summer grasses dotted here and there with trees, the cottonwood-lined Escalante River curving gracefully through the whole scene, its beaver ponds burnished like mirrors by the sun, its rills and rapids glitter-

ing like crinkled foil. I stayed there for a long time, wondering why it had taken me so long to discover such wonder, before starting back down to the valley, past the piñon and junipers, through the blue-green groves of sage, inhaling their scent as if I were trying to intoxicate myself forever with the essence of the place.

I like to roll the names along my tongue—Dirty Devil, Comb Ridge, Escalante, San Rafael, Mancos Mesa, Waterpocket Fold, Boulder Mountain, the Henrys, the Burr Desert, a hundred more. We all should know them, for they are the last of the wildness as the Beehive State, like the rest of the West, becomes more of what it has always been in human terms, an urban place where the engines of extraction desecrate the land even while industrial tourism celebrates it to death.

We can save the best that is left; we have the tools, and all we need now is the wit to accept the fact that in the saving of these last uncorrupted rivers and canyons and mesas and fine empty places in the land of stone time, we can learn once again the lesson written in the eyes of lizards and the hearts of trees—that wilderness is not a threat to be conquered, but a protection to be embraced.

(*Photo on previous spread*) View from Boulder Mountain across Capitol Reef National Park to the proposed Henry Mountains Wilderness.

Basque-American Identity
Past Perspectives and Future Prospects

What are the future prospects for Basques as a discernible ethnic group within the American experience? I would note at the outset that we social scientists do not have a particularly distinguished record as prognosticators. If you doubt that, try reading economists' predictions regarding the future of the American economy in the year-old copies of *Time* or *Newsweek* that your dentist provides in the waiting room. I am also reminded of the admonition, attributed to Samuel Goldwyn: "Never engage in forecasting, particularly regarding the future!"

Nevertheless, I find a certain attraction in discussing the future. When you analyze the past or comment upon the present you are forced to work within the limits of obvious constraints. That is, in large measure, the data shapes the analysis. If the interpretation becomes too farfetched, you are vulnerable to the criticism that alternative explanations are more plausible and satisfying. Speculation regarding the future can be more exhilarating and challenging. It is also safer, since you cannot really be proven wrong, at least not immediately.

Is it legitimate to ask what basis I have for speculating about the future of Basque-American ethnicity? My answer is that for the last quarter-century I have devoted much of my life to trying to understand both Old World and New World Basque life (Douglass and Bilbao 1975). As coordinator of the Basque Studies Program of the University of Nevada, Reno, I have also become what might be called an "intimate outsider" within Basque-American reality, one of the architects of its academic expression. I have therefore been both your observer and fellow traveler. At the same time, in my capacity as a social anthropologist I have devoted my life to the study of emigration and ethnic-group formation throughout the world. Therefore I bring to the task some appreciation of the intricacies of past and present Basque-American reality, as well as a comparative knowledge of how other groups have confronted similar issues in different times and places.

Space does not permit me to tell the full story of Basque settlement in the United States. But it is necessary to underscore those aspects in the Basque-American past and present that I believe to be particularly relevant to any projections concerning its possible future.

Basque Demographics

The first point that needs to be made is that the Basque-American community has a unique demographic history that militated against its persistence as a distinct ethnic group within American society. Most Basque immigrants were recruited from rural settings in Europe and entered the United States as single males. Most planned to spend a few years before returning to the Basque Country with their savings. The obvious implication was that the Basque-American community lacked the necessary female dimension for the formation of family life. Over time this impediment diminished as Basque women entered the United States to work as domestics in the emerging network of Basque hotels and boardinghouses, where they met and married countrymen. Also, an occasional immigrant became committed to an American future and either went back or sent back to the Old Country for a bride. However, the point remains that Basque-American family life developed slowly, which meant that the Basque-American community remained relatively small and but shallowly rooted in American society.

A more subtle, but no less real, implication was that the Basque-American community lacked the leadership that quickly emerged in at least certain other immigrant groups. Drawn from an Old World farming background and poorly educated in a village school, the typical Basque immigrant was not in a position to shape opinion or forge unity among his fellow immigrants. As mostly single young men in their late teens and early twenties, few of the immigrants could lay claim to either the life experience or moral authority conferred by marriage and age. The early Basque Americans, therefore, largely lacked a professional class of journalists, priests, educators, doctors, lawyers, and politicians, in short, opinion makers, who might have provided the initiative and vision to found the publications, voluntary associations, and religious and financial institutions that defined ethnic life for some other American immigrant groups.

Parenthetically, we might note that the Basque emigrant diaspora did not lack these familial and professional dimensions. Rather, in the nineteenth century when established families and trained professionals opted to leave the Basque Country, they were likely to choose a Latin American destination, where knowledge of the Spanish language and customs facilitated adaptation. A family opting for Buenos Aires could expect its children to make a smooth transition, particularly regarding schooling; a Basque lawyer or doctor choosing Havana could practice his profession. In contrast, Basques in the United States faced an alien land with an unfamiliar tongue, a place of opportunity only for those persons who were unattached and who lacked the formal skills to opt for an alternative to the lonely life of the sheepherder on the frontier margins of American society.

Consequently, as much as any immigrant group within the American experience and more than most, Basques became identified with a single industry—sheep husbandry. While Basque Americans also engaged in mining, cattle ranching, construction, and small-scale commerce in the towns of the sheep-raising districts of the American West, it is also true that by the turn of the present century throughout much of the region to say "sheepherder" was to mean "Basque."

This profound involvement in the sheep industry impeded the formation of a Basque-American ethnic group in three ways. First, by its very nature the occupation precluded population concentrations of Basque Americans. Rather, a few thousand individuals were distributed throughout the open-range districts of all thirteen western states, an area of literally hundreds of thousands of square miles. Therefore we have no rural communities or ranching districts dominated by Basques comparable to the Scandinavian settlements of Minnesota or the German colonies of Texas. Nor do we have examples of "Basque towns" in cities such as Boise, Reno, and San Francisco, settlements comparable to the urban ghettoes formed by the Poles in Chicago, the Italians in New York, or the Irish in Boston.

Second, within the broadly disseminated Basque-American population there were internal distinctions that further curtailed the emergence of a collective identity. There is a sense in which "Basque" and "Basque American" are generic rather than specific categories. They gloss over a hierarchy of subidentities with their attendant loyalties and emotions. There is a "French Basque" versus "Spanish Basque" distinction that has more meaning as a primordial identity for the former than for the latter. Rather, Spanish Basques tend to see themselves as Navarrese, Arabese, Gipuzkoans, or Bizkaians.

Emigration from all of these Basque regions was not distributed evenly throughout the American West. Rather, French Basques and Navarrese established what might be called the southern tier, extending across California, central Nevada, Arizona, Utah, Colorado, Wyoming, and Montana, while Bizkaians constituted the northern tier, which encompassed parts of northern Nevada, eastern Oregon, and southern Idaho. Nor did these two broad communities develop simultaneously. Rather, one grew out of largely French Basque involvement in the California gold rush of the mid-nineteenth century, whereas the Bizkaian infusion was a late nineteenth- and early twentieth-century development. In short, the vagaries of their immigration history meant that the few thousand individuals who came to the American West from the Basque Country were further internally segregated in both space and time, which reduced their capacity for collective action as "Basques" or "Basque Americans." It is not at all hyperbolic to say that as recently as forty years ago the Basques of Boise and the Basques of Bakersfield shared virtually no ties, maintained no contacts, and were but dimly aware of each other's existence.

The third consequence of the sheepherding legacy was the imagery surrounding it, an imagery that did not, at least until recently, lend itself to ethnic pride. Sheepherding was one of the most denigrated occupations in American society, an interpretation of which Basque Americans were keenly aware. I do not wish to belabor the point, since I have found little evidence that Basques were ashamed of sheepherding. In fact, most took personal satisfaction and pride in a job well done. However, it is equally true that until recently this remained a private sentiment, one to be shared only within Basque-American circles or with a few "safe" American sympathizers. It is only as a part of contemporary Basque ethnicity that the sheepherder tradition has been put on public display as a facet of ethnic identity, whether through the sheepherders' ball, certain aspects of the Basque festival, or today's town-dwelling Basque's tendency to stress his family's sheepherder origins.

The negative image of the sheepherder that prevailed until recently may be regarded as the Basques' particular version of the immigrant's lot. In this regard, they differed but little from most emigrants in other times and places, almost all of whom have had to struggle to gain acceptance in the host country. There were additional factors, however, that reinforced the Basques' reticence to display their ethnic identity. First, they had entered a society that was prejudiced against Latins—Hispanics in particular. While the linguistic, cultural, and genetic evidence suggests that Basques do not even qualify as a Latin population, in the average American's reckoning the southern European location of the Basque Country and the fact that Basques entered the United States as either French or Spanish nationals were likely to make them Latins. At the same time, Basques by and large did not fit the Latin stereotype of short, dark persons and could therefore easily "pass" as generic Europeans as long as they maintained a low ethnic profile. Again, I don't want to overstress this point, since it tended to play itself out differently in different parts of the American West. For instance, wherever there were large concentrations of Mexicans, Spanish Basques were at more pains to distinguish themselves from Latins, and, to a lesser degree, French Basques distinguished themselves from Spanish Basques.

The Basques of Boise, virtually all Bizkaians, provide an interesting case. It might be argued that Boise was one of the few areas of the American West where a Basque identity was well established prior to the Hispanic one. If Boise Basques escaped the Latin legacy they were less fortunate regarding certain political pitfalls. As *the* Spanish Basque community in this country, Boise Basques are most affected by events in Spain, events which on at least three occasions have all but compromised their group image.

The Spanish-American War at the turn of the century placed Boise Basques, most of whom were recent arrivals and virtually all of whom retained Spanish passports, in a particularly vulnerable position. Deportation or internment as enemy aliens were certainly not out of the question. Unfortunately, we have scant evidence regarding the specifics, but what little we do have suggests that Boise Basques maintained the lowest possible profile throughout the conflict and its immediate aftermath. It was a particularly delicate period in light of the negative press that Basques were already receiving. At the time they were regularly vilified as usurpers of the public lands with their nomadic or "tramp" sheep bands. The outbreak of World War I again called Boise Basque loyalties into question. While Americans were off to the conflict in Europe, Spanish nationals were insulated, since Spain remained a nonbelligerent. From an American viewpoint the potential enemy of the Spanish-American conflict was thereby converted into the draft dodger of the global one.

The second delicate period for Boise Basques was the Spanish Civil War. Franco's uprising was touted in America, and particularly by the Catholic Church hierarchy, as a sacred crusade to save Spain from godless communism. Bizkaia and Gipuzkoa, however, remained loyal to the beleaguered Spanish Republic and fielded their own army. At the same time, the defenders declared the Basque Country, or Euskadi, independent and elected a president and parliament. The pro-Franco press denounced the Basques as "red separatists." Boise Basques were placed in an anguished and delicate predicament. Virtually all had relatives in Bizkaia suffering the pains of war. Some Boise Basques, though only a few, shared the political dream of an independent Basque Country. However, sentiment in the wider American public clearly favored Franco. The Boise Basques' response was to raise money for humanitarian assistance, but not arms, and then to call a press conference to underscore the fact to their fellow Boiseans. However, once again it was obviously a period in which Basques preferred a low ethnic profile.

Finally, there is the question of Euskadi ta Askatasuna (ETA) and its political violence, as well as the broader issue of Basque nationalism. In part this is an ongoing concern. Again, while some persons sympathize with Basque nationalism generally, and a few with ETA and its tactics in particular, for most Boise Basques the whole nationalist agenda is poorly understood, confusing, and remote. Few Boise Basques have the interest or the means of following Old World Basque politics closely, and most are one or two generations removed from a firsthand exposure to the Old Country and its problems. At the same time, international press coverage of Basque issues runs to the sensational. A single bombing or kidnapping by ETA receives far more attention than, for example, do the electoral results for the Basque parliament. Thus, for many Basque Americans there is ambivalence or even resentment over Old World Basque politics. Like Italian Americans forced to bear the stigma of the mafia, Basque Americans struggle with the terrorist label, or at least with the fear that such might become established in American public opinion.

Collective Consciousness

We have considered several demographic, economic, and political factors that militated against conversion of Basque immigration into an established Basque-American ethnic group, and it is important to keep them in perspective. At no time were their negative effects truly decisive; in fact, some Basques decided to stay in this country and formed families. Wherever several households became established there was the basis for interaction predicated upon a combination of Old World and New World factors.

The entry of Basques into a particular area of the American West was seldom random but rather entailed chain migration from one village, a few contiguous villages, or two or three clusters of villages in the Old Country, as new emigrants joined previously established kinsmen or fellow villagers in the New World. After a generation of American-born Basques emerged, the local Basque community was further cemented by their marriages, a high percentage of which were within the ethnic group. In short, individuals formed families, and families formed clusters that, in places like Boise, Elko, and San Francisco became sufficiently large so as to facilitate collective activity among Basque Americans.

In several districts of California, Nevada, and Idaho this critical threshold had been reached by the turn of the present century. Indeed, by the 1890s there was a Basque-language newspaper, *California'ko Eskualherria*, being published in Los Angeles, California, a sign that this country's oldest Basque colony had developed a group awareness that transcended the local community. More typical of Basque collective action at the turn of the century was the creation in Boise in 1908 of a Mutual Aid Society to provide medical care to needy Basques and a ticket back to Europe for indigent ones.

We could cite a few more examples of collective action in particular Basque-American communities during the first half of the present century, but the truth is that they were few and far between. In many western towns and regions Basques had pretty much entered, struggled, triumphed to some degree, founded families, and raised their children to be Americans. For their part the

American-born Basques, like the offspring of most other hyphen-
ated Americans, sought full acceptance in the wider society. They
were more likely to be mildly embarrassed by their parents' English than proud or knowledgeable about their ethnic heritage. In
this regard they were simply responding to the relentless assimila-
tion pressure in this country, the vaunted melting-pot philosophy
of national integration. When I interview people who lived through
this period, the two themes that recur constantly are the playground
fights over being called a "Black Basco," or some other insult, and
the constant pressure to excel in school and athletics—a pressure
exerted by parents but also from within as individuals sought to
demonstrate their worth in American terms.

Throughout the first half of this century, then, concentrations of
persons of Basque descent emerged in several parts of the American
West. However, for these several collectivities to catalyze into a self-
conscious Basque-American ethnic group, with activities that transcended particular localities, there had to be developments within
the wider society.

On the one hand the image of the Basque as an alien and unfair
competitor for the resources of the western range had to change. Beginning about the turn of the century with creation of the national
forests and culminating in the Taylor Grazing Act of 1934, federal
control of grazing on the public lands was extended throughout
the American West. Much of the legislation was pointedly aimed at
excluding Basque tramp sheepmen, that is, the outfit owned by a
noncitizen with no private land. While this inflicted major hardship
on many individual Basques, for the Basque-American collectivity
it removed the major source of its negative stereotype. Indeed, the
group image actually benefited as many tramp sheepmen sold out
and returned to Europe and, beginning in the 1920s, restrictive U.S.
immigration laws all but cut off the flow of Spanish nationals into
the United States. By the 1940s there was such a shortage of sheepherders in this country that Congress enacted special legislation to
exempt intending Basque herders from the Spanish national quota.
In short, by 1950, the Basque sheepherder had been transformed
from villain to hero in the public eye.

The second development that improved the climate and thereby
enhanced the prospects of display of their ethnicity by Basque
Americans was the "roots" phenomenon. That is, beginning slowly
after World War II and peaking in the 1960s Americans have cele-

brated their ethnic differences. Indeed, this has been so much the case that there is almost a sense today in which an American who has no ethnic identity suffers from a certain impoverishment of the spirit. In this regard, WASP has become the saddest ethnic designation within the lexicon of American ethnic relations.

By the late 1940s Basque Americans were poised on the threshold of conscious public display of their ethnic heritage. I consciously avoid the expression "ethnic resurgence," which used to be common in the scholarly literature and even in the popular press. The term invokes, quite wrongly in my view, the notion of a recapture or return to some former state. I hope that it is clear from all that I have said thus far that there was no Basque-American ethnic identity to be reclaimed; rather, the very concept as well as its content had, in several senses, to be invented. Indeed, social scientists and historians alike are now more prone to speak of the invention of tradition rather than its rediscovery or resurgence, whether when talking about ethnic group formation or the emergence of whole nations such as France or the United States (Hobsbawm and Ranger 1983).

Boise and San Francisco played key roles in the creation of Basque-American identity. The establishment of the San Francisco Zazpiak Bat Club in 1924 is the earliest evidence that we have of the successful formation of a Basque club. In 1951 construction of the Boise Basque Center provided Boise Basques with a physical locale for their club's activities, and provided both a challenge and a dream for most of the other Basque clubs of the United States. Establishment of Boise's Oinkari dancers in 1960 was another precedent subsequently emulated by most other clubs, and the performances of the Boise dance group at the Seattle World's Fair in 1962 and the New York World's Fair in 1964 were early public displays of Basque-American ethnicity.

Publication in 1957 of Robert Laxalt's novel *Sweet Promised Land* (1957), an account of his father's life as a sheepman in the American West and his return to his French Basque village of birth, gave the Basque-American community a literary spokesman. Dominique's story provided Basque Americans with a text with which all could identify to some degree. The book became a best seller and thereby communicated the essence of the Basque legacy in this country to a national readership.

Partly in response to interest engendered by Laxalt's book, the first national Basque festival was held in Sparks, Nevada in 1959.

Its content was truly an invention, since the organizers incorporated folk dances and athletic events from more than one Old World Basque region and married them to such western Americana as the barbecue and the sheepdog trial. While the festival thereby differed from its counterpart held in any village of the Old Country, it was quickly emulated in several of the Basque colonies throughout the American West. Today there is a Basque festival cycle in the region, which begins in late May and lasts through early September, providing the Basque-American community with the opportunity to display a version of both its European folk and western American legacies. An additional spin-off of the Nevada festival was the creation of Basque clubs in several locales, the main purpose of which was to sponsor and organize an annual festival (Douglass 1980a).

In 1967 the University of Nevada founded a Basque Studies Program. The program provided the Basque-American identity with its scholarly dimension, although this was not its prime purpose. More to the point, it organized summer study tours to the Basque Country, giving many young Basque Americans a chance to experience Old World Basque culture firsthand. In the early 1970s, Boise State University conducted several yearlong study programs in the town of Oñate. Subsequently, Nevada and Boise State joined forces and presently run summer, semester, and yearlong programs at the San Sebastián and Bilbao campuses of the University of the Basque Country and at the University of Pau near the French Basque area. Many of the Basque Americans who have attended the European programs presently play active and key roles in particular communities of the American West.

The creation of North American Basque Organizations (NABO) in 1973 was another watershed event in the invention and maintenance of a Basque-American identity. NABO overarches the Basque clubs of the United States, facilitating sponsorship of activities and events that transcend the local clubs. These include organization of annual national handball and *mus* (a card game) championships. Until recently there were practically no *txistularis*, or Basque drum and flute players, in the United States, which meant that few of the dance groups could perform to live music. NABO has sponsored several summer music camps at which Basque-American children from throughout the American West are taught the *txistu* by an instructor brought over from Europe for the purpose. Other noteworthy developments include construction of a cultural center in

1983 by the San Francisco Basques, creation of the Society for Basque Studies in America, celebration of the first Jaialdi in 1987 in Boise and the recent establishment of a Basque museum and Cultural Center there, the visit to the United States in the spring of 1988 by José Antonio Ardanza, president of the Basque Autonomous Community in Spain, and dedication of a national monument to the Basque sheepherder in Reno in 1989. The list is not exhaustive, since there were other significant developments on the Basque-American scene. Rather, it is meant to illustrate the range of activities that in one way or another celebrate Basque-American ethnic identity and project it to the wider, non-Basque public.

The Future of Basque Identity

Indeed, after four decades of intense effort it is fair to say that there are presently more vehicles for expression of Basque-American identity than at any time in the nearly 150 years since Basques first began to enter the American West. How, then, might we view the future? A rosy interpretation would consider the recent past and present circumstances of Basque-American ethnicity and conclude that they have never been more robust and that the future is even brighter. I would, however, play the devil's advocate and suggest that what we may be actually witnessing is the Indian summer of Basque-American culture, a brief if glorious period before its demise, at least as presently constituted.

I base this conclusion upon three interpenetrating circumstances in contemporary Basque-American reality. First, there is the changing demographic profile of the ethnic group, due partly to cessation of Basque immigration into the United States and partly to intermarriage between Basques and their non-Basque neighbors. Second, there is the erosion in the use of the Basque language as the vernacular. Third, there is the externalization and commercialization of the ethnic identity.

Regarding changing demography we should remember that for the individual Basque immigrant who became committed to an American future, life in this country remained highly conditioned by Basque ethnicity. The rate of endogamy, or marriage with fellow Basques, among the immigrant generation was well into the 90th percentile. Both the Basque-owned ranch operations and the Basque hotels of the open-range sheep districts were ethnic enclaves, and it was within such settings that the first U.S.-born generation of Basque Americans was formed. Its own ethnic persona was shaped not only by the direct influence of Old World–born parents but also by contacts with the steady stream of Basque sojourners who worked on the ranches and boarded at the Basque hotels when in town.

As I have noted, beginning in the 1920s, the flow of Basque immigrants into the United States, and particularly from the Basque provinces of Spain, was impeded, though not entirely interdicted, by restrictive U.S. immigration legislation. By the late 1940s and 1950s there was a perceptible labor shortage in the sheep industry and the U.S. Congress passed several laws exempting Basque herders from national origins quotas. During the 1960s and early 1970s the Western Range Association, a sheep ranchers' organization, recruited several thousand Basques for three-year sheepherding contracts in the American West. Until about twenty years ago, then, there was a constant flow of Old World–born sojourners to reenergize the Basque-American ethnic scene.

By the mid-1970s, however, several factors conspired to all but choke off Basque herder immigration in the United States. Sheep numbers on the western ranges plummeted drastically because of adverse economic factors and the efforts of environmentalists to limit access. Recovery of the Spanish and French economies made sheepherding wages uncompetitive with employment alternatives in the Basque Country itself. The Western Range Association decided to shift its recruitment of herders from Europe to Mexico, Peru, and Chile (Douglass 1980b).

Consequently, today there are half as many sheepherders in the American West as there were two decades ago, and fewer than one hundred of them are Basque. This means that since the mid-1970s the Basque-American community has been largely cut off from its traditional source of Old World–born fellow ethnics. One of the noticeable effects is the present dearth of what had become a marriage pattern among Basque Americans, namely, the union between the Old World–born, former sheepherding male and a first-generation Basque-American female born on a sheep ranch or in a small western town.

The second marker of ethnic decline mentioned earlier is erosion of the language. Basque is unrelated to any other human tongue and is seldom learned by outsiders. It therefore provides its speakers with what is tantamount to a secret code. Most Basques who entered the American West were bilingual in Basque and either French or Spanish. However, the former was the language of intimacy and became the vernacular of both the sheep camp and the Basque hotel. For Basque Americans raised in such contexts, bilingualism meant Basque and English. Insofar as the ethnic bases of the ranch and hotel were being renovated regularly by the presence and passage of non-English-speaking sojourners, the Basque language skills of Basque Americans were reinforced. Indeed, the language was neither a curiosity nor a luxury, but rather a necessity. With the decline in Basque immigration the language has lost its major *raison d'être*.

Many Basque Americans, Old World– and New World–born alike, bemoan the loss of the language. Periodically, a few members of a Basque social club attempt to implement language courses for their children. At the Basque Studies Program in Reno we receive several requests annually for a self-taught Basque method. But the reality is that formal Basque language courses have little real attraction and even less staying power, whether initiated by concerned private parties or by institutions such as the University of Nevada, Reno, or Boise State University.

In part the situation is exacerbated by the perception that learning Basque is a difficult task with the small payoff of personal satisfaction. Upon enrolling in language classes Basque Americans often express the sentiment that they are doing so in order to be able to converse with their grandparents. This is telling commentary on the former role of Basque as the language of intimacy, on the one hand, and its limited horizon on the other. Indeed, we can now discern among Basque Americans a stronger tendency to choose Spanish or French, should they opt for language learning. This is clear in the student profile of the yearlong courses that we offer at the San Sebastián campus of the University of the Basque Country. About half our students are Basque Americans. They can opt for either Spanish or Basque language training. Only a handful choose the latter.

In sum, Basque no longer functions as either the language of intimacy in the Basque-American home or as the vehicle of commerce in ranching or hotelkeeping. In conceding its former functions it has been reified into an object of nostalgia. For most Basque Americans the cost of attaining and then maintaining fluency is simply too great in light of the practical considerations.

Anthropologists have long underscored the close relationship between language and world view in human affairs. One can therefore only surmise that the loss of the language among Basque Americans portends other far-reaching modifications in their culture. Old World Basques are acutely aware of this issue and currently expend millions of dollars annually to foment the use of Basque in the European homeland. The rhetoric of this defense of the language characterizes it as the soul of Basque culture and equates language loss with cultural suicide. In the American West this particular battle has been all but lost.

The third symptom is commercialization of Basque culture. Today it is not uncommon to see bumper stickers proclaiming "Basque Power" or "Basque is Beautiful." The Basque hotels, which formerly were the semiexclusive, no-nonsense, workingman boardinghouses of the sojourning sheepherders, are now extolled in television ads and on highway billboards as ethnic eating establishments. Some postdate the era of open-range sheep raising and simply trade on the reputation of the original boardinghouses for hearty Basque cuisine served family style. However, most of the longstanding establishments have been transformed as well. Lacking the flow of sojourners that were once their lifeblood, and conscious of a loosening of the dependency of Basque Americans upon these ethnic havens, the hotels now cater to a non-Basque crowd. To enter them, then, is to experience a world of studied ethnicity in which imagery is carefully staged. The walls are adorned with Old World paraphernalia and scenes of sheepherding on the western ranges in palmier days. The bartender and waitresses wear Basque folk costume and are coaxed to provide stock answers to the tediously reiterated question "Who are the Basques?"

Then there are the festivals. Prior to the first Basque festival in 1959, Basques of a particular area might gather once or twice annually to have a barbecue or picnic restricted to insiders and their intimate associates. Today's Basque festival is regional in scope, highly publicized by the media, and open to the general public. While this provides Basque Americans with an effective venue in which to display certain aspects of their identity, it also runs the risk of trivializing it.

In short, the Basque-American ethnic identity *created* in the postwar period is clearly in crisis. To the extent that it is inspired by a European peasant heritage and an American sheepherding legacy it elicits two worlds that have all but disappeared. Today the Basque Country is a modern, urban-industrial society and open-range sheep ranching is vanishing from the American scene. Consequently, to the extent that Basque-American identity remains predicated upon such symbols it runs the risk of becoming more show than substance. Its twenty-first-century representative may come to have more in common with the drugstore cowboy or the cigar-store Indian than with his forebears who tilled fields in Europe or herded sheep in the American West.

The question then becomes: Is the race over in any meaningful sense? My answer would be—maybe. There is reason to hedge since, in my judgment, Basque-American culture stands at a critical crossroad. The Basque-American identity that we have been considering was a recent and conscious creation—and one that I am suggesting may have played out most of its useful life span; however, American Basques are just as capable of creating a new cultural reality more suited to the twenty-first century. Indeed, the vague outline of such developments may actually be discernible. The Jaialdi held in 1990 in Boise, which attracted 30,000 visitors, may in fact be both its metaphor and harbinger.

That which most distinguished Jaialdi from the standard Basque festival was its wide-ranging cultural expression, on the one hand, and a profound integration of Old World and New World Basques as participants on the other. As cultural expression Jaialdi began with a film festival in which Boiseans were exposed to the cutting edge of contemporary Old World Basque cinema, it continued with cultural exhibits at the Basque museum and formal lectures at Boise State University, and it concluded with the performances of some of the Basque Country's leading artists.

Among the participants was a charter flight of European Basques who came to Boise expressly for the occasion, including a delegation of high-level officials of the Basque government. Jaialdi also served as a magnet for Basque students studying in the United States, as well as for several Basque-American students and scholars with an interest in their heritage. San Francisco Basques have instituted their own Basque Cultural Day, which, though obviously on a smaller scale, nevertheless reflects the spirit of Jaialdi.

So if the earlier interaction between the Basque Country and the American West was primarily economic, this is no longer the case. Today the relationship is characterized less by job opportunity and cash flow than by an exchange of people and ideas. The labor contract between the Western Range Association and the aspiring herder has been replaced by the cultural agreement between the president of the Basque Country and the governors of Idaho and Nevada, as well as the sister cities accord between San Sebastián and Reno, Gernika and Boise. Another example is the José Miguel de Barandiarán chair of Basque Studies at University of California, Santa Barbara. Similarly, the marriage between the former sheepherder and the rancher or hotelkeeper's daughter is being replaced by the union between Old World and New World Basques who met while one was studying in the other's country.

In retrospect we can say that in the Basque case, as with every other immigrant group in American society, contacts between the Old World homeland and its New World emigrant diaspora were highly conditioned by what an Australian historian has labeled the tyranny of distance (Blainey 1966). Until well into the twentieth century emigration was a difficult and expensive endeavor. Emigrants went out for years if not forever, and their continued contacts with home were sporadic at best. After World War II the situation has been colored by what might be phrased the tyranny of dollars. That is, while startling advances in transportation and communications became available, in fact they were only affordable by the American side. Our students could travel there, while their businessmen and professionals found it prohibitively expensive to come here. However, in the last ten years there has been a dramatic reversal in the equation. The flow is now two-directional and is growing in magnitude. Furthermore, compared to the earlier wave, Basque immigration into the United States is now broad-based, ranging from the students seeking instruction in American universities to the Basque trade delegation and performing artists. It is out of this new reality that the Basque-American identity of the twenty-first century is likely to emerge—if it is to emerge at all.

REFERENCES

Blainey, Geoffrey. *The Tyranny of Distance.* Melbourne: Sun Books, 1966.
Douglass, William A. "Inventing an Ethnic Identity: The First Basque Festival." *Halcyon* (1980):115–30.

————. "The Vanishing Basque Sheepherder." *The American West* 17, no. 4 (1980):30–31, 59–61.

Douglass, William A., and Jon Bilbao. *Amerikanuak: Basques in the New World.* Reno: University of Nevada Press, 1975.

Hobsbawm, Eric, and Terence Ranger, eds. *The Invention of Tradition.* Cambridge: Cambridge University Press, 1983.

Laxalt, Robert. *Sweet Promised Land.* New York: Harper, 1957.

Inside the Glitter
Portraits of Workers in Nevada's Casino Industry

Nevada is at the forefront of labor changes in the West. The service sector is the fastest growing segment of the American economy, and tourism, entertainment, and gambling lead the growth.

Yet surprisingly little research has been done on casino industry workers. For most of us, they are outshined by gaming's glitter. In the past, photographers and writers went to factories, docks, and farm fields to document work in America. These days one must look to casinos, theme parks, and restaurants.

The casino industry has changed from a white labor force to one as diverse as the streets of New York. Like the East Coast factories a century ago, the tourist meccas of the American West are creating jobs into the next century for thousands of immigrants from around the globe. For many, gaming offers steady work, sometimes bolstered by union wages, stock options, flexible hours, and community support. Within a generation, immigrant casino workers are becoming middle-class Americans in this service economy.

The workers I have photographed are the fabric of American community. They are gay and straight, parents and grandparents, graduate students and high school dropouts. Maids and managers alike bring a professionalism to their work. And in their off-time, casino and hotel workers attend college, practice their religions, create music and art, spend time with their kids, and discover plants new to science. Their stories reflect how work life is changing in America today.

Carmen Rios
Busgirl

My mother had sixteen kids; twelve of us are still living. And she worked outside the house too! So we're used to working.

I came to Reno last year from Guanajuato, Mexico. I was a tour guide in Mexico, so my English is pretty good. I'm 21 years old. My mother was working here for the past few years, and she loves it. So I decided to come on up.

I live near downtown in an apartment with my mother and little brother. My brother is fourteen—his name is Pablo, as in the Pope. We all get up at 6:00 so that my mother and I can get to work by 7:00 and my brother can leave for school. Sometimes I have to be at work by 5:30 to set up for brunch. My mother is a supervisor of maids at the Eldorado.

Today I'm tired. I worked a double shift yesterday, sixteen hours on my feet bussing tables. First it's brunch, then lunch. At breaks, I sit down and talk to people. Working a double shift was my choice. I need the money. We just moved from a place with furniture to a place without, so we had to buy some. And then there's the rent— $350 a month. I split that with my mother.

Bussing tables I make $4.75 plus tips. We get time and a half if we work more than eight hours. Some days I make $40 in tips, sometimes less than $10. If you're smiling, asking about the weather, just a little conversation, they'll tip you.

At work sometimes people bug you. We had a Mexican lady come in yesterday and she said, "Do you speak Spanish?" Then she began to command me, "Well, I want a table near the window, non-smoking, etc., etc." As if I were her maid or something. Sometimes, if you're from their country, they treat you worse.

I'm usually speaking English. They don't like us to speak Spanish between ourselves on the job, because then they can't understand us. I am almost thinking in English now, but to me it's a relief to speak Spanish.

When we're done with work we come home and relax. We watch TV, have some dinner. And we listen to music—Edie Gorme is my favorite. I love the romantic stuff.

(*left*) Carmen Rios
bussing tables. (*below*)
Carmen Rios at home
with her family. (All
photos in this essay by
Kit Miller)

Marilyn Jackson at the Committee to Aid Abused Women.

Marilyn Jackson
Laborer

I've been through so many changes. I was born in 1954, grew up in Seattle. There was the Panther Party, the Free Breakfast Program, everything was happening. In this day and age no one even wants to stop and give you the time of day, let alone ask you, "Are you hungry? Do you have a place to stay?"

I'm working as a day laborer cleaning up the Silver Legacy before it's turned over to the owners. I found out about this program called Goals Unlimited from a friend who came by. He has all these construction clothes on and I said, "Dang, Bernard, I need a job!" He said, "Here, this lady will get you in construction." I thought, "Yeah, sure." You always hear something. And then when it comes down to it you can't qualify for some reason. But Jackie said, "Yeah, you can come to class."

In my class there were young women, older men, a white guy. Jackie told us how to get along on the job, conflict resolution. What causes people to lose their jobs is mostly their inability to get along with others or their attendance. Jackie even showed us how to get healthy food at a fast food restaurant to make fuel so that we can be productive.

Marilyn Jackson cleaning windows during construction of the Silver Legacy.

Goals Unlimited pays us seven dollars an hour. They don't think it's possible to live on minimum wage, so they pay us what they think is right.

When I first came to Reno I worked cocktailing for years. There was a lot of sexual harassment. That was one of the reasons I quit. The girls that had the best stations and Fourth of July off were the ones sleeping with the boss.

I'm getting kind of distressed, cause it doesn't seem like people care—even my daughter doesn't have a sense of community and putting something back. She tells me, "Mama, this is the 1990s." What does that mean? The more things change the more they stay the same. People still hungry, coming out of abusive situations. Kids ain't getting good medical care.

I've been staying at the Committee to Aid Abused Women. I made some cool friends there, like my counselor, Gina, who is a Shoshone woman. There's other women you can talk to and there's kids. We've done art, gone to lectures. This week I'm moving into my own apartment. I'm hoping my little four-year-old granddaughter can visit me there.

My dreams are—I'd like to have a car that's not almost as old as my daughter, with a warranty. I want a piece of property! And a pet. Someone glad to see you when you hit the door, who thinks you're wonderful! "Hey, I missed you today."

Phan Dang
Pai Gow Poker Dealer

There are a lot of Vietnamese here. But we don't see them too much because many of us work two jobs. It's because they have to pay too much money. Big house. New car.

I am forty-five years old. I deal Blackjack and Pai Gow poker at the Comstock.

I come from Vietnam, from a city on the mountains about four hundred miles from Saigon. At university I studied Chinese-Vietnamese history. I learned English in school, I also speak some French. Here I watch TV and talk to everyone.

My husband was a captain in the army. In 1975 after South Vietnam lost, they gather every officer and take them away. After that I take care of my two boys and sell vegetables from a cart. In 1982 they release my husband. No job for him in Vietnam after prison.

I came to the United States because my husband is political refu-

Phan Dang dealing at the Comstock.

Phan Dang shops at the Asian Market in her free time.

gee. The United States government bought airplane tickets for the four of us. We arrived in Reno without even a dollar! I just think it is beautiful, quiet, and very large, quite different from my country.

Three months later I got a job working banquets at the Peppermill. Then I went to dealer school. I took a six-week course for 21, four weeks for poker, about ten months of practice before I got the job at the Comstock. I concentrate all the time when I'm working. If I thought about anything else I could make a mistake.

I make $5.02 an hour before tips and I have benefits. I make a lot less than I used to, and the IRS still takes $15 a day tip money. I'm taking another dealer's job so I'll be working graveyard and day shift. My husband works swing. It's OK. Less fighting.

On my days off I sleep, clean house, wash clothes, go to the beauty shop. I shop at the Asian Market, and cook eggrolls for my family.

I have a better life than my parents, and my children have an American education. One son is a keno writer, the other is a change person. They both go to college, and get support from Job Corps—one studies auto mechanics, the other electric mechanics.

Last month I bought a condo—I paid out 20 percent—$16,000. I had the money in the bank because everybody work, everybody save money. In Vietnam you work hard, but you can't make anything. Here, if I work I can have something. All my family have green card. In five years we will apply for citizenship.

We celebrate New Year. I hope my sons keep that tradition. In Vietnam New Year's is the time they sit together and remember the ancestors.

Sheldon Craig
Entertainer

One luxury we have is that we get to be ourselves in our bubbliest form. I put this on, and it's silvery and shivery, and it makes me happy. It's like Christmas.

We do two shows a night, six nights a week. The opening of the show hits you like a freight train. The second the lights come on we have to run in and keep that high energy going.

You don't want to miss the show ever. If you get sick you do your best to get back in as soon as possible. Doctors always say, "You need two weeks off." Well, for us that's absolutely unreal.

The first show is at 7:00. We get here by 6:00 and that gives us time to say "Hey we're all here, are there any problems today, is somebody sick?" After the first show we have a two and a half hour break, then we come back and work for another hour and a half. By 12:30 everything's packed away and we're ready to go. Afterwards we go to the bar upstairs, or we go out together to American Bandstand.

My daytime is spent teaching a dance class, practicing voice, going over new music, sewing. On my days off I like to go shopping, just hang out with friends, see the area. On weekends someone will have a birthday and we'll have a barbecue.

Some people in the show are married with families, some are just totally single. We have all types and it's like a family. When we're rehearsing sixteen hours a day, we don't see anybody else, so the show is where we make our close bonds. And we share our dream.

My father was military, so I grew up all over the country. Putting on these shiny clothes was something I always gravitated to. I had always just loved entertainers and liked singing. I went to college and got my degree in music and my minor in dance. Now I make $1,000 a week.

Sheldon Craig preparing for a show.

Sheldon Craig at the mall with his friends.

I have a lot of things going. I'm writing a show, designing costumes, and putting choreography together. I'm trying out for a
show in Las Vegas, and I have my own little nightclub show. I'm
very lucky, because what makes me happy and what was so thrilling for me to do with all my friends ended up being my job. Not
everybody gets that.

Jerry Tiehm
Bellman

When I have free time I do botanical consulting work. This plant is one of eighteen I've discovered new to science, and one of five that's named after me. It's called *Stroganowia tiehmii.*

I've been a bellman three years. We're concierge, information service, and bellman, all in one. People from out of town ask you where to rent a car, where the closest beauty salon is, how to get to Mustang Ranch.

I needed a job, and I wanted something people-oriented. I have a Master's in botany, and I had worked at the New York Botanical Garden herbarium. But there aren't any botany jobs in Nevada and the jobs out West tend to be seasonal. You have to eat. So I found this job.

The customers are very responsive as long as things with the hotel have gone OK. Occasionally someone will yell at you, and you have to just let it go by. Next person that comes up, put a smile on your face, and treat them like you treat everyone else.

We're paid minimum wage. And we get a commission if we sign people up for tours—anywhere from $5 to $9. The IRS says my tips are two-fifty an hour. If people are winning they aren't necessarily tipping. We've had people that won ten thousand dollars that tip nothing.

I grew up in Reno, so the casinos were always there. We all thought it was more glamorous than it actually is. Now I see what I call the dark side of the casinos. A certain percentage of people that work here, this is also their social life. They go sit at the bar, and somebody has a few drink tokes. Pretty soon they've been there for hours. Sex is also a commodity in the casino. It can be tough on marriages.

You have to have a life away from the casino. Otherwise, it's going to get to you. Booze, clothes, and casinos. To me it's just a waste of time. Most days I'm out the door at three o'clock, and I'm busy till ten-thirty at night.

Reno's gotten so big now. I liked it when it was a nice little hick town of fifty thousand. I graduated from Reno High. My father was a mechanic and a Shriner, also a drinker. He knew everybody in town. We never took the keys out of cars, never locked the doors on the house.

(*above*) Jerry Tiehm delivering efficient service to hotel guests. (*below*) Jerry Tiehm with *Stroganowia tiehmii*.

Anwar Masud
General Manager

One of our big challenges is to keep the customers coming back. So we offer Polynesia Night, where everyone dresses Hawaiian and we have Polynesian dancing. Many of our clients are older people from Canada, and they love it. Part of my job is helping them have fun.

I was born in West Pakistan. My family are Muslim. My father imported goods from China and Singapore. Ever since I was a very young child I wanted to come to the United States. I spoke English from kindergarten and at ten spent time at United States Center reading comic books. I felt I knew Donald Duck, Porky Pig, Wylie Coyote.

I came to San Francisco in 1974 to attend college. My father let me come, though he couldn't help me financially. I had no contacts. The second day I found a small apartment over a grocery store for $60 a month.

I asked people what jobs can an 18-year-old do, and they told me restaurants. I got a graveyard job as a busboy/dishwasher, wore my best clothes, and was just buried in dishes. My family had servants and I never had to work a day in my life, much less at a crazy hour

Anwar Masud at Polynesia Night, Riverboat Hotel and Casino.

Anwar Masud and family.

washing dishes. I contemplated quitting, but decided no, I'm gonna make it, and it got easier.

I decided to go to college in Kansas and the Greyhound stopped for an hour in Reno. I had dinner with a friend here and he convinced me to stay and go to UNR.

I worked as a busboy, then a waiter. When I turned 21, I got into the gaming side by getting dealers to teach me at empty tables. I was a supervisor at the Eldorado for six years and dealt at the Comstock at the same time. When the Riverboat opened I was offered casino manager. I moved into it naturally, like I was born to do that, and just enjoyed the heck out of it.

Our business is so dynamic, more so with the proliferation of gaming. If someone in this industry can't rise to the top it's only because they really didn't want to.

In my free time I like to be with my son, who is ten. Now I am remarried to a Pakistani woman. She came to Reno only last December, so we are still showing her the sights—Lake Tahoe and the mountains. My mother lives with us too.

The *Valley Times*
A Personal History

Philip Graham, the late publisher of the *Washington Post,* called journalism "the first rough draft of history" (Halberstam, *The Powers That Be,* 161). Anyone who writes the history of Nevada in the 1960s, 1970s, and early 1980s should turn to the state's many newspapers, and particularly to one born in 1959 as the *North Las Vegas Valley Times.* Its founder was Adam Yacenda, who was Hank Greenspun's editor during the *Las Vegas Sun*'s most controversial days. Later shortened to the *Valley Times* and expanded from a weekly to a triweekly, Yacenda's paper evolved from a key player in North Las Vegas affairs into one of Nevada's most important and influential newspapers under the later ownership of Bob Brown, the former editor of the *Las Vegas Review-Journal* and one of the state's most knowledgeable political journalists. The *Valley Times* lived only for twenty-five years, dying of debt on June 22, 1984, but it was a great influence on other newspapers of its time, and a clearing-house and home for some of the greatest reporters in Nevada's renowned journalism history. It became a crucial source for news and analysis of Nevada's political economy, making it important for our understanding of the evolution of the Sunbelt and its society—how the postwar boom transformed Las Vegas, the state of Nevada, and, indeed, the West. The story of the *Valley Times* is also an opportunity to look inside the life of a newspaper and its people—how they affected their times, and how the *Valley Times* affected them.[1]

I

Adam John Yacenda brought vast experience in politics and journalism to his newspaper. He was born on December 17, 1915, in Jersey City, and to the end retained his eastern accent and his curiosity, always asking "What do you think is behind that?" and usually coming up with the correct answer. He began his career as a stringer for the *New York World-Telegram*, one of the many New York City dailies that died in the mid-1960s. After working for newspapers in New Jersey, he came to California in World War II for his health, and soon began publishing the *Beverly Hills Bulletin* for its owner, Will Rogers Jr. But Yacenda was a political animal, and a Republican: in 1950, he served as a press secretary for a young California congressman, Richard Nixon, in his successful Senate campaign against another representative, Helen Gahagan Douglas, whom Nixon painted as the "Pink Lady." Seeking a warmer climate, Yacenda moved on to Las Vegas. He recalled that when he interviewed at the *Las Vegas Review-Journal*, editor John Cahlan never looked up at him from his desk. So, Yacenda went to the newly founded *Las Vegas Sun* as a reporter and was promoted to editor two years later. In that job, Yacenda trained a staff of outstanding journalists who went on to become leading editors, publicists, and advertising executives in Las Vegas, and oversaw a crusading paper, aiding Greenspun with a combination of encouragement and caution.

Yacenda's ambitions extended well beyond the *Sun*. In 1954 he left to work for the reelection campaign of his fellow Republican, Governor Charles Russell. He planned to run Russell's Las Vegas office during the governor's second term, but late in the campaign his old boss, Greenspun, broke a story alleging possible corruption surrounding Vail Pittman, Russell's opponent, and Cliff Jones, the Democratic national committeeman and outgoing lieutenant governor.[2] When the ensuing controversy helped assure Russell's reelection, the governor told Yacenda that naming him to a position would look too much like a payoff to Greenspun, so they set it up for him to return as managing editor. Yacenda laughed cynically as he recalled saying to Russell, "Thanks a lot." But Yacenda went back to the *Sun* until late in 1958, when he grew tired of interference from Greenspun (Yacenda may have been the only editor who ever was able to stand up to him) and other *Sun* executives. He also wanted to own his own paper, in his own town—North Las Vegas, where he lived and which he considered ripe for a community newspaper to compete with the weekly *North Las Vegas News*, which Greenspun owned.

The *North Las Vegas Valley Times* was born as a weekly on Thursday, March 26, 1959, and sold for ten cents a copy. Its first issue reflected the careful planning that Yacenda put into the project. It was full of advertising from merchants in Las Vegas and North Las Vegas and offered ample news. But in the boosting fashion common to small-town papers, the banner headline announced, "NO. VEGAS GROWTH LOOMS," with details on new homes and business permits. The front page featured pictures of Progress Days and park improvements, a report on the ultimately unsuccessful efforts of Yacenda and a hotel publicist to locate an atomic museum in North Las Vegas, a list of voting precincts for the pending municipal election, and a salutation letter to the paper from Mayor Earl Hartke. Yacenda waited until the next issue, which also reported his involvement in forming a North Las Vegas Rotary Club, for the customary statement of purpose. On April 2, 1959, beneath the heading "A Newspaper Dedicated to Serving the People," Yacenda made clear his differences with—and from—Greenspun:

> The VALLEY TIMES—your only Home-Owned newspaper—is here to serve North Las Vegas—by presenting constructive community news, by adding to the cohesiveness of community spirit and by supporting the local merchants. . . .
>
> Investments in the future of this city can be made through patronization of the community paper. Our aim is to build North Las Vegas into a great and prosperous city. Mutual support—between the community newspaper, the merchants and the citizens themselves—is the key to that future. . . .
>
> The needs and demands of the people of North Las Vegas are felt and recognized by the VALLEY TIMES since it is in every respect a North Las Vegas paper which, as part of the community, has of necessity the same needs, desires and interests as the people it serves. . . .
>
> The VALLEY TIMES reaffirms its sincere desire to serve as the instrument of the people and not, as others might have it, to make the people the instrument of the paper.

For most of the nearly fifteen years Yacenda published it, the *Times* grew consistently and sought to wield influence. On November 11, 1959, it merged with the *News* "to give the third largest city in Nevada a strong, aggressive and sparkling newspaper dedicated to serving the people." Greenspun, overtaken in their competition, provided printing facilities for several years. "A Politically Independent Newspaper," it began publishing twice weekly as 1963 began, and Yacenda continued his locally oriented front-page column, "Adam's Atoms," which later gave way to "The Lantern by Diogenes." Yacenda kept the *Times* on the course he set for it. "He really understood how to make a small community newspaper succeed," one of his reporters, Bruce Hasley, recalled. "I will never forget his hammering away at photos of children and dogs and getting as many names of local people in the paper as we could." He worked both behind the scenes and in print for "progressive city government," joining in the quest for physical and fiscal growth and development with City Manager Clay Lynch. As Yacenda explained after the defeat of one of his council slates, "This newspaper takes a special interest in city government because North Las Vegans have so often proven their concern with city business. We pledge to continue that policy and to report the facts of city business for our readers to judge" (*North Las Vegas Valley Times,* May 8, 1969).

Yacenda also remained politically active in Las Vegas and throughout Nevada. He switched his affiliation to Democratic, finding that he and that party had grown more compatible, ideologically and personally. Once, he came within striking distance of running for office himself. In 1966, when the first election after reapportionment created a state senate seat for North Las Vegas, several party leaders asked him to run in the largely Democratic district; Yacenda promised to think about it, and apparently had little trouble deciding against it (ibid., May 30, 1966). He was a close adviser to Republican Oran Gragson, a Las Vegas businessman, on his four successful campaigns for mayor of Las Vegas and his predictably unsuccessful race for governor in 1962 against Democratic incumbent Grant Sawyer. Yacenda also tried to aid Lieutenant Governor Ed Fike when he opposed Senator Alan Bible for reelection in 1968 and eventual victor Mike O'Callaghan in the 1970 gubernatorial election, only to find himself blocked by party leaders, who considered Yacenda too independent and actually may have wanted Fike to lose. Hasley, one of the last reporters Yacenda hired, recalled, "He had one of the shrewdest political minds around. He didn't get the credit he deserved for his political advice behind the scenes. A lot of people in office today owe their careers to him." Gragson agreed: "I followed his instructions to the T" (*Las Vegas Sun,* June 14, 1986).

The *Times* and Yacenda did all of this, and often did it well, but not without increasing difficulty. While the paper expanded to tri-

weekly in 1973, North Las Vegas never grew, physically or govern-
mentally, as Yacenda wished. The city council often was in turmoil,
with recalls and threats of recalls, while Lynch's efforts in behalf
of growth made him a controversial figure, despite the support he
received from Yacenda and many in the community. Nor did Yacenda receive the support that he thought necessary from government, business, and private citizens. North Las Vegas simply lacked
an identity unique from its neighbor. Worse, Yacenda increasingly
had to yield control to his staff because he suffered from a defective heart valve that would require surgery. Thus, Yacenda began
looking for a buyer, and he found one. The November 7, 1973, front
page announced the sale of the *Times* to Robert L. Brown. Yacenda,
the *Times* announced, "had known Brown, a longtime resident of
Nevada, for many years" and was "confident that he will provide
integrity and newspaper know-how to continue to build the fine
paper this community deserves." Brown praised Yacenda as "one of
Nevada's outstanding newspapermen. He has done an amazing job
of building the *Valley Times* against tremendous odds. It is a tough
job because you just don't build a newspaper overnight. But Adam
Yacenda has made the *Valley Times* a very successful and widely
read newspaper." In turn, Brown promised "a number of personnel
additions and political changes at the paper, but the *Valley Times*
will continue to be politically independent" (*North Las Vegas Valley
Times*, November 7, 1973).

Indeed, Yacenda had found a kindred spirit: a veteran newspaperman, a political and business maneuverer, and a conservative
in the good sense of the word. Robert Lloyd Brown was born on
November 25, 1930, in Glendale, California, where his father was a
newspaperman. His road to Las Vegas was a long and winding one:
from his first job as a nine-year-old cleaning a press and the office
at his father's San Pedro paper, Brown worked his way through the
University of Michigan as a pressman for the school's daily, and on
papers in Los Alamos, New Mexico, and Rock Springs, Wyoming,
before serving in the Korean War as an MP and then as a reporter
for *Stars and Stripes*. After the war, he spent five years with United
Press in Korea, Japan, India, and Pakistan. But he put his career as a
foreign correspondent behind him to return to the United States in
1958 to edit and manage papers for publisher Donald W. Reynolds
in Arkansas and then Alaska (*Valley Times*, June 10, 13, 21, 1984).

Brown's career changed significantly when Reynolds imported

him to edit his flagship paper, the *Review-Journal*, early in 1961. At the time, most evening papers were in decline because of television; the *Sun*'s circulation was catching up to the *Review-Journal*'s; and Brown was taking over for Al and John Cahlan, who had run the paper from the 1920s until Reynolds forced them out. But Brown quickly won over the staff, which included several reporters who once had worked for Yacenda at the *Sun*, and built on it. The *Review-Journal* began pulling away from the *Sun*, which faltered badly when a fire destroyed its plant in 1963. Thus, as Jim Seagrave, a reporter whom Brown imported from Alaska and who became one of the leading hotel publicity executives in Las Vegas, recalled, Brown "found himself in a town dizzy with growth and prosperity, a raucous amalgam of carpetbagging city slickers and good old boys, grifters and drifters, saints and scoundrels. The city cried out for a conscience. Brown, ever-bristling with idealism, matter-of-factly assumed it was his responsibility to heed the call" (*Valley Times*, June 21, 1984; Highton, *Nevada Newspaper Days*, 233–68).

Conscience ended Brown's career at the *Review-Journal*. In 1964, Brown backed Lieutenant Governor Paul Laxalt, a Republican, in his race against first-term senator Howard Cannon, a Democrat allegedly linked to a scandal involving Bobby Baker, a close friend and former aide to Lyndon Johnson when he was Senate majority leader. When Brown devoted considerable space to the story in the *Review-Journal*, Johnson called Reynolds and pressured him to back Cannon, apparently threatening his Federal Communications Commission licenses for television and radio stations in Reno and Las Vegas. Reynolds ordered Brown to kill all stories about the scandal and to keep Laxalt out of the paper unless he could be mentioned unfavorably. Brown resigned and, for the next decade, became the kind of itinerant journalist and publicist he often hired: a speechwriter for Laxalt, who lost to Cannon by 84 votes; city editor of the *Nevada State Journal*; chairman of the Nevada Tax Commission — an ironic stint, given his later problems; editor and general manager of the *Tucson Daily American* from 1969 to 1971; owner and publisher of the *Lacey Leader* in Washington from 1972 to 1973; in Las Vegas, partner from 1971 to 1973 in May Advertising, then the state's largest such firm. But it was wrong for him: Jude Wanniski, a onetime *Review-Journal* reporter who became a leading national journalist and adviser to Ronald Reagan, recalled that when Brown was with May, "he would apologize to me for having a big car."

Brown was, above all, a newsman; as *Times* publisher, he would drive a Honda (*Valley Times*, June 10, 13, 21, 1984; Highton, *Nevada Newspaper Days*, 160–62).

Under Brown, the *Valley Times* would reflect not so much his biases as his belief in what kind of news mattered. Shortly after taking over from Yacenda, Brown became convinced that North Las Vegas was incapable of supporting its own newspaper. Like Yacenda, he felt that the city was too much a satellite of Las Vegas, lacking its own identity, not to mention sufficient prosperity. That left Brown with the option of reducing the thrice-weekly publication schedule, or expanding to a daily and into Las Vegas. Choosing, as he put it, to go forward rather than backward, and hoping to dislodge Greenspun's *Sun*, he turned the paper into a Monday-through-Friday daily in March 1975, with an emphasis on politics—Brown's expertise—and on gaming, which, he felt, neither the *Review-Journal* nor *Sun* covered as a serious industry. Indeed, when the *Times* added a Sunday edition in October 2, 1977, not only did it present a regular page of gaming news and features—the first local paper to do so—and a week-in-review page, but it even dared to be a tabloid. In this way, the Sunday edition would look thicker— it would take more than two tabloid pages to fill a page of a broad-sheet—and different, without succumbing to the sensationalism that characterizes so many tabloid papers.

In only one area did Brown indulge himself: attacks on Green-spun, of whom he wrote, "There has never been a more power hungry man in the state of Nevada than Hank himself. And there are few that can top him at wheeling and dealing. Those who've watched him use his newspaper as a blackjack to advance his own personal ends know the truth thereof." Aware that he was Brown's editorial and financial target, Greenspun declared, "I don't believe *The Valley Times* is properly constituted as a newspaper." Given Greenspun's power and wealth, Brown had taken on a herculean task; asked whether Greenspun and his *Sun* could be overcome, a local advertising executive replied, "It can't be done. But if anyone can do it, Bob Brown is the man" (*Valley Times*, March 1975, August 11, 1977, October 2, 1977; Toll, "Three's Company," 20).

In the process, Brown relied, as he had at the *Review-Journal*, on a peerless staff of reporters and editors. He hired A. D. Hopkins, an outstanding *Sun* reporter, as managing editor in 1974. But Brown and the less politically inclined Hopkins had an edgy relationship, and while promoting Hopkins, Brown had appointed as his city editor Hasley, a *Times* reporter since June 1973. Hasley proved more compatible with Brown personally and journalistically, and his desire to remain behind the scenes complimented Brown's political maneuverings. As a result, in May 1977, Brown promoted Hopkins to executive editor, a job from which he could supervise and write feature and investigative stories, and run Brown's weekly gaming tabloid, *Las Vegas Today;* Hasley became managing editor, responsible for the daily news operation. Little more than a year later, Hopkins was at the *Review-Journal* and Hasley became, as *Times* reporter and city editor Linda Faiss wrote, "the heart of The Valley Times" (*Valley Times,* June 21, 1984).

Brown, Hopkins, and Hasley developed an exceptional group of reporters, and the *Times* indeed became, as Brown hoped, must reading for Nevada's power brokers. Working from what one writer called a "stucco cheesebox" of a building across from a truck stop in North Las Vegas, Brown gave his editors and reporters freedom to operate while Hopkins and Hasley nursed them along (Toll, "Three's Company," pp. 18–21). While Seagrave wrote a popular television column—the only one in Las Vegas at the time—David Dearing and Dick Odessky provided thoughtful, incisive coverage of the gaming industry; eventually, former *Review-Journal* news editor Dave Verbon succeeded them as gaming expert and became Hasley's aide as news editor. Norma Staley served as Hasley's right hand and the newsroom's mother hen, proofreading and editing many of the paper's syndicated features. After several editors and writers came and went, two journalists became fixtures in the sports department: Ed Koch, a daily columnist and leading boxing writer, and Ken White, a writer and columnist who handled most of the layout. And chances were that a major political story appearing without a byline and announcing, "*The Valley Times* has learned . . . ," " came from Brown's typewriter. He also generated a daily editorial, "As We See It," which combined his incredible number of inside sources on both sides of the fence, his deep knowledge of Nevada politics and economics, his conservative inclinations, and his desire to be a player.

The most important of the daily's reporters and columnists was Ned Day, who is generally considered the greatest investigative reporter Las Vegas has ever known. A native of Wisconsin, Day went to work for the *Times* in 1976, soon after it became a daily. His coverage of law enforcement and the mob was not only sound, but often awe-inspiring; colleagues recalled the night that five different major sources were on hold to tell him about the day's events while he talked with a sixth. Day broke an incredible number of stories: the scandals surrounding Argent Corporation, its ownership of the Stardust Hotel, and hidden interests from Chicago; and federal wiretaps of alleged mobsters in Kansas City and Las Vegas, to name his biggest ones. His columns varied from those topics to his personal life, which included equal amounts of debauchery and wenching; his nocturnal activities became legendary, and provided often hilarious column material. He made a point of attacking Jerry Lewis on the day of his telethon for muscular dystrophy, just to set off readers. Until Day left for more money and circulation at the *Review-Journal* in 1981, his column occupied a starring role on page two of the *Times*; after he left, Brown started an insider column, "Morning Line," made up of contributions from himself and the staff, because he reasoned that to bring in a new columnist would only build up someone else for the competition to hire away (*Valley Times* during Day's tenure, 1976–81; *Review-Journal* and *Sun*, September 1–15, 1987, on Day's life and death).

Brown and Day were involved in what became the most controversial story in the history of the *Valley Times*—a story that reflected their journalistic talent, Brown's involvement in politics, and the paper's shaky finances. In 1978, they found out that Attorney General Robert List, a Republican candidate for governor, had received assorted free services—"comps"—from the Stardust, yet had billed the state for his room and board. Brown met with List before the election and chose not to print the story, believing that it would be perceived as a smear. But Brown wrote an uncharacteristic editorial endorsement of moderate Democratic Lieutenant Governor Bob Rose. He said, "The editorial philosophy of this newspaper has been to support conservatism in government," but he accused List of increasing his budget too rapidly, failing to fight crime, and having "played politics with the office of attorney general in an almost unconscionable manner." After the election, the *Sun* reported that Brown offered to withhold publication of the story, for a price: a gaming license for Stardust executive Frank Rosenthal, who had the kind of background that state gaming officials were unlikely to tolerate. The *Times* finally published Day's heavily documented story ten days after the election and followed up with Rosenthal's charges that several major Nevada politicians had asked him to use his influence with Brown to kill the story. In an editorial and news stories, Brown attacked List's "big lie" and "phony, politically inspired" charges and demanded a grand jury investigation, his picture making a rare appearance on the front page of his paper in the process. (*Valley Times*, November 1978; *Las Vegas Sun*, November 9, 1978; "The Mob on the Run").

But thanks to Rosenthal and other bad decisions involving business, Brown ended up on his front page more often than he wished —he looked askance at Greenspun for that sort of thing—and for reasons neither becoming nor seemly. While growing too close to Rosenthal, Brown also expanded the size and staff of the paper. He hoped to beat the *Sun* in the battle for second place behind the *Review-Journal* but lacked the advertising revenue to pay for it. This prompted Brown to agree to two illegal actions. One was a check-kiting scheme tied to Argent and May Advertising, where Brown once had been a partner: they would buy advertising at high rates, and he would kick back to them most of what they paid. The other involved the payment of payroll taxes: one of Brown's business managers convinced him that if he held off on paying these to the Internal Revenue Service until the paper was profitable, the government would simply accept back payment (*Valley Times*, December 1, 1978; Toll, "Three's Company," 18–21).

The kind of trust that Brown put in his editorial staff proved badly placed when applied to business. Eventually, a federal investigation of Argent and its nefarious connections led to Brown's indictment, guilty plea, and punishment of a $5,000 fine, 1,000 hours of community service, and his testimony in federal court against May. As for the payroll taxes, the IRS led Brown to believe at the beginning of July 1982 that he had two weeks to work out a payment plan. Less than a week later, he arrived to find his building at 1007 E. Cheyenne in North Las Vegas padlocked. That night, editors and reporters put out a smaller version of the paper at Brown's dining room table, and the *Times* survived "with a lot of help from our friends," as Brown put it. Friends and supporters gave or loaned Brown money, which he used to finance the printing, retain some semblance of a staff, and fight the IRS, which later seized the paper's newsracks, prompting the normally even-tempered Brown finally to attack the IRS for "petty harassment" that "could have serious First Amendment implications." Eventually, the *Times* became the only newspaper in the United States to survive an IRS seizure, and it won back its presses in court (*Valley Times*, July 7–12, August 5, 1982, June 9, 1983, January 13, 1984).

Meanwhile, Brown remained a significant figure in Nevada journalism and politics. His editorials and columns still were "must reading," and the state's leaders wore out his telephone line and office carpeting talking or visiting with him for advice and ideas; although Brown was a Republican, his endorsements often crossed party lines—he traditionally preferred incumbents, observing that if they did their jobs properly, they deserved to be retained—and members of both parties turned to him. Recognizing his financial problems, Brown named a new publisher, but they disagreed over the paper's future direction and Brown fired him. A parade of reporters served briefly in the newsroom; most of them were in between jobs and looking to keep busy, while others had foundered personally or professionally and needed a job. By the early 1980s, the *Valley Times* was not competitive with the older, more established, and richer *Review-Journal* or *Sun*, but it continued to wield influence and won sympathy, if very little money, for its plight. When the IRS moved in, Greenspun wrote that "if Las Vegas is not destined to have three print media, we prefer that Bob Brown and his Valley Times be the one to survive along with us. He happens to be a good competitor in the best newspaper tradition" (*Valley Times*, July 7–12, 1982, September 20, 1983).

II

But the *Valley Times* was clearly in decline. Most of its staff left for other publications or for better-paying jobs outside of journalism. Brown and Hasley still managed to attract talented reporters to work for them, but paying them was another matter. As a result, they had to rely on those who had other sources of income or simply wanted to work for next to nothing—for fun, experience, or something to do. One was a high school student who impressed Brown with his oratory in a Rotary Club speech contest. Brown invited him for an interview and told him, in a classic understatement, "I can't pay you very much." He became known as "The Kid" to Hasley and the other senior staff who remained. It was a mark of the paper's financial straits that when Hasley took a three-month leave of absence in 1983 to work at a television station, Brown turned to the then-eighteen-year-old kid to put out the paper each night. He designed the news section, wrote occasional stories and editorials, and earned a wealth of experience then and after Hasley's return.

I was that teenager, and the chance to work at the *Valley Times* changed my life. Until then, I had planned to pursue a communications degree and a journalism career. Given the experience that I was getting at the *Times,* I felt that I would be better served by a different major and went into history. Brown planned to use me in the sports department, and I wound up filling in as sports editor when Ken White was on vacation or off, but Hasley, desperate for every semi-breathing body he could get, commandeered me for the news department. Just before joining the *Times,* I had won a high school journalism contest in which the judge was Ned Day. He visited the paper shortly thereafter and apparently told Hasley that I had talent; Hasley and I have joked since that it was the first time he noticed that I worked there. I thought of telling this story when I was writing my master's thesis in 1987 and 1988, but my late adviser, Ralph Roske, told me, "You're still too close to it." He was right, and he may still be right. But what follow are impressions and memories, anecdotes still fresh but filtered through what I hope is a more adult, liberal, and historical mind.

From my first months at the paper, three news stories stick out in my mind. One was the first story I obtained on my own, about efforts by the Clark County School District to force out the most experienced—and thus highest-paid—high school teachers by sending them to teach lower grades. The local media jumped on the story, and I beamed as Hasley bounced around the newsroom saying, "That's the way it used to be around here—they followed us." The other was a story about a political debate. I took the notes and, as the debate finished, in rat-a-tat style, Hasley ticked off ten subjects that he wanted me to cover in one story. I wrote it and gave it to Bruce for his editing. The next morning, I basked in praise from other staff members who told me how brilliantly the story under my byline was written. When I read it, I found that it bore no resemblance to the original account, except for that precious byline. If Hasley's editing genius required testimony, I could now provide it. (Indeed, one of the few stories that Hasley wrote while I was there was an account of an interview with Rosenthal when someone blew up his car; Day wrote the same story for the *Review-Journal,* and it is no disrespect to Day to say that Hasley wrote rings around him.)

The other story was of far more significance in the paper's history: President Ronald Reagan's speech at a rally for Nevada's Republican candidates in 1982. Chic Hecht was running against Howard Cannon. Few knew then that Brown was one of Hecht's top advisers, that he had helped push Hecht into the race and design his successful campaign. Hasley chose me to write the main story about the rally. I was too nervous and concerned at the time about "getting it right" to know or care about Brown's involvement in creating the story, but Hasley had enough confidence in me to give me the assignment—and too small a staff to have much of a choice. Brown and Hasley were happy with the results, and that was good enough for me. Opportunities like that rarely come along—Hasley once grinned at me and said, "You know, kid, if you were at a bigger paper, they'd have you writing obituaries."

Simply by remaining at the *Times,* I had the opportunity to design the paper each night. By 1983, the news pages had shrunk to about thirteen a day, filled mostly with copy from our ancient Associated Press teletype machine, a few syndicated columns, occasional stories by occasional reporters, the editorial page, and Brown's "Morning Line" column. The composing room had become adjusted to Hasley's high speed, and I referred to each evening as a "crash landing." I was allowed to make mistakes, some colossal: I ran the same syndicated column twice on the same page, once chose a color scheme for the front page that nearly gave readers retina burn, and was the editor responsible for a misspelling in the banner headline. But I also had to make editorial judgments that, I suppose in retrospect, no eighteen-year-old should have been asked to make. But Brown was desperate and I was willing, and I gained an understanding of how a newspaper reaches the public, and why it contains what it does.

An interesting example occurred early in 1984 while Brown and Hasley were away at a journalism convention. Chief Justice Warren Burger was coming to Las Vegas to address the American Bar Association. I assigned a reporter to find out about Secret Service plans to protect Burger; she learned that none had been made. As she prepared to write her story, an FBI agent called to talk to me and explained that while he had no inclinations to be a censor, a question had come to mind: if we printed that kind of story, would we be encouraging someone to try something? The answer was simple, and I killed the story, for which Brown, Hasley, and others praised me. Part of my reasoning was that the agent had a point; another was that I had dealt with the agent before, knew him to be a thoughtful and decent man, and saw no reason to doubt or desire to antagonize him. Only later did my more mature mind grasp that my decision on a potential life-or-death situation had been based in part on friendship or self-interest, rather than on sound journalistic ethics. To this day, I wonder whether any inexperienced—or even experienced—editor or reporter would have thought any differently.

The *Times* had journalistic ethics, but we also understood what the First Amendment really, and unfortunately, means: that freedom of the press belongs to the owner of the press. Jim Joyce, a former journalist who was close to Brown, told a class at the University of Nevada, Reno, that the key to good journalism was financial independence; only then could a reporter afford to write a controversial story. Thus, unlike the staff of the halcyon days of the late 1970s, we of the early 1980s never were much inclined to look into some stories that might offend the few advertisers who remained with the paper. Once, Brown published a report that cast an unfavorable light on one of his closest friends, but only after talking with him and helping him work out a response to the story. After Brown was indicted, I interviewed U.S. District Judge Harry Claiborne for a school project, carefully informing him that I was there as a history student, not as a reporter. He asked about Brown, whom he was to sentence, and said, "I like Bob." I told Brown this, joking that he was home free. Brown shook his head and explained that a few years before, Claiborne had asked him not to print a story about him, but Brown went ahead and did so anyway. Then he laughed and added, "Now I think I should have listened to him!"

As with most of those who worked for him, I loved Bob Brown, no matter his legal and financial entanglements, as I loved Hasley, White, and the other editorial staffers I worked with. But, as in any family, we tussled. When Brown was short of funds to meet the payroll, Hasley believed in the Marine policy—and he was a former Marine—that the commander is the last one into the mess tent; accordingly, Brown would pay everyone else first, leaving Hasley in an understandably unhappy frame of mind. One night, Hasley stomped in without saying anything and closed his office door, the surest sign that he was in a bad mood. Brown came down the hall leading to the newsroom, scurrying in his slightly stoop-shouldered way, looked at Hasley's door, leaned into the newsroom, and asked, "Mike, could you give Bruce the editorial?" I looked at him and said, "Oh, listen to the big brave publisher, afraid to face his managing editor." When everyone, including Brown, stopped laughing, the publisher replied, "OK, you've had your fun. But I didn't pay Bruce today, so he's mad at me, not you." I did as Brown asked. He was right, of course—when it came to understanding what made people tick, he usually was.

Still, Brown and I had one fundamental disagreement: politics. At each election, Brown wrote an editorial in which he endorsed a candidate in almost every race and announced that it was legal—and, to him, logical—to take that page into the voting booth. When I registered to vote in 1983, I became a Democrat by inclination and ideology, and told Brown that I would vote against his selections, thus assuring that my votes would be liberal and Democratic. He laughed, and I continued to write occasional editorials for him.

Several of these reflected Brown's supportiveness, his activities as a political player, and my naïveté. When he and Hasley were away one weekend, I wrote an editorial critical of state Attorney General Brian McKay. The next day, I chose as my topic the federal Small Business Administration's unwillingness to make loans to the gaming industry. Later I found out that Brown had promised McKay that he would refrain from further criticism, that one of Brown's best friends was the head of the SBA's Nevada office—and that Brown called both to take the heat for what I wrote. Later, I suggested an editorial urging the Reagan administration to keep its nose out of El Salvador, and he agreed. I wrote it before he could change his mind, and he published it. The next day, his friend Hecht was calling Brown, chiding him for failing to understand the importance of El Salvador, for taking an untenable position, and so on. Brown laughed heartily as he told me the story.

When it came to money, especially the lack of it, we still managed to find something to laugh about at the *Valley Times*. No one doubted Brown's journalistic ability—my favorite example was the day I called his office, but he was unavailable; Tom Wicker, the columnist for the *New York Times,* was on a political scouting trip, and the person he sought out in Las Vegas was Brown—but we questioned his business acumen, for good reason. However, even fiscally, he revealed considerable artistry. One of the legendary newsroom stories involved Ned Day's quest for a raise. Brown replied that he lacked the money but would do his best. A few nights later, Brown walked to Day's desk and told him that as a top reporter and columnist, he deserved a title. Could Brown name him associate editor? Day accepted, visibly pleased. A few more nights passed, and then Day looked at Hasley and said, "I blew the raise, didn't I?" I doubted this tale until I was putting out the paper six nights a week, for a $150 weekly paycheck, and Brown called me in and proudly announced that he wanted to name me news editor. My paycheck remained the same.

I have enough memories to fill a book—as I plan to do someday. I remember Yacenda, who became a dear friend and in politics a mentor, stopping in often to find out if Brown would pay him (Adam was owed, we guessed, nearly $100,000). Adam would tell me about his day while waiting for Brown, who would hide in his office or try to sneak past. I remember emulating the editors by occasionally screaming and throwing things when something went wrong: I kicked a copy machine and left a large dent in the side. Ken White nearly burst trying to keep from laughing when Brown later came downstairs and asked, "What happened to the machine?" I just shrugged. I remember the night the wire machine acted up and Hasley and White told me of how when he was sports editor, Koch grew so angry that he tried to throw the machine, which must have weighed 100 pounds, and getting it to move six inches, a *Times* record. I remember the day Hasley ordered me to let an irate subscriber talk to Brown, who came out complaining that his editorial would have been completed an hour before if not for "some crazy woman" berating him about the paper's circulation. I remember the gossip, the inside information, the largely unjustified sense that I, too, was a player. Actually, I was just a kid, getting a million dollar's worth of experience and having more fun at a job—and making less money at it—than I could ever hope or expect again.

III

I remember Brown talking to me early in June 1984 about the future of the paper, how he wanted the *Valley Times* to be known as more than just "Bob Brown's paper" and for it to continue after he was gone. I thought it strange at the time, but it turned out that Brown had just learned the extent of the paper's debt, and hindsight suggests that he had a premonition that its demise might contribute to his own. Less than a week later, on the night of Friday, June 8, 1984, Brown, who suffered from high blood pressure and was a Christian Scientist, died of a heart attack. Hasley and a stunned *Times* staff paid tribute to Brown the next day with his biography, eulogies from Nevada leaders of both parties, and an editorial promising to continue what Brown had begun. Four days later, more than one thousand mourners crammed into a chapel and heard the recollections of Brown's children, Mark and Stephanie; one of his closest friends, Jude Wanniski; and Florence Lee Jones Cahlan, a longtime Las Vegas journalist and historian. Brown's widow also received in his name UNLV's Distinguished Nevadan award, which Brown had declined to accept because he feared that his legal problems would reflect unfavorably on the university.

Meanwhile, the *Valley Times* kept publishing, with Hasley and me designing the paper and writing the editorials and the "Morning Line" column. But the *Times* had filed for federal bankruptcy protection when the IRS clamped down, and now the court-appointed controller found no money in the till and a debt of nearly $2 million looming. (The depths of Brown's problems were apparent in my being owed $2,700 on a $150 weekly paycheck). The court named a trustee, Berkeley Bunker, a former U.S. senator from Nevada who had written a column for the *Times* in the 1970s. Bunker called together the staff and informed them that he could not, in good conscience, continue publication when they had no hope of being paid. The *Valley Times* of June 22, 1984, was the last. While Yacenda remained active in the North Las Vegas community until he died in 1986, those who had remained at the *Times* scattered: Hasley into television news production, then to the *Review-Journal* as assistant city editor, then to a California publication; Koch to the *Sun;* White to the *Review-Journal;* and Staley to *Las Vegas Today,* which was sold, and then to edit several suburban monthly papers.

Clearly, then, this article cannot be considered an exclusively historical retelling or interpretation. But other critics have cited the importance of the *Valley Times.* Behind the scenes and in print, Yacenda and Brown greatly influenced the development of southern Nevada from the 1950s until the 1980s. Brown's editorials from 1974 to 1984 represent an example of thoughtfully conservative reporting and analysis of a tumultuous era of Nevada history and politics. The journalists whom Yacenda and Brown trained went on to positions of influence (especially those outside the historical profession). The reporting of the *Valley Times* in general, and Ned Day in particular, did a great deal to expose hidden interests in the gaming industry and to contribute to changes in how it was regulated and how it saw and sold itself. For a decade, Las Vegas was the only city other than New York with a population of more than 100,000 and three competing daily newspapers. Today, two newspapers, under joint ownership, publish daily, but usually without the investigative skills, editorial judgment, or inside knowledge that could only have been available to those who, like Yacenda and Brown, were longtime political players and observers.

The *Valley Times* affected its times and times to come and needs to be remembered—affectionately, critically, and accordingly. To this day, I believe that if Bob Brown and the *Valley Times* had lived, Hasley still would be managing editor, White the sports editor, Koch the sports columnist, Staley editing and proofreading—and I still would be news editor, supervising an editorial staff that probably would comprise mainly college students and young reporters. Yet I would be wondering, at age thirty, why everyone still called me "the kid."

NOTES

1. On the history of journalism in Nevada and Las Vegas, see Jake Highton, *Nevada Newspaper Days: A History of Journalism in the Silver State* (Stockton: Heritage West, 1990), especially 233–68; Michael S. Green, "The Las Vegas Newspaper War of the 1950s," *Nevada Historical Society Quarterly* 31, no. 3 (fall 1988): 155–82. The important factual data also may be found in Richard E. Lingenfelter and Karen Rix Gash, *The Newspapers of Nevada: A History and Bibliography, 1854–1979* (Reno: University of Nevada Press, 1984), 158–59.

An excellent contemporary account of the competition between the three Las Vegas papers is David W. Toll, "Three's Company: The paperchase in Las Vegas where three newspapers slug it out on the streets each day," *Nevada* 38, no. 2 (April–June 1978): 18–21. For background on Las Vegas in the era in which the *Valley Times* published, see Ralph J. Roske, *Las Vegas: A Desert Paradise* (Tulsa: Continental Heritage Press, 1986), 144 and *passim*; Eugene P. Moehring, *Resort City in the Sunbelt: Las Vegas, 1930–1970* (1989;

reprint, Reno and Las Vegas: University of Nevada Press, 1995). Ned Day later wrote and anchored a documentary on KLAS, "The Mob on the Run," an excellent account of the gaming industry in Las Vegas, and extremely good on issues affecting the *Valley Times.*

The heart of this article is based on conversations—*interview* would be too formal a word—with many friends from the *Valley Times.* I wish to acknowledge my debt to them: Bruce Hasley, Dave Verbon, Ken White, Linda Faiss, Terry Care, A. D. Hopkins, and Jim and Jan Seagrave. I also am indebted to Brown's widow, Shirley Shupe, and her husband, Lew, and to Brown's children, Mark and Stephanie, for their assistance. I would especially like to thank Hasley, Verbon, and White for reading this paper in draft form.

Obviously, I went through many issues of the *Valley Times,* especially those from April 1, 1982, to June 22, 1984, my tenure with the paper. Three dates from 1984 pop up frequently in the section on Brown: June 10, when his obituary appeared; June 13, when an account of his funeral was published; and June 21, when a section of tributes from friends and former employees appeared in the paper. These issues provide much of the background on Brown himself.

For a sense of the paper's early days, I am most grateful to the late Adam Yacenda. We talked often in the last two years of his life about his career at the *Sun* and the *Times,* and he did a great deal to help me understand the life of an editor and political activist; his obituary in the June 14, 1986, *Las Vegas Sun* also was useful. I was able to talk at some length with Bob Brown about the *Times* and his career. An interview with the late Hank Greenspun (March 27, 1986) provided background on the press and politics in Nevada, and on his dealings with Yacenda and Brown. Also helpful is Greenspun's autobiography, with Alex Pelle, *Where I Stand: The Record of a Reckless Man* (New York: David McKay, 1966).

Many excellent works are available to enhance one's understanding of the relationship between the press and politics. For a national perspective, see David Halberstam, *The Powers That Be* (New York: Alfred A. Knopf, 1979). Many of the oral histories produced by the University of Nevada Oral History Project have been with editors and publishers whose recollections underscore the many hats they wore in their communities; without listing a ream of publication information, let me bow toward the two oral histories by John Cahlan and to those of Joseph McDonald, John Sanford, Paul Leonard, Charles Russell, and especially Jack McCloskey. Besides the aforementioned studies, see Marilee Joyce, ed., *The Gentle Giant: How Jim Joyce Helped Shape Nevada Politics for a Generation* (Las Vegas: Nevada Publications, 1994).

The body of literature on the growth of the postwar West and Nevada is exciting, occasionally daunting, and growing. I have been influenced greatly by Peter Wiley and Robert Gottlieb, *Empires in the Sun: The Rise of the New American West* (New York: G.P. Putnam's Sons, 1982). Three works on the postwar era, related to Nevada and Las Vegas, have been especially useful for facts and/or interpretations: Mary Ellen Glass, *Nevada's Turbulent '50s: Decade of Political and Economic Change* (Reno: University of Nevada Press, 1981); John M. Findlay, *People of Chance: Gambling in America from Jamestown to Las Vegas* (New York: Oxford University Press, 1986); and Gary E. Elliott, *Senator Alan Bible and the Politics of the New West* (Reno and Las Vegas: University of Nevada Press, 1994).

2. The story has been recounted in many of the works cited above, especially Greenspun and Glass. Greenspun had alleged corruption against Glenn Jones, the local sheriff. Jones filed a defamation suit, and Greenspun's source became unavailable, leaving the publisher in the lurch. He and reporter Ed Reid set up a "sting" operation in the Thunderbird Hotel and hired a private investigator, Louis Tabet, to pose as an investor. They recorded conversations with the sheriff and several other political and business leaders. In one of these, Lieutenant Governor Cliff Jones (no relation) bragged to Tabet that he would control gaming licenses when his fellow Democrat, Vail Pittman, was elected governor. When Greenspun published the story in the weeks before the election, Glenn Jones dropped his suit and Cliff Jones had to resign from his post as Democratic national committeeman. The controversy also helped defeat Pittman and reelect Russell.

The Changing West
Urban and Rural

This article is a set of edited remarks from a panel discussion at the American Society for Environmental History's 1995 biennial conference, in Las Vegas. The public event was held at the Marjorie Barrick Museum of Natural History on the campus of the University of Nevada, Las Vegas. The discussion was sponsored by the Nevada Humanities Committee and moderated by Jon Christensen, Great Basin regional editor of *High Country News*.

The panelists were:

Robert Gottlieb, author of *Empires in the Sun: The Rise of the New American West, America's Saints: The Rise of Mormon Power, A Life of Its Own: The Politics and Power of Water,* and *Forcing the Spring: The Transformation of the American Environmental Movement,* and coordinator of the Environmental Analysis and Policy Division of the Department of Urban Planning in the School of Public Policy at University of California, Los Angeles;

Ed Marston, publisher of *High Country News*, a biweekly newspaper that covers Western environmental issues and is based in the small fruit-growing and coal-mining town of Paonia, Colorado;

Hal Rothman, professor of history at the University of Nevada, Las Vegas, and author of *America's National Monuments: The Politics of Preservation, On Rims and Ridges: The Los Alamos Area Since 1880,* and the forthcoming *Devil's Bargain: Tourism and Transformation in the 20th Century West;*

Mike Davis, who teaches urban theory at the Southern California Institute of Architecture and is author of *Prisoners of the American Dream* and *City of Quartz: Excavating the Future of Los Angeles* and a contributor to the *Nation* and the *Los Angeles Times*.

JON CHRISTENSEN: I would like to start by thanking everyone for coming here to share their ideas about the changing West with us. In a city that has a new come-on every day, it's nice to see that the humanities can draw a good crowd.

For me, coming from Carson City, where I live, to Las Vegas is like traveling through a time machine. I'm never quite sure where I've landed. Las Vegas seems like a city out of place and out of time. I often find myself feeling dazed and confused about the changing West when I'm here.

Robert Gottlieb, you've been exploring empires in the sun for many years. Las Vegas seems to be growing into that title with the Luxor's pyramid, Excalibur's medieval castle, and MGM's Emerald City now sharing the Strip with Caesars Palace. What do you think about coming into Las Vegas these days?

ROBERT GOTTLIEB: I have images of Las Vegas that are permanently imbedded in my memory from the first time I came to this community when I was doing research for *Empires in the Sun*. I was here during the great floods of the late '70s. In Las Vegas they forgot that it *can* rain and it *can* rain heavily in the desert. There was a flood in the parking lot at Caesars Palace. And it was quite a sight to watch the Rolls Royces going down out of the lot, down Las Vegas Boulevard, floating as if on that kind of special quality that Las Vegas has that you never quite hit the ground.

I also spent time, not on the Strip or in one of the hotels that are the centerpiece of this community, but in a totally run-down courtyard complex in North Las Vegas that was the center for Franciscan activists dealing with social justice issues. They introduced me to a very different experience of Las Vegas that had to do with questions of how people lived who were outside the spotlight.

Another part of my research was looking at *roots*. And in this community you have to start with the very different kinds of Mormon communities that have inhabited and passed through and shaped Las Vegas and other parts of the West. I interviewed a dealer, a working-class guy with a good job, who was told by his bishop that there was a reevaluation of the policy of whether those in the church would have the right to have jobs on the floor in the casinos. The word on high was it might be all right to encourage this industry, as had been done over the years, and to have high-level executive positions in the gaming industry, but it wasn't all right to be on the floor.

Those are images that don't go away for me of what this community is all about. They get reinforced each time I come here.

JON CHRISTENSEN: Ed Marston, you seem to love Las Vegas because it's everything your hometown is not. How does Las Vegas grab you?

ED MARSTON: By the pocketbook.

I realize lately that I've turned into an old-fashioned boomer and booster. In some sense I hate the changes. But really I love what's going on, and I think Las Vegas is the most vital large city in the region. There are a lot of vital small communities in the mountain West and in the deserts like Moab. But Las Vegas is doing things on a large scale.

It's certainly not leading the way, in any sense, because Las Vegas, like Steamboat Springs, like Aspen, like Moab and Sun Valley, is focused in on itself. Each of these places thinks its experience is unique. But they're all going through somewhat the same thing. And this is a vital time in the West.

This is a historians' conference so I probably shouldn't say this, but whenever I meet a person who is interested in Custer or in the old railroads or mountain men—you know, these modern mountain men get together and try to recreate the old West—I always think they're a little foolish. What's happening now is *much* more interesting than the West of a century ago, even as we've mythologized that. We are fortunate to live now. I have a saying that there are people here now who someday will look back on this era and wish they had been alive *now*. You know, the "be here now" thing of the hippie era. So I am a fan of Las Vegas and the West today.

JON CHRISTENSEN: Hal Rothman, you seem to be setting down roots here. How have your first impressions of Las Vegas changed since you began calling this home?

HAL ROTHMAN: The salient feature of my first experience in Las Vegas was when people asked my wife and I where we were from, we said, "We're from Kansas." They asked us, "What part of California is that in?"

Our first real experience here was looking for a home. We looked at thirty-four homes in one day. And the most astonishing thing about those homes was that they were all identical: They were all within about $10,000 in price; they were all built in the same way, in the same style, with walls around them, with very small patches of grass. It looked as if somebody had taken a carpet and rolled that carpet out along with the dogs and fire hydrants and an occasional sapling. And they said, "You can have the sixth one on the left or the tenth one on the right." There was really almost no difference among them.

Looking around at homes, we found out that a lot of the developers were New Yorkers. What they were building were little Brooklyns in southern California style. You got these houses that look southern Californian in architecture but that are placed close together in the manner of the streets in Brooklyn.

We were ready to put an offer down on a house until the agent pointed out that the streets were peculiarly narrow. She said, "Imagine what happens if any of these families have more than two children who are teenagers. Imagine what your street is going to look like with cars. You're not going to be able to get a car down the middle of it." I went back to that neighborhood recently and looked around, and sure enough it looked like an old street. It had the spatial dimensions of a street in the interior of Philadelphia or the oldest parts of New York City.

It's ironic that there's so much space around us, and still we cram ourselves into progressively smaller and smaller and smaller parcels of property. I think you can hear people snore in the next house in a lot of the newest developments. Yet people flock to these things. They're not interested in the older homes. They're not interested in the homes built in the '60s or the '70s, the early '80s or even the late '80s. They're interested in the ones built today.

This creates enclaves. While the neighborhoods don't necessarily have walls around them—some of them *do*—they are walled off by an attitude. And they strangle older, viable neighborhoods in the city. They turn neighborhoods that are homeowner based into rental based. They turn places that have some measure of stability into places that are fundamentally transient.

JON CHRISTENSEN: Mike Davis, you drove into town in your truck like millions of other road warriors from Los Angeles do every year. How does that shape your impression of Las Vegas?

MIKE DAVIS: My favorite film is a movie called *Lady from Shanghai*, in which Orson Welles is a left-wing Irish American sailor who gets seduced by Rita Hayworth. They're having this scene of decadence on a beach and she asks him, "What do you think of it?" And he says in a brogue, "Sure, it's a bright and guilty place." Every time I come to Las Vegas it seems both brighter and more guilty than the time before. It seems brighter, literally, in the sense that the megawattage here keeps getting turned up. If you come in on I-15 at night you can see the reflection from the casinos at Stateline, 30 miles before you get to Baker. It seems more guilty because every time I come to Las Vegas there seem to be more poor people and more social inequality.

The questions that Las Vegas begs are the same questions that southern California begged for most of the twentieth century: Is the boom sustainable? What is there to hold the culture and society together when the boom ends?

In southern California, jobs and rapid growth—the most astonishing regional boom in the twentieth century, fifty years of unbroken prosperity—substituted for culture, identity, sense of place, any kind of equilibrium between groups. You have nothing here like you do in Pittsburgh or Cleveland or New Orleans, where people, almost regardless of class or ethnicity, have a patriotism of place. People in L.A. have a patriotism to jobs and a standard of living.

It seems to me that Las Vegas has become a more grotesque but also more desperate version of this. This is everybody's last chance in America. And the best thing about Las Vegas is that through incredible hard work and militancy, tens of thousands of people have gotten a second chance here and created a decent way of life. The Culinary Workers Union, more than any single force in Nevada, is responsible for the fact that there is a high wage standard of living for working people here.

That's the best thing in the city. But this is a city that is addicted to a belief, as southern California was until recently, in its infinite prosperity and infinite growth. Now, you see what's happening in southern California. I think the decline of southern California is probably the biggest single event in the West in this decade. There's no cultural preparation for it. There's no cultural immune system in southern California to deal with slow growth, to deal with structural unemployment, to deal with all the nasty stuff that crawls out into the sun when there aren't a lot of jobs.

So that's the issue to be faced about Las Vegas, particularly in the context of Nevada history. There's simply nowhere on the face of the earth that's been shaped more by the boom/bust cycle than Nevada. This is a civilization of abandoned dead cities and dreams. No boom has ever lasted in Nevada. Part of Nevada's charm is that it remains in many ways an uninhabited place, a place defined by its ghosts.

What's interesting is that when you talk to people in the Culinary Workers Union, you find there's a kind of stratigraphy. You can go all the way back and find people from Butte who came to Las Vegas in the '50s, people from the recession in New England in the late '50s, on down to the latest generation of reverse Okies from Los Angeles, people whose lives were built around steel or mining or big factories. They keep kind of instinctively raising this question of the law of value: What are we creating here? What are we adding to the national product? They think: You know, thank God I have a job. Thank God I have a strong union to defend my wage. But where is the American economy going?

In that sense Las Vegas is more than just a fast-forward version of Los Angeles. It's a symptom of a national economy. At the end of the twentieth century, major growth sectors are prisons and gambling and theme parks. What kind of world is this we're creating? This is what deindustrialization has given us.

There seems to me to be an incredible hubris right now that somehow the gaming industry is going to continue to expand for the next ten or twenty years. But if it doesn't (and I'm not talking about anything apocalyptic), but when it comes time to pay the costs of super growth, when you have the overcapacity in the hotels and the industry stops growing, what's going to happen in the city? Will it be any different than the kind of malign symptoms you see happening in Los Angeles right now?

JON CHRISTENSEN: Hal Rothman, you've described tourism as a devil's bargain. In Nevada, we've won some pretty good bets wagering with the devil. But are we selling our souls?

HAL ROTHMAN: In an economic sense, Nevada has won a significant number of bets. I have a student who argues that Las Vegas is the example where the rising tide raises all ships. She's someone who came here in the early 1960s in her late twenties and whose family came from poor roots, who worked in the casinos and had a very nice middle-class income. As Mike points out, the process works because there is a strong-enough union contingent here.

On the other hand what she doesn't count are the transients. People forget that of every three people who come to Las Vegas, two leave. So you've got a success rate here of one in three. Now, that'll win you the National League batting crown in most years, but it's hardly the basis for building a society.

When state legislators and governors embrace tourism, they are offering a panacea. They aren't fully aware of the consequences.

Tourism is really the most colonial of colonial economies. The devil's bargain is that tourism is transformative. It will change you.

When I was working in the National Park Service, I became very conscious of tourism as an industry. When we think about tourism, we think about the 22 million–plus people who come to Las Vegas every year and what they see. We don't think as much about *how* the people who live here experience that process. When you live in a national park, or when you work in what is fundamentally a service industry, you begin to see how service industries are transformative.

About the same time I was thinking about this issue, I started to hear a lot of talk from state legislatures in places where things had gone bad, where they had lost their base industry. They were saying: "Tourism is a wonderful thing. It will solve all our problems. We've got some feature we can market here, something people want to see, something they'll pay to see. And the great thing about tourism is we don't have to give anybody tax abatements. We don't need a particularly skilled labor force. We can take people who have lost unskilled jobs and give them new jobs that are equally as unskilled, that will pay them equally well."

Well, there's a transformative process here. You see it in the Aspens and you see it in the Sun Valleys, the places Ed seems to like so much. You see that there's a process by which native people— people who are native to the region, no matter what their ethnicity, no matter what their race—end up at the bottom of the heap. Unless they have land to sell, unless they have marketable skills, they end up literally cleaning the bathrooms and cleaning the rooms of people who come to visit and later build trophy homes. You see this process throughout the West. It's not only in Nevada.

I would argue that Bill Janns—whose family is responsible for Westwood and Thousand Oaks and for the transformation of Sun Valley and the creation of Snowmass—is one of the pivotal figures in the twentieth-century West. Here is a man who was raised in wealth, became a champion skier, and built ski resorts that transformed not only recreation but also the very nature of those communities.

In bleaker moments I've come to think that people who sell their natural resources and let their ground be torn off are better than people who sell tourism, because tourism is ultimately the marketing of your identity and you cease to be who you think you are in

some fashion in that process. That's the devil's bargain of tourism.
Yes, you make a lot of money. But you make a lot of money at the
price of things that to some people are at least equally important.

JON CHRISTENSEN: Robert Gottlieb, you've done a lot of work
exploring two critical issues in the West: water and environmental justice. Is there an environmentally just way for Las Vegas, the
fastest booming metropolis in the West, to get the water it needs
from the rural West?

ROBERT GOTTLIEB: No.

It used to be a kind of a common-sense notion in the water industry, among the water agencies and the communities where the water
agencies dominated, that the way to develop water was to get new
water. The way you got new water is that you took the water from
where it was plentiful and brought it to where it wasn't. And you
used instruments like federal taxpayer dollars and engineering staff
of the Bureau of Reclamation to get your way or you duplicated that
(as we did in California) with your own state infrastructure. That,
in turn, created allocations, an infinite system, a cycle of expansion
that allowed water to come to where it wasn't sufficient, wasn't
available, where you didn't have a local supply for practices such
as agriculture or mining, or, more recently, urban development.

You had the water and you could grow. You could create the development that you needed. You put more acreage in irrigation. You
created more developments in the outlying areas. Then you just
went to your next source. There was a saying in the water industry
that water that flows free is water that is not used.

Well, that system doesn't work anymore. You can't do interbasin
transfers. It's too expensive. You've got too much opposition. You
have a political framework that doesn't work anymore.

So what's the next step? Well, you've got your allocation system
in place, so you then go out and you take the water that's already
been allocated, that already belongs to someone. And you buy it.
You come out with your wad of bills. That's the notion that Las
Vegas has now.

Las Vegas got maxed out at 300,000 acre feet on the Colorado
River system, so it was one of the first to look around and say,
"We've got to create a new system for taking water from where it's
already allocated." The obvious places to look are where there are
not a lot of people—rural areas. Or you go to where Indians live,

because after all, that's the great history of the West: We took the land away, now we'll take the water away. But now we're going to do it with a wad of bills.

Then you discover that you can't do it with the rural areas, because all of a sudden, they're up in opposition, and you've got some pointy-head environmentalists in Las Vegas who are saying that this is reduplicating the Owens Valley experience here in Nevada. And you maybe aren't able to cut the deals with the Indian tribes, because there are some fanatics there who believe that water has a community value and not a commodity value.

Your next step becomes to rewrite the law of the river. That's what Las Vegas is doing, but there are going to be limits in doing that. You can put out as much money as you can and address all the kinds of impacts that you assume will occur if you take the water from where it already belongs, but what you can't do is to mitigate the fact that the water has a value that's separate from that wad of bills. Nor does that answer the question of what you're going to do with the water when you get it here.

Las Vegas has to go through the debate of what it wants to do with the water before it starts thinking about how it's going to pay for it.

Water doesn't act as a constraint on growth in the West. It never has, whether it's for agriculture, mining, or urban areas. Water *does* highlight the issues.

JON CHRISTENSEN: Ed Marston, you travel all over the West. Is this common for communities in the West to be agonizing over change?

ED MARSTON: Yes. But first I have to address some of the issues others have raised. I think the boom is *not* sustainable; it will go bust.

I've lived through one incredible bust in which my town became literally half empty. I sometimes pray for another bust.

Boom and bust is the nature of the desert West. That's what's going to happen and there's no way around it.

Yes, we're all obsessively talking about change. Every community is talking about it. But we lack the tools to talk about it.

We lack a free press almost everywhere in the West. We certainly lack a regional press, because papers in the West that used to be regional have mostly become city papers. The *Denver Post* used to literally cover the region. It had more Sunday circulation in Colorado and the five states around it than all the other papers combined. It played the role of uniting the region. That does not exist anymore. We lack those media.

We also lack independent universities. Every major university in the West, with the exception of Brigham Young, is a state-supported institution. And BYU is a church-supported institution. We do not have many small, independent, liberal arts colleges. We have state institutions, and they are micromanaged by their state legislatures and by the special interest groups to an incredible degree.

We lack a citizen reform movement, a broadly based citizen reform movement. Environmentalism has a wonderful vision, but it's limited as a citizen reform movement. So we're still in many ways parts of an uncivilized society that can't communicate with each other. Each community obsessively talks about the change, brings in the experts, and sort of goes through the process all by itself.

JON CHRISTENSEN: Robert Gottlieb, how did we get here? Is this tension and conflict over change something new in the West?

ROBERT GOTTLIEB: It's not new. And it's not the same in the sense that we have many Wests, not a single West. We don't have a region that has a single identity. Those many Wests and those many regions have histories of conflicts, of tensions, of very sharp divisions along class and ethnic lines. We've had very different Wests when you think of a relationship to the land that is experienced differently by different groups, different cultures, different histories.

We've had a West that has had a labor movement that has fought for its very existence because of the interest groups that plowed through it, whether it was mining, whether it was the railroads, whether it was any of the extractive industries. Now it's the urban-based industries that have fought to maintain their domain, without yielding an inch to basic human rights. In exchange we've had groups of workers forming and trying to create their identity amid these sharp kinds of conflicts. We've had the Wobblies. We've had the Western Federation of Miners. We've had Mine, Mill, and Smelter Workers. That's part of the history of the West that helps you understand the kinds of conflicts here in Las Vegas.

It's important when we think boom/bust that we also think about history of conflict that comes in and out of those boom-and-bust sequences. That cycle gives a very different sense of what it means to define place or community.

The West is not singular. It's many places, and it still has the tensions between communities and groups and classes and races, between urban and rural.

JON CHRISTENSEN: Mike Davis, can we get anything new and useful out of this discussion?

MIKE DAVIS: I think we can if those of us who are environmentalists, self-declared environmentalists, start by admitting that we've lost the most important battle of all. I'm not just talking about the Clinton administration's collapse over things like grazing fees or casino taxes or the general rout and retreat of environmentalism over the last few years. There's something more fundamental: The environmental movement, with very, very few exceptions, has no dialogue with the granddaughters and grandsons of the I.W.W. or the Western Federation of Miners or the working-class westerners, whether they're up in Forks, Washington, or in some small uranium town in southwestern Colorado. These are the people who paid the price for the great dislocations in the West over the last generation.

The reality here is that since the mid-'60s there have been at least a half million and possibly more academically well-endowed people with some kind of lifeline better than welfare or an employment check who have moved to those last best places, and they've made those places into luxury goods. The newcomers act with a sense of noblesse oblige, that only somebody with a mountain bike and a backpack has the right to wilderness. They haven't defended the working-class West against what is really one of the most complete economic catastrophes in the short history of the West.

You can probably date it with the collapse of the copper industry in the '70s and go through one resource industry after another. This economic decline has taken away peoples' lifelines; it has taken away their pride; it has taken away their dignity. But they're resourceful people and they fight on. The tragedy now is that when they can't afford to make the payment on their motorcycle, they think that their worst enemies are the environmentalists, that their worst enemies are the people who moved in two years ago with the modem.

I think there's an urgent need for an open, frank, critical discussion within the environmental movement about how it tends to alienate that blue-collar West, which should be its essential ally in populist struggles against capital and the corporate domination of the West.

There's one other point that is seldom brought up. Increasingly in the cities of the West there's an urban population that has no access whatsoever to everything that I'm sure most of us love about the West. For instance, L.A.'s Department of Water and Power, as one of its many empires, controls the Owens Valley, one of the most beautiful landscapes. Thanks to them, it is now preserved without fast-food franchises or development in perpetuity. But as far as I know, they've never even thought of building camps up there to let inner-city kids come out in the wilderness. I think the environmental movement has failed in not making a kind of wilderness experience a basic democratic right, in not really thinking hard about the questions of how to provide access to all of those things to the people in the city.

To me, those are the two essential allies that we need to have before the environmental movement can emerge from what I think is actually now a period of very deep defeat in the West.

JON CHRISTENSEN: Ed Marston, *High Country News* calls itself a paper for people who care about the West. Are there things Las Vegas can learn from the rest of the West?

ED MARSTON: That's a good question. But first I need to address some other things that have been said. I love the image of the modem and the motorcycle, Mike.

But it sounds like the mining industry is being enshrined here. We should remember what the mining industry was like in its early days. In Telluride, half the miners who went into the mines were either killed or crippled. I think that's how we're living now, in a way. We're seeing the beginning of an industry. We don't really know where it's going.

And remember, this new industry of the late twentieth century replaced something else that was in decline. The West was in structural decline; it was in cultural decline. The community I live in was on its deathbed, no matter what would happen. We new people, of the '70s and '80s, obnoxious and overeducated though we are, *didn't* really push anyone out. Those people were gone. What pissed off the people we moved in among was that their kids had left and we came in and were willing to try to live in these communities. They didn't like us. They missed their children. But their communities *were* going down.

There are certain moral judgments I can't buy into much. I don't see why gambling is any less necessary than beef or gold. I mean, frankly, forced to choose between gambling, beef, and gold, I'd have to think about it. I'd throw out gold right away, and then I'd have a struggle. I like video poker. I can have more fun on a couple of dollars than I can eating a hamburger.

I think that both in the United States and globally we're at a point where most of our economy is sort of unnecessary. I don't really need the next generation Macintosh in my office. I don't really need modems and faxes. In fact, I don't like them. They speed up my life. I moved to this little town to kind of disconnect. Suddenly, between FedEx and modems and faxes, I'm racing as fast as I was when I lived in New York.

I think gambling and life-style and recreation and skiing just haven't been mythologized yet. They aren't old enough to have legitimacy.

The other quarrel I have is with Robert Gottlieb. The West is absolutely a region, a *singular* place. My region, my West, the inter-mountain West (the East to Californians) is the states that are a third or more public land, and the presence of that public land, the federal presence, along with the incredible landscapes—the fact that you can be driving down I-70 and be buried in an avalanche or be killed by a falling rock—makes this region different. Westerners are loyal to their region in a way that I never was when I lived in the East. Perhaps southerners are, but I don't think anyone else is.

I also feel that we haven't worked hard enough. Ben Read has said that people who live in the Jackson Holes of the world must realize that they're like the people who lived next to Chartres and the other great cathedrals in medieval Europe. We haven't taken on that responsibility yet. We haven't grown yet, and I don't know that we *can* grow. I don't know that we can accept that responsibility for being the caretakers of a wonderful landscape and for interpreting that landscape, not just selling t-shirts with its name on it.

We have to understand what is possible and what we're shooting at for the future. What is gone is gone. It's dead. The old West died culturally first; then it died economically. We moved into dying communities.

JON CHRISTENSEN: Mike Davis, what can the rest of the West learn from Las Vegas?

MIKE DAVIS: Before I answer that let me refer to two other points. One is that I thought Hal's remarks on tourism were brilliant. Of course there's another part of the West that you could describe as the "sub-tourist" West. It doesn't have any romantic history or spectacular landscape that it can turn into local capital. That's the part of the West that right now is going through the prison boom.

A number of years ago when I was driving a truck for a living, I pulled into Pecos, Texas, which was one of the great energy boom-towns of the late '70s and early '80s. The population went up to about eighty thousand, dropped down to about forty to fifty thousand, with 40 percent unemployment. I walked into a Mexican restaurant. The young guy who was the proprietor had a button with his picture on it. He was running for mayor. He explained to me that although the population of Pecos was 70 percent Mexican, there had never been a Latino on the city council. He was going to be mayor, and he was going to whip the ass of those old Anglos.

It seemed really great, so I asked, "What's your program?"

He said, "I'm gonna save Pecos with mean bitches."

"Excuse me," I said. "Did you say, 'mean bitches'?"

"That's right," he said.

Pecos was on the short list for a federal women's prison. For a town like Pecos this was the second coming; there wasn't anything better in the world than to have a bunch of mean bitches who would create four hundred jobs in Pecos, a town that describes probably a hundred other towns in the American West.

In rural California, the Department of Corrections is becoming the major employer. The biggest growth industry in rural California, the California of dying lumber and agricultural towns, is that of storing the underclasses of California's cities.

It's no different in Nevada, which has the highest incarceration rate in the United States, or in Arizona. I've been shocked by how many new prisons or camps I've seen.

There is also a danger that the whole Great Basin, having been the national sacrifice zone for purposes of the Cold War, is now going to become the nation's toxic disposal site. In other words, the places that can't be turned into Moab (and the local people turned into cigar-store Indians), are going to get prisons or they're going to get plutonium or the solid waste from Los Angeles.

All this raises in my mind a question that scares me, because I consider myself a Westerner: Is there any stability? You can describe western history by using catastrophe theory, seeing it as a series of booms and busts that leave more and more debris. Are we capable of creating any equilibrium here?

On the other hand, it's also interesting to consider the effects of resource constraint on economies and urban growth. For example, look what's happened in Israel and Japan, two countries that face massive resource constraints. Their brains get bigger. Instead of solving everything just by importing more of the same, they changed their way of life. They became inventive. They raised the productivity of their civilization in relationship to their environment. It's very interesting that in the history of L.A., the two most creative times in terms of urban design and urban way of life were in the beginning of the century, before the aqueduct, during the bungalow period, when people had a kind of water ethic. They were water scarce, and it made them very creative. Then again briefly in the period of droughts and energy crisis in the '70s under Jerry Brown, they suddenly discovered alternative sources of energy.

It's amazing how restraints on resources can wake up brain cells even in a brain-dead civilization like ours. A major potential source of new economic growth and new jobs in the American West could come from making our civilization socially just, and putting it into equilibrium with its environment.

JON CHRISTENSEN: That sounds like a good, hopeful note on which to end this discussion of the changing West. I would like to thank the panelists for stimulating our brain cells.

I would also like to thank the Nevada Humanities Committee for making such thought-provoking discussions a public part of our changing state. There is no more important and committed sponsor of public discussion of the important issues of our day. The committee enlarges, enriches, and enlivens public debate by getting scholars, journalists, and the public to mix it up, share our knowledge and concerns, embrace our commonalities, and confront our differences. The humanities help us understand the changes the old West went through and grasp the changes coming in the new West, so that we will be better able to shape how our communities and our lives change in the future of the West.

Tumbleweeds and Toenails
Weed Abatement in Silver Springs

Out here on the carrion highway
three men, two semis and a propane
torch to kill the devil weed
the only vegetation
on this black stretch that hooks
Mule Flats to Leetville Junction.

In one more month they'll blow away
and by Christmas, snow will light
their tails at first sun. Were it not
for the occasional mask of motion
I'd drive to Austin before seeing
the orange men move.

But why turn back skeletons
with their tools? Is it that rain
simply won't do or the frenzy
of fired gun at so wicked a thistle?
Either way, they pour it on, as if at play.
Highway 50 will never be bordered again.

Wyatt Earp and the Exterminators

The place looks like hell. Charlie Prinup stands at the curb leaning against his old '57 Mack truck. He shakes his head and tilts the can to his lips. The beer washes over his cheeks, slopping onto his t-shirt. For the past year or so he's let everything go. The lawn's covered with oil spots, littered with trash, and dead. The house is empty— no curtains on the windows, no pictures on the walls, no furniture, no people sitting around the fireplace talking, laughing, drinking. Maybe there were more important things to do. Maybe not.

Charlie tosses the empty onto the lawn and pushes away from the truck. He follows a narrow path through the shrubs along the side of the house and emerges in the backyard. The trees in back are bigger than those in front. There are three of them: two elms and a weeping willow. Diesel engine parts are scattered under the elms. The willow, the largest of the trees, stands in the middle of the yard next to an old stone well. Charlie stops at the well, steadies himself, and looks up at the willow. Beneath it, in the enclosure formed by its drooping branches, his younger brother and Julie are sitting at a red-wood picnic table. The table is covered with beer cans, a large paper sack, and two gallon bottles of wine—one empty, the other half full. His brother Phil has passed out again. Julie is watching him.

Charlie looks over at Phil. Twenty years ago, when their father died and left them the old Mack, Phil and he had moved to Sacramento. Plenty of work in California, everybody said. They were going to kick everybody's ass in the trucking business. They even made a little money—bought the house, bought another truck. A new one. God, it was nice—air conditioning, chrome wheels, double sleeper. Phil moved in with him and Julie after his fourth wife left him. "I'm through with marriage," Phil said then. "What the hell is wrong with me, Charlie?"

Charlie uncaps the wine bottle and takes a long pull. His eyes are watering when he sets it down again.

"Why don't we go over to my mother's and I'll fix you guys some breakfast?" Julie is saying. "The two of us should be able to get Phil in the car."

"I'm not hungry."

"It's hot under here, Charlie."

He shrugs. He feels sweat trickling down his sides.

"Have another beer," he says.

The heat doesn't bother him. And he has always liked sitting under the tree. During the winter when it rained, he used to crawl under the table with the kids. They called it their fort and would hide there until Julie called them back into the house. The kids loved it here. Now he can't even afford to rent, let alone buy, them another home.

"Those assholes," he says. "Those dirty sonsabitches. Who the hell do they think they are?"

"What's that?" Julie asks. "Was it a car door?"

"Goddamn them to hell."

Charlie stopped making the house payments after they lost the new truck. It was okay for a while—some letters, a few threatening phone calls. Then the off-duty cop showed up at the door. Phil and Charlie were drinking beer, watching a ball game. The mortgage company was giving them thirty days to vacate the premises. If they weren't out by then, they would be forcibly removed from the house. When the man left, Phil asked Charlie why he hadn't told the son-of-a-bitch to get screwed. Charlie told Phil not to worry about it. He'd take care of things just like he always had. But by the end of the month it looked real bad. Julie's mother wouldn't lend them any more money. Finally, the old woman let them store their furniture in her garage and took in Julie and the kids. Charlie and Phil have been camping out under the willow.

"It's not right, goddamnit. It's just not right."

Charlie has one hand wrapped around the neck of the wine bottle. Every so often he makes a fist and slams it to the table. Phil is awake now and after each hit on the bottle Charlie passes it over to him.

"They're out to get us, Phil. All the money-grabbing assholes are out to get us." Charlie leans across the table and grabs Phil by the arm. "We're family. We've got to stick together."

"What're we gonna do, Charlie?" Phil asks.

"Forget about it," Julie says, touching Charlie. "Let's go to my mother's."

"They got theirs and the rest of us are screwed. I should've kicked his ass when I had the chance. Should've pasted the sonuvabitch where he stood." Charlie takes another gulp from the bottle and points up at the tree. "We'll stay right here under this goddamn tree. Wait for the bastards to come to us."

"There's somebody in the house," Julie says, shaking him.

"What?"

"They're in the kids' bedroom."

Charlie sets the bottle down and turns to look at the house. Phil reaches below the table. When Charlie faces them again he sees the .38 next to the wine bottle.

"Go show the bastards that cannon," Phil says. "Just like you said, Charlie. They can't fuck with us."

"No, Charlie," Julie says and stands.

"Come on, Charlie. Pick it up."

Charlie hasn't seen the old piece in years. Phil once lent the gun to an old girlfriend for protection, but she had given it to another boyfriend. After a night of drinking, Phil had talked Charlie into going with him to get it back. The woman lived out in the country. When he and Phil got there, she came out of the house in her bathrobe and started screaming at Phil. A few minutes later the boyfriend stepped outside with the .38 in his hand. The moon was full that night, and Charlie could still remember how unreal everything seemed in the pale light. The man stood there in the yard telling them to get the hell off the property. Phil broke his beer bottle on the bumper of the car and started for him, but the woman stepped between them. The boyfriend was so busy watching Phil and his girlfriend that he never noticed Charlie moving closer. And then Charlie stepped right up and took the gun away. Just reached out, snatched it, and pointed it at the man's head. The woman had begged Charlie not to shoot him. When the boyfriend started crying, Charlie finally let him go.

Driving back to town, Phil told him, "Big brother, you looked just like Wyatt Earp, walking up and grabbing the gun like that."

Charlie is staring at the gun and thinking about how close he came to killing that sonuvabitch.

"Sit down, Julie," he says, grabbing the .38 and shoving it in his pants.

"I'm coming," Phil says and falls over backwards. Charlie helps his brother back onto the bench.

"You just stay here with Julie in case they get past me, little brother."

Charlie goes to the back door, opens it a crack, and sticks his head inside. Gun in hand, he steps into the house. He can't see them but he can hear them. Their voices echo through the empty rooms:

"What'd you find in there?"

"I'll have to go back out to the truck for some more juice. There's a whole nest of the little bastards inside this wall."

Charlie wipes the sweat from his eyes with the back of his hand and suddenly realizes he has to pee. He glances over his shoulder at the back door. He thinks about Julie and Phil waiting for him under the tree. Then, dancing from one leg to the other, he makes his way to the kids' bedroom. At the doorway he stops and looks inside. There are two of them dressed in white coveralls. One of the men has a shiny metal canister strapped to his back. There's a hose leading from it attached to a wand. The other man is wearing a black New York Yankee ballcap.

"Drop it, you sonsabitches," Charlie says.

The two men look at him. The one with the canister holds the metal wand loosely at his side.

"Jesus," he says to Charlie. "Drop what?"

"This is my home, goddamn you."

The man raises the wand, points it at Charlie, and says, "Don't point that at me, you old fart."

"Easy, Dave," the Yankee fan says.

Charlie groans. He feels the wet warmth spreading in his crotch. When he looks down at his pants, the Yankee fan steps up and snatches the gun out of Charlie's hand.

"This old piece isn't even loaded," the man says. "Christ, he smells like a brewery."

"I've peed my pants," Charlie says.

They grab Charlie under the arms and carry him to the rear of the house. At the back door they shove him outside. Charlie staggers a step or two, loses his balance, and falls onto his side. The Yankee fan walks over and throws the pistol into the stone well beside the willow.

"Lady, you better get this old drunk out of here before I call the cops."

Julie is kneeling beside Charlie.

"Oh, baby," she says and puts her arms around him. Charlie tries to push her away, but she holds him tight. Finally he gives in and allows her to help him to his feet.

"Let's get Phil to the car," she says. "He's out again."

Charlie nods and dries his eyes on his sleeve.

"Did you shoot the bastards, Charlie?" Phil asks when they wake him.

Julie says, "Shut up, Phil."

After they get Phil in the car, Charlie looks up at the house. The two exterminators are going back inside. The man with the canister is almost through the door when he glances over his shoulder. Pivoting on his heels, he whips up the metal wand and points it at Charlie. The Yankee fan begins to laugh. Charlie starts around the car.

"Get in here, Charlie," Julie says.

Charlie continues on toward them. He's a tall man about fifty-five with a pot belly, curly silver-black hair, and a square jaw. Reaching the tree, he pushes the branches aside and settles on the bench opposite Julie and his brother. The air inside the willow is humid, and it smells of stale beer and sweat.

"What the hell kind of world lets people take your house away from you?" he says.

"Forget it," Julie tells him. "There's nothing you can do about it. Have another beer. Phil, give him a beer."

Julie reaches over and shakes Phil. She appears fresher, less rumpled than the two men. She's big, about thirty-five, and her large breasts are stuffed into a skimpy halter top. Phil doesn't move.

"He never could handle his liquor," Charlie says, taking a warm beer from the bag. He looks past Julie at the trunk of the willow. There's a bare spot about halfway up the trunk where he helped Julie's kids carve their initials into the tree.

"You look tired, baby," Julie says. She opens his beer.

"You and me got married in this house, Julie. Remember? Phil and the kids tied cans to the back of the Mack."

"It doesn't run anymore," she tells him.

"What?" He's still staring at the tree.

"The truck," she says. "It doesn't run."

"What the hell difference does that make? It'll run as soon as me and Phil fix it."

Bill Abrams is English coordinator for the Nevada Department of Education and a member of Ash Canyon Poets.

Katrine Barber is a Ph.D. candidate in American studies at Washington State University. Her primary emphasis is on cultural studies and the western United States.

Teresa Baumeister works on her Ph.D. at the University of Nevada, Reno. She has one daughter, Beatrice. She also has indoor plumbing.

June Johnson Bube is at the University of Washington, completing her dissertation on women's sensational adventure tales about western settlement published between 1840 and 1880. Her project examines this fiction as both social criticism and an imaginary site to play out gender conflicts and fantasies. Her article is part of her larger exploration of Frances Fuller Victor's compilation of nineteenth-century women's "border tales."

J. Edward Chamberlin was born in Vancouver, British Columbia. Since 1970, he has been on the faculty of the University of Toronto, where he is now professor of English and comparative literature. His books include *The Harrowing of Eden: White Attitudes Towards Native Americans*, *Ripe Was the Drowsy Hour: The Age of Oscar Wilde*, and *Come Back to Me My Language: Poetry and the West Indies*. His essay was originally written as a lecture for the Center for the American West.

Jon Christensen is the Great Basin regional editor of *High Country News*.

Bill Cowee is an accountant by vocation and a poet and fiction writer by avocation. He has served as poetry editor on the *Bristlecone* and as co-director of the Western Mountain Writer's Conference. He is a founding member of the Ash Canyon Poets.

Before arriving in Nevada, **Sheri F. Crawford** taught humanities at San Francisco State University and a California community college. Currently she teaches history and western traditions in the University of Nevada system.

William A. Douglass is coordinator of the Basque Studies Program at the University of Nevada, Reno.

Cheryll Glotfelty is associate professor of literature and the environment at the University of Nevada, Reno. She is co-editor with Harold Fromm of the *Ecocriticism Reader: Essays in Literary Ecology* (Athens: University of Georgia Press, 1996).

In 1995, **Michael S. Green** became tenure-track professor of history at the Community College of Southern Nevada. He is completing a Ph.D. in history at Columbia University. He has published many articles on Nevada history and has previously appeared in *Halcyon*. True to *Valley Times* tradition, he has been a columnist for *Las Vegas Weekly* and a political consultant for A*Track*Tions Compaign Conductors.

Shaun T. Griffin lives with his family in Virginia City, Nevada, just west of the Dead Camel Mountains. His last chapbook of poems was *Under Red-Tailed Sky* (Reno: Black Rock Press, 1995).

Laurie Macfee is a writer and visual artist living in Reno. She teaches beginning photography at the University of Nevada, Reno, and divides the rest of her time between the Black Rock Press and her twin daughters, Sarah and Eva.

Kit Miller's photographs have appeared in the *New York Times*, the *San Francisco Chronicle, High Country News*, and many other publications.

Paul Morris worked in television for twenty years before enrolling in the M.A. and Ph.D. writing programs at the University of Nevada, Reno. His fiction has been published in *Red Neck Review*, and he is co-author (with Stephen Tchudi) of *Schooling for a Literate Society* (San Francisco: Jossey-Bass, 1996).

Wesley Reid has lived in the Great Basin his entire life and is currently pursuing a Ph.D. at the University of Nevada, Reno.

Lee E. Scanlon is associate professor of mass communication at Eastern New Mexico University, Portales.

T. H. Watkins, a former senior editor of *American Heritage,* has been editor of *Wilderness,* the magazine of the Wilderness Society, since 1982. He is the author of twenty-four books, including *Righteous Pilgrim: The Life and Times of Harold Ickes, 1874–1952,* a finalist for the National Book Award and the National Book Critics Circle Award and winner of the *Los Angeles Times* Book Award; *The Great Depression: America in the 1930s;* and with Dyan Zaslowsky, *These American Lands: Parks, Wilderness, and the Public Lands.* Most of the photographs and much of the text for this article were taken from *Stone Time: Southern Utah, a Portrait and Meditation,* recently issued by Clear Light Publishers, Santa Fe. Reprinted by permission of the author.

Dorothy Zeisler-Vralsted is an associate professor of history at the University of Wisconsin–La Crosse.